Emergency Management and Tactical Response Operations

D1616648

THE BUTTERWORTH-HEINEMANN HOMELAND SECURITY SERIES

Other titles in the Series:

- **Biosecurity and Bioterrorism** (2008)
  ISBN: 978-0-7506-8489-7
  Jeffrey R. Ryan and Jan F. Glarum

- **Maritime Security** (2008)
  ISBN: 978-0-12-370859-5
  Michael McNicholas

- **Introduction to Emergency Management, Third Edition** (2008)
  ISBN: 978-0-7506-8514-6
  George Haddow et al.

- **Terrorism and Homeland Security: An Introduction with Applications** (2007)
  ISBN: 978-0-7506-7843-8
  Philip P. Purpura

- **Introduction to Homeland Security, Third Edition** (2008)
  ISBN: 978-1-85617-509-8
  Jane Bullock et al.

- **Emergency Response Planning for Corporate and Municipal Managers, Second Edition** (2006)
  ISBN: 978-0-12-370503-7
  Paul Erickson

Other related titles of interest:

- **Introduction to Security, Eighth Edition** (2008)
  ISBN: 978-0-7506-8432-3
  Robert J. Fischer, Edward P. Halibozek, and Gion Green

- **Background Screening and Investigations** (2008)
  ISBN: 978-0-7506-8256-5
  W. Barry Nixon and Kim M. Kerr

- **The Corporate Security Professional's Handbook on Terrorism** (2008)
  ISBN: 978-0-7506-8257-2
  Edward P. Halibozek et al.

- **Design and Evaluation of Physical Protection Systems, Second Edition** (2008)
  ISBN: 978-0-7506-8352-4
  Mary Lynn Garcia

- **Vulnerability Assessment of Physical Protection Systems** (2006)
  ISBN: 978-0-7506-7788-2
  Mary Lynn Garcia

- **Introduction to International Disaster Management** (2007)
  ISBN: 978-0-7506-7982-4
  Damon Coppola

- **Risk Analysis and the Security Survey, Third Edition** (2006)
  ISBN: 978-0-7506-7922-0
  James F. Broder

- **High-Rise Security and Fire Life Safety, Second Edition** (2003)
  ISBN: 978-0-7506-7455-3
  Geoff Craighead

- **Investigative Data Mining for Security and Criminal Detection** (2003)
  ISBN: 978-0-7506-7613-7
  Jesús Mena

Visit **http://elsevierdirect.com/security** for more information on these titles and other resources.

Emergency Management and Tactical Response Operations

Bridging the Gap

By Dr. Thomas D. Phelan

AMSTERDAM • BOSTON • HEIDELBERG • LONDON
NEW YORK • OXFORD • PARIS • SAN DIEGO
SAN FRANCISCO • SINGAPORE • SYDNEY • TOKYO

ELSEVIER   Butterworth-Heinemann is an imprint of Elsevier

Butterworth–Heinemann is an imprint of Elsevier
30 Corporate Drive, Suite 400, Burlington, MA 01803, USA
Linacre House, Jordan Hill, Oxford OX2 8DP, UK

Library of Congress Cataloging-in-Publication Data
Application submitted

British Library Cataloguing-in-Publication Data
A catalogue record for this book is available from the British Library.

ISBN: 978-0-7506-8712-6

For information on all Butterworth–Heinemann publications
visit our Web site at http://elsevierdirect.com/security

Printed in the United States of America
08 09 10 11 12 10 9 8 7 6 5 4 3 2 1

Dedication

This book is dedicated to my wife, Catherine Waite Phelan.

Her expertise in writing, editing, and nutrition have supported me throughout my time away responding to disasters and sequestered in my home office to write this book.

Table of Contents

Foreword		**xiii**
Acknowledgments		**xvii**
Introduction		**xix**
Chapter 1	**There Never Used to Be a Gap**	**1**
	Introduction	2
	Traditional Career Paths to Emergency Manager	2
	Changing Demands on Emergency Managers	6
	Declining Membership in Volunteer Emergency Response Units	8
	The Influence of Business and Industry in Emergency Management	9
	Summary	12
	Discussion Questions	12
	References	12
Chapter 2	**Tactical Operations vs. Management Skills**	**13**
	Introduction	14
	Skill Sets for Tactical Operations	14
	Skill Sets for Emergency Management	21
	Acquisition of Skill Sets	26
	Training vs. Education	28
	Summary	30

Discussion Questions   31

References   31

**Chapter 3   The Demands of Managing According
to the Incident Command System (ICS)   33**

Introduction   34

ICS Command Staff   34

The Role of the Operations Section Chief   37

How the Operations Section Chief is Supported
by Command Staff   40

Role Clarification and Skill Sets for Command Staff   42

Summary   46

Discussion Questions   46

References   47

**Chapter 4   The Incident Commander:
A Chief or a Manager?   49**

Introduction   50

Traditional Roles for the Chief   50

The Shift from Tactical Response Operations to Management   58

Management Roles of the Incident Commander   58

Experience, Education, and Training: How They Contribute
to Competency   65

Management by Objectives   66

Summary   70

Discussion Questions   70

References   71

Chapter 5   What Colleges Have to Offer   73

Introduction   74

The Growth of Emergency Management
College Programs   75

Curriculum for Emergency Management   77

Prerequisite Skills and Practice   81

Education vs. Training   84
Research   86
Summary   89
Discussion Questions   89
References   90

Chapter 6   The Career Path in Emergency Management   91
Introduction   92
Entry-Level Positions   92
Gaining Experience as a Volunteer   95
Local, State, Regional, and National Positions   98
Career Development Skills for Emergency Managers   112
Summary   115
Discussion Questions   115
References   116

Chapter 7   Case Study: Ground Zero   117
Introduction   118
Tactical Operations   118
Emergency Management   122
Summary   128
Discussion Questions   128
References   129

Chapter 8   Case Study: The Tsunami Response in Sri Lanka   131
Introduction   132
Tactical Operations   132
Emergency Management   135
Summary   142
Discussion Questions   142
References   143

**Chapter 9   Case Study: Private
and Public Perspectives from Katrina**   **145**

    Introduction   146

    Tactical Operations   146

    Emergency Management   150

    Summary   154

    Discussion Questions   156

    References   157

Chapter 10   The "Manager" In Emergency Management   **159**

    Introduction   160

    Management by Objectives   160

    Command and Control   164

    The Role of "Manager" in the Case Studies   166

    How Crisis and Emergency Management Expertise Aid
General Managers   172

    Summary   174

    Discussion Questions   174

    References   175

Chapter 11   Resistance   **177**

    Introduction   178

    The Growing Gap between First Responders
and Emergency Managers   178

    Overcoming Resistance to College Preparation for
Emergency Managers   180

    What Research and Study Have to Offer Tactical Operations 186

    Understanding the Different Requirements of Emergency
Management and Tactical Response Operations   188

    Summary   190

    Discussion Questions   190

    References   191

Chapter 12   Working Together   **193**

Introduction   194

Partnering between College Programs and Community
First Response Organizations   194

The Administrative Chief Model   200

The Role of Emergency Management on Scene   201

The Best of Both Worlds for the Safety of the Nation   204

Lessons Learned   205

Summary   209

Discussion Questions   210

References   210

Appendix   **211**
Index   **285**

FOREWORD

I picked up the phone, and it was Dr. Tom asking if I would answer a few questions from some students he was teaching. I was expecting to speak with a small group and reply to perhaps three or four "softball" questions concerning my experience in responding to global disasters. Instead, I was on speakerphone with a full classroom of students who were interested in the details. They wanted to know what worked, what went wrong, the emotional stress factors, political issues, social challenges, levels of effectiveness, and more. These students were highly motivated and our discussion went on for well over the scheduled hour. Tom had motivated his students to reach well beyond the standard textbook answers. Tom knew that real world crisis situations require customized solutions with a good dose of practical experience mixed in. As we ended the session, I commented to Tom how much I enjoyed speaking with his students and looked forward to his sharing his extensive practical knowledge and first hand experience in emergency management with practitioners, consultants, and students worldwide. Tom then reminded me I had agreed to write the "foreword" to his book.

Tom's position concerning the importance of proven skills among emergency managers and first responders is absolutely correct. Simply watching a video on how to perform CPR (cardiopulmonary resuscitation) does not qualify an individual to be a paramedic. To be qualified you must have hundreds of hours of combined classroom and first-hand field experience including responding to emergency calls with certified paramedics. You must pass a series of difficult tests, professional evaluations, and update your skills on a regular basis. Only proven, qualified individuals are legally allowed to be designated as certified paramedics. The same requirements for obtaining appropriate education, field experience, and testing should hold true for individuals holding the position of city, state, or federal emergency manager. When unqualified individuals are placed in a position of having to make critical decisions with little or no experience the results can be catastrophic. This was clearly demonstrated in the Hurricane Katrina disaster where many of the senior government emergency management leaders we would expect to count on in a crisis were ineffective and failed to properly execute their responsibilities.

The responsibility for the Katrina leadership failure lies with those who have the authority to make political appointments or assign individuals to critical leadership positions without taking into consideration the qualifications needed to be successful (education, certification, and proven experience). There are several good examples where common logic guides our leaders to make the right choice. Appointees to the position of United States Surgeon General have consistently been experienced medical doctors. This passes the logic test since the key responsibility of the Surgeon General is to focus on the health of our citizens, and a medical degree seems like a necessary requirement when issuing medical advice. The same logic should be applied when appointing an individual to be responsible for emergency management where a mistake in judgment could cost lives and increase suffering instead of reducing the disaster impact, maximizing response efforts and accelerating recovery. Political appointments are a key component of our democratic process. It is not without reason to expect those appointees to be qualified for the job they are being asked to take.

Another challenge in emergency management is convincing businesses leaders, government officials, and citizens to invest some of their time, effort, and money in predisaster risk assessment and mitigation. We understand that wearing a seat belt and driving a car with air bags could help save our lives. We learned that preventative medicine can help us to live longer and more productive lives. Most of us agree with a well-known quote: "An ounce of prevention is worth a pound of cure." The U.S. Congressional study conducted by the Multi-hazard Mitigation Council on the benefits of investing in predisaster mitigation yielded the following: For every US $1 invested in structural (physical improvements) and nonstructural (education, aware-ness, and community programs) mitigation there was a benefit to society of $4 or greater. A 4:1 payback sounds like an excellent investment to me. Unfortunately, very little funding is made available by the U.S. Government or individual states for that purpose.

Oxfam International, a major nonprofit organization focused on humanitarian relief activities, released their "Climate Alarm" study stating,

Natural disasters have quadrupled over the last two decades, from an average of 120 a year in the early 1980's to as many as 500 today. The number of people affected by all disasters has risen from an average of 174 million a year between 1985 and 1994 to 254 million a year between 1995 and 2004.

Knowing that the number, magnitude, and impact of natural disaster events continue to increase, we need to find better ways to educate and motivate our politicians, businesses, and communities to invest in predisaster mitigation.

Dr. Tom has been directly involved in some of the most promising efforts to build awareness, skill, and expertise in emergency management and first response. He has successfully applied the lessons learned from his first-hand crisis management experience to his teachings and writings. Tom has addressed the issue of disaster preparedness complacency and worked on the development of global crisis management systems successfully implemented in 17 countries. I am very pleased to have worked with Tom on a number of crisis events, including the World Trade Center 9/11 terrorism attack, the Indian Ocean Tsunami, and Hurricane Katrina. With Tom's help, individuals seeking a career in emergency management will have the opportunity to become the most qualified professionals the industry has ever seen.

−*Brent H. Woodworth*

Acknowledgments

This book could not have been completed without the editorial assistance of my wife, Catherine Waite Phelan, my students at Elmira College, and my colleagues who encouraged me to share my thoughts. My office was professionally managed by Lynda Mura while I took time to write. Inspiration was offered by many close friends and associates, including Richard Arnold, David J. Arrington, Alexander Charters, Ed Devlin, Glenn Fried, Julie Galdo, Roger Hiemstra, Terri Pond, Scott Ream, Tom Shepardson, Deidrich Towne, Jr., and Brent Woodworth. Appreciation is due to my students at Onondaga Community College, Victoria Ladd-de Graff at National Grid, and my clients who all worked diligently without me while I was at Ground Zero, in Sri Lanka, or in New Orleans. It was helpful to receive feedback from all those who attended and commented on my presentations at conferences sponsored by Disaster Recovery Journal, the Canadian Centre for Emergency Preparedness, the FEMA Emergency Management Institute, and several regional and professional organizations from the U.S. to Singapore. I am especially grateful to Patrice Rapalus of Elsevier Butterworth-Heinemann who took an early interest in this project and remained supportive throughout.

Introduction

Emergency management consists of a special set of concepts and principles that differ greatly from the technical expertise applied by first responders. Where those involved directly in tactical response operations require specialized, focused training to perform their duties safely and effectively, emergency management personnel benefit from education in concepts, principles, and practices of management, not operations. Both operations and management have critical roles to play in preparing for, responding to, and recovering from disasters. Emergency management has the important responsibility of supporting operations through overseeing safety, communication, liaison with all stakeholders, planning, logistics, finance, administration, intelligence, and information. Management of these functions is complex, especially during a disaster. Emergency managers, however, have duties to perform in mitigation and preparedness before disaster strikes, and in recovery and restoration, long after the disaster response is over.

This book addresses the apparent gap between emergency management and tactical response operations. It is written to stimulate discussion among all those engaged in professional development, regardless of their roles in emergencies or disasters. The book poses ideas and questions to promote discussion and thought about how emergency managers and operations personnel work together.

Three case studies are provided from the author's experience at Ground Zero following the September 11 attacks, in Sri Lanka following the Indian Ocean Tsunami, and in New Orleans following Hurricanes Katrina and Rita. The observations provided are solely the views of the author, not the organizations in which he served. They are limited to only those aspects of the emergency response and management directly observed.

Each chapter includes learning objectives and discussion questions designed as guides for adult learners in emergency management studies or degree programs. A brief summary of the contents of each chapter follows:

- Chapter 1, There Never Used to Be a Gap, defines emergency management and tactical response operations, discusses the gap between the two over time, and reviews the traditional paths to emergency management positions. It discusses the changing roles of emergency managers and the ways in which business and the military have accepted leaders educated in colleges rather than coming from within their own ranks.

- Chapter 2, Tactical Operations vs. Management Skills, illustrates the different skill sets required for operations and emergency management. The difference between training and education is explored.

- Chapter 3, The Demands of Managing According to the Incident Command System (ICS), presents the notion that the Operations Section Chief is supported by all other command and general staff and describes their roles and responsibilities. The chapter is not intended to be a course in ICS.

- Chapter 4, The Incident Commander: A Chief or a Manager?, describes traditional expectations of a command and control model and contrasts them to the managerial role recommended for incident managers.

- Chapter 5, What Colleges Have to Offer, presents the added value of a college degree program in emergency management, the variety of programs in existence, and the accessibility for students using new instructional technology. The chapter further explores differences between education and training.

- Chapter 6, The Career Path in Emergency Management, identifies the types of volunteer experiences available and the job titles of positions in local, state, and national emergency management agencies. Career development skills are also addressed.

- Chapter 7, Case Study: Ground Zero, contains the author's observations of emergency management from three weeks in New York City immediately following the attacks. As a member of the Disaster Mortuary Operational Response Team (DMORT) logistics support unit, not as a forensics professional, the author participated in managerial and logistical support for a tactical operational response unit. Direct observations of the emergency management functions are presented.

- Chapter 8, Case Study: The Tsunami Response in Sri Lanka, reports the response and recovery efforts of the Centre for National Operations (CNO) at the capital of Sri Lanka, Colombo. The observations include strategies, coordination efforts, and technology used to manage the disaster.

- Chapter 9, Case Study: Private and Public Perspectives from Katrina, includes observations made by the author who served in both the private and public sectors in response to Hurricane Katrina. The chapter focuses on those areas where the author served directly and is not a commentary on the roles of various branches of government.

- Chapter 10, The "Manager" in Emergency Management, speaks to the managerial concepts and principles applicable to emergency management. The roles managers played in the three case studies presented in Chapters 7–9 will provide the evidence of the need for emergency managers as well as general managers to be educated in crisis and emergency management.

- Chapter 11, Resistance, addresses the perceived resistance to college-educated emergency managers, who may lack years of experience in operations. The content of college degree courses in emergency management is explored to illustrate its applicability to emergency management roles and responsibilities.

- Chapter 12, Working Together, emphasizes the need for emergency management personnel and tactical response operations personnel to work together. The chapter examines the role of emergency management personnel on scene during a disaster response. It concludes with the point that natural disasters will continue to occur regardless of how we educate ourselves. The chapter attempts to put into perspective the enormity of the challenges that lie ahead and the need for both managerial expertise and operational excellence in handling those challenges.

My goal in writing this book was to provide readers with evidence that knowledge of management concepts and principles is valuable to emergency managers, even those with years of experience in tactical response operations. Another goal was to introduce the idea that learning the relevant managerial concepts and principles is better acquired through college degree programs than in other ways. Finally, the challenge to those interested in emergency management careers is to become educated for the betterment of all in documented, credible, and professional emergency management practices. The reader is invited to accept the challenge.

Chapter 1

There Never Used to Be a Gap

Objectives of this chapter:

- Define emergency management and tactical operations.

- Discuss the gap created over time between emergency management and first responders.

- Review the traditional paths to the role of emergency manager.

- Demonstrate the changing demands for emergency management.

- Discuss how the declining number of volunteers is impacting training of emergency managers.

- Show how business and the military have accepted management specialists.

☑ Summary

☑ Discussion Questions

☑ References

Introduction

The premise of this book is that emergency management skills are necessary to provide support to those engaged in tactical operations when responding to an emergency. The skill sets possessed by those in tactical response operations, whether in fire service, law enforcement, emergency medical service, or another specialty, are technical in nature. Such skill sets do not include the skills of emergency management such as planning, liaison, public information, logistics, purchasing, finance, administration, or gathering information or intelligence. When first responders are engaged in tactical operations, particularly in larger incidents, they will benefit from the support of emergency managers who can coordinate those services supportive of, but not necessarily directly involved in emergency response tactics. The growing demands for administrative support, from grant writing to planning, are the responsibility of management personnel, not first responders. The need for skilled administrative personnel has grown as emergency response has become more regional, and in some cases, national. In case after case, certainly from the attacks of September 11, 2001, to Hurricane Katrina, the most closely reviewed and often criticized aspect of the emergency response was not focused on the actions of first responders, but on how the incident was managed. A gap is growing between those involved in tactical operations and emergency managers. The gap will be resolved when the supportive role of emergency management personnel is examined for their contribution as coordinators who provide critical support to operations personnel, rather than for the degree to which they may be involved in command and control.

Traditional Career Paths to Emergency Manager

There never used to be a gap. Chiefs were customarily veteran firefighters or cops who had earned their stripes in the trenches of the fire service or law enforcement. It was unheard of to have a chief from anywhere else. Respect came from years of service, side by side with the personnel you were to lead. You knew what they did and how they did it. And more importantly, they knew you knew. Firefighting and law enforcement were, for the most part, local activities. You fought your own fire, alone. You apprehended your own criminals, alone. On occasion, you reached out to the neighboring town or village, or to a neighboring precinct or district in the cities, for additional apparatus or manpower. It was the early beginning of mutual aid, or the "all points bulletin." "Put out an APB," you would order when a suspect fled outside your jurisdiction. Things were simpler. There were not as many routes out of town, not as many hazardous materials to deal with, certainly not the complications that exist today in emergency management. The Chief knew what he had, and who he had. There was not anything or anybody else. Local fire departments stood alone as did local law enforcement departments.

What is changed? Why is it we say, "Every emergency is a local emergency," when, in fact, few of them are? Yes, they require immediate local response to suppress the fire, respond to the automatic alarm, or 9-1-1 call for emergency medical service; and they always will. The change is in the source of the response. It may not be as local as it used to be, hence, the source of the complexity. There are many more roads in a community, communications systems, absentee volunteers, greater threats, less isolation, and greater awareness of connections and interdependencies. Can you remember a time when firefighters were alerted by the ringing of a bell at the fire house or in the village square? Later there were loud sirens on the roof of the fire barn, and even later sirens positioned across town for better coverage. A fog horn blasted numbered combinations or codes indicating the location of the fire, or the fact that schools were closed for the day (7-7-7 in my community, my favorite signal as a child). Not only every firefighter, but every residence had a list posted with the numbers and the locations they signaled.

These early forms of callout systems succeeded because all of the responders were within the sound of the horn or siren. They were men and women who lived and worked in the community. As communities grew, and bedroom communities developed in the surrounding areas, responders either moved too far away to hear the callout, or they formed smaller, volunteer departments on the "outskirts" of town. Each had its own callout systems and signals. They were well staffed with ample numbers of volunteers and apparatus. In law enforcement, city jurisdictions concentrated within the city limits, while sheriff's departments and constables provided law enforcement to the surrounding areas. As the suburbs grew, local law enforcement departments were created, some by towns, some by villages. In the rural areas, sheriff's patrols and even the State Police provided protection.

As the systems for fire protection and law enforcement expanded to serve a more distributed population, the need for mutual aid systems developed. Smaller departments, fire or police, could support each other, saving the need for duplicating apparatus and specialists. There was also the need to communicate amongst departments more rapidly than in the past when all services were centralized in the city, town, or village.

Sharing resources required coordination, communication, and cooperation. When the shared services arrive on scene, they require direction and information.

As the complexity of working together increased, so did the requirement that chiefs devote full attention to managing those resources, taking their attention away from tactical operations.

Over the years, the complexity has grown—mutual aid systems, 9-1-1 dispatch, technological advances in callout systems (from plectrons, to pagers, alphanumeric pagers, radios, cell phones, rapid notification systems).

Key Terms

A Plectron is a specialized VHF/UHF single-channel, emergency alerting radio receiver, used to activate emergency response personnel, and disaster warning systems. Manufactured from the late 1950s, through the late 1990s, by the Plectron Corporation in Overton, Nebraska, hundreds-of-thousands of these radios were placed in homes of first responders across all of North America. This included ambulance crews, full-time and volunteer firefighters, off-duty specialized police response teams, Civil Defense members, and search and rescue teams. (http://en.wikipedia.org/wiki/Plectron retrieved 8/12/2007)

Though departments may be geographically dispersed, the callout systems have far-reaching capabilities, often dispatching multi-jurisdictional responders. When responders are dispatched from multiple agencies, coordination on scene is required. Today, outside the cities, this is the norm rather than the exception. Even within cities, resources from multiple disciplines—fire, law enforcement, EMS, public works, Red Cross, and the media—assemble with a need for coordination at the scene. And in many cases, the Chief doesn't know all the responders. The complexity requires following some sort of standard, direction, command and control.

The Need for a Coordinated Response

As emergency services grew in complexity, the need for greater coordination also grew. Response to a single incident, though handled thousands of times daily across the nation at the local level, now may involve multiple disciplines, agencies, departments, or jurisdictions. In fact, the greatest numbers of incidents are local—small fires, domestic disputes, ambulance calls, traffic accidents, burglaries.

NFPA Overview on the U.S. Fire Problem[1]

In 2005, US fire departments responded to an estimated 1,602,000 fires. These fires caused 3,675 civilian deaths and 17,925 civilian injuries. In the same year, 87 firefighters were fatally injured while on duty (R. Fahy and P. LeBlanc, 2006) and 80,100 suffered non-fatal injuries.

Often, only one responder is involved, particularly in law enforcement, but many times, multiple agencies are dispatched to the scene of an incident. Along with the first responders come the crowds and the media. Perimeters need to be established, crowds must be controlled for safety purposes, and the media requires our attention. Many of the activities in an emergency response have nothing to do with fire suppression, apprehension of a suspect, or caring for the injured. They pertain to safety, public information, liaison, planning, logistics, or finance and administration. These efforts, in addition to tactical operations, require coordination, leadership, command, and control. If the fire chief is to concentrate on fire suppression, the chief cannot be distracted with coordinating resources other than those directly involved in tactical operations. Examples are coordinating a Joint Family Assistance Center or warming or feeding the responders. Someone else needs to be available to handle coordination. Such coordination needs only to be supportive of the efforts of those in tactical operations—fire suppression, suspect apprehension, search and rescue, care of the injured.

Over time, as callout systems have made resources from multiple agencies more readily available to respond, the likelihood of several response organizations arriving on scene has increased. Electronic monitoring systems, scanners, for example, have even increased the number of non-responders, volunteers, and curious members of the public who arrive on scene. Even the highway system and the increased volume of traffic have increased the number of people who might just pass by the scene of an incident. Media response has changed from the local newspaper reporter, photographer, or the local radio station, to the arrival of media choppers overhead, dish antenna vehicles, and network connectivity. These make your local incident a national news story in minutes.

Is the fire chief to be so distracted that tactical response operations will suffer? Not on your life! Either the chief will simply ignore anything other than fire suppression, or someone else will handle coordinating all these entities. Who, you ask? Emergency managers can offer the support that chiefs need, or for that matter, support for anyone responsible for tactical operations.

Changing Demands on Emergency Managers

Some argue that Noah was the first emergency manager. He built the ark before the flood, an excellent example of preparedness. Would Noah's task have been accomplished more efficiently if he did not have to be concerned about gathering the animals, the feed, and documenting his magnificent story for publication? Similarly, first responders must focus on the emergency—putting out a fire, rescuing a trapped miner, apprehending a masked robber.

Early forms of emergency management were evident following World War II, focused on Civilian Defense. The job was largely preparedness. People were concerned with the threat of nuclear attack during the Cold War period. Local offices of Civilian Defense inspected facilities for suitability as fallout shelters. Supplies left over from the Korean War were distributed and stored in such facilities. Local governments created offices of Natural Disaster and Civil Defense whose responsibilities were to locate, inspect, and stock fallout shelters in case of nuclear attack. Prior to this time, sheltering, feeding, and otherwise providing for victims of natural disasters were the responsibilities of the American Red Cross. In many cases, the role of emergency manager was an additional responsibility assigned to fire chiefs, police chiefs, or experienced retirees from emergency services departments.

> Emergency Management is one of a number of terms which, since the end of the Cold War, have largely replaced Civil Defense, whose original focus was protecting civilians from military attack. Modern thinking focuses on a more general intent to protect the civilian population in times of peace as well as in times of war.[2]

A major difference between the role of the chief of a first responder unit and the role of an emergency manager is the duty related to preparedness or protection. Where the chief of a tactical operations unit focuses on response to a specific emergency, the emergency manager has a wider focus on planning and preparing for all hazards, in addition to those that have already occurred. Where first responders may transfer command and leave the scene of an emergency once the fire is out, for example, the role of an emergency manager may extend beyond fire suppression to such matters as providing shelter for the victims, responding to the media, conducting debrief meetings, and preparing after-action reports. This is not to ignore the work first responders perform following an incident. They, too, are busy with such matters as fire investigation, restoring apparatus, and equipment to a state of readiness, and, in some cases, conducting debriefs for personnel. Law enforcement officials have enormous responsibilities for compiling evidence, conducting interviews, and filing paperwork or reports in support of their investigations. What is important to note is that the responsibilities are different, and the skill sets are different. When compared, side by side, the skill sets of emergency managers have little in common with those of first responders involved in tactical operations.

According to B. Wayne Blanchard, Ph.D., CEM, Higher Education Project Manager, FEMA Emergency Management Institute,

> One would think it apparent by now that emergency managers at all levels of government need to have emergency management competencies when obtaining their positions. It should no longer be accepted that anyone, at any level of government, be put into a lead emergency management position without having such competencies as those described herein.[3]

The emergency management competencies referred to above have been the subject of an on-going project since 2003 wherein several professionals in emergency management have commented, edited, and refined a comprehensive list. As new developments, such as the response to Hurricane Katrina in 2005, have occurred, the list has been reviewed and rewritten. Emergency managers from across the country and from several foreign countries have contributed to identifying the core competencies. This will be presented in detail in Chapter 2. These competencies do not resemble those of first responders in tactical operations. Special training and education are required to ensure that emergency managers have mastered the core competencies. The core competencies required of emergency managers differ from those of tactical operations responders enough to require different education or training.

It is in addition to what may have been taught to or learned by experienced tactical operations responders. Emergency management supports tactical operations, and requires different competencies.

Declining Membership in Volunteer Emergency Response Units

In many instances, emergency responders and managers have gained valuable experience as members of volunteer organizations such as fire departments, ambulance corps, and Red Cross chapters. Some have gained such experience in the military. There was a time when several industries depended upon the military to train men and women who later accepted technical positions in industrial settings. Examples include the recruiting of technical specialists for the nuclear power industry from veterans of the nuclear Navy; radar technicians and engineers from military units; pilots for commercial airlines; and institutional bakers and chefs with prior military food service experience. When the military draft was discontinued, the availability of prospective employees with such training declined. The career management fields suffered the same condition. Many learned leadership skills in the military as officers. Certainly law enforcement and fire services careers benefited from recruiting those with prior military training in weapons handling skills, fire apparatus skills, and physical conditioning and agility.

Many former military personnel volunteered in their local communities, transferring their skills to become valuable members of volunteer fire departments, rescue squads, or Red Cross chapters. Emergency volunteer organizations depended upon local residents who could be called upon at any hour of the day. As residents in "bedroom" communities or rural areas migrated to employment in the nearby cities, their availability for emergency response declined. In some instances, rural or suburban volunteers fell to levels below those required to provide adequate fire or rescue services. Today, many such volunteer departments are forced to use mutual aid callout systems to muster the resources necessary to respond to even the smallest fire or accident. The declining membership in voluntary organizations is approaching the crisis level in many communities.

Just as the military served as a training ground or "farm team system" for many businesses and industries, the volunteer fire departments have been a type of "farm team" for emergency management. Those who accumulated valuable experience fighting fires in the volunteer departments acquired high degrees of transferable skills to emergency management positions. Of particular value, in addition to tactical operations skills, were those skills related to leadership, communication, command and control. Volunteers work with these skills as they advance in their departments from firefighter to lieutenant to assistant chief to chief. Some of my most accomplished students in associate, bachelor, and master's degree programs in emergency management are volunteer firefighters. They have chosen to study emergency management in order to prepare for emergency management careers. Above all, they recognize the different skill sets required when learning about emergency response planning, emergency exercise program design, or emergency communications. Their experience on the fire ground makes the education extremely relevant for them.

With the decline in membership in the volunteer departments, the pool of potential emergency managers with valuable first-responder experience is also declining. This is removing the traditional career ladder progression from volunteer to chief to emergency manager and making the need for emergency manager preparation more critical than in the past. Even though the skill sets are different, there is no denying the value of first-responder experience for prospective emergency managers. It contributes to their familiarity with terminology, equipment, standard operating procedures, apparatus, and personnel.

In summary, if the traditional "farm team system" is declining, emergency managers must be developed through other avenues. The education and training of emergency managers in college classrooms is replacing the "farm team." This is creating some resistance, just as it did in business and industry and in the military. *Also adds to credibility*

The Influence of Business and Industry in Emergency Management

In business, industry, and the military, adjustments were made to accept the leadership of college or academy educated leaders where, in the past, leaders rose up through the ranks. It was formerly inconceivable to have a plant manager who had not worked on the plant floor making or building the company's product. Similarly, it was formerly inconceivable to have a lieutenant, captain, or colonel who had not served in the enlisted ranks. There are educational institutions and military academies whose focus is on educating and training students for leadership. In American business, factory workers, many of them World War II veterans, applied their skills during the greatest expansion of industrialization in world history. They started at the bottom and worked their way up: journeyman, craftsman, supervisor, manager, superintendent, plant manager, vice president, president. They crossed over from union positions to management positions. They did not want the same path for their children, however. Following World War II, these hard-working Americans wanted something better for their sons and daughters. They worked hard and long so their children could attend college, preparing for management positions. One only needs to follow the transformation of an economy based in heavy industry to today's information economy to see that the education of post World War II citizens has created more "white collar" jobs than "blue collar." In this process, plant workers were required to accept the leadership of individuals who had never served on the plant floor. They knew business, finance, organizational development, human resource management, benefits administration, technology, and marketing, but not manufacturing. They knew how to market, sell, manage, budget, organize, lead, and negotiate, but not how to design, build, construct, or repair the product. Seasoned plant floor workers resisted this transition. They did not welcome the leadership of individuals who had never served on the plant floor. That resistance has been demonstrated in union negotiations, labor agreements, executive compensation packages, and succession plans. But somehow, business has adjusted. Corporations have recognized the critical need for educated employees, those who have learned about leadership, communication, technology, and scientific methods. Corporations are so intent on building an educated workforce that college recruiting, once in decline, has had a resurgence. Tuition assistance programs have supported employee attendance at colleges. Degree requirements have increased in job postings.

Similarly, the military has accepted the graduates of military academies as leaders. West Point, Annapolis, the Air Force Academy, the Coast Guard Academy, and college ROTC programs have produced military officers who assume leadership roles upon graduation, leading enlisted personnel with years of tactical experience. Why? Because the skill sets differ.

Case Study: My Daughter, the Lt. Colonel

When my daughter graduated from Fordham University, she spent a year working the graveyard shift in the Bureau of Criminal Justice in Brooklyn dealing with the release of prisoners in their own recognizance. She was interested in urban social work, and had rented a small apartment in Park Slope. When she called to tell me she had enlisted in the Marines and would soon be attending Officer's Candidate School at Quantico, I was relieved that she would be safer than in Brooklyn, but concerned because she had no prior military experience, not even ROTC. She graduated from OCS, and is today a Lieutenant Colonel. Her military career has helped me to learn the amount of administrative support required to field a combat military. For more than twenty years, she has served in a leadership position, doing necessary work, required to support our troops in both Desert Storm and the war in Iraq. She has never mentioned a weapon to me, nor any disrespect from those in her unit. She is a female officer, trained in leadership, management, social work, and discipline. Those skills are just as necessary in the military as the valued skills of tactical operations. One can't succeed without the other.

If business, industry, and the military have adjusted to the leadership of those trained outside the tactical operations generally associated with their manufacturing or combat environments, so may the fire service, law enforcement, emergency medical services, and others involved in responding to disasters and other emergencies.

Summary

The role of the emergency manager has become increasingly crucial as incidents and response capabilities have grown in complexity. First responders may be dispatched from multiple departments and disciplines. Fire and police chiefs must concentrate their efforts on tactical operations, often as Operations Section Chiefs under the Incident Command System. As support is requested by Operations Section Chiefs, the activities in public information, liaison, planning, logistics, finance, administration, information, and intelligence, often from multiple agencies, must be coordinated. Since the expansion of incident response staff has occurred over time, the need for specially trained emergency managers has increased.

Discussion Questions

1. Define emergency management and tactical operations.
2. Explain how emergency management supports tactical operations.
3. Describe the reasons that incident response is more than just local.
4. Why has business and industry grown to accept managers who did not rise up in the ranks or who do not have direct experience on the "assembly line"?
5. Explain how technology has played a part in creating a need for emergency management at the scene of an incident.

References

1. http://www.nfpa.org/assets/files//PDF/Research/USFires05.pdf retrieved October 23, 2007.
2. http://en.wikipedia.org/wiki/Emergency_management retrieved August 20, 2007.
3. Blanchard, B. Wayne. October 7, 2005. Top ten competencies for professional emergency management. http://www.training.fema.gov/EMIWeb/edu/docs/Blanchard%20-%20Competencies%20EM%20HiEd.doc retrieved 8/27/2007.

Chapter 2

Tactical Operations vs. Management Skills

Objectives of this chapter:

- Identify differences in skill sets of tactical operations and emergency management.

- Examine typical skill sets used in tactical operations.

- Examine typical skill sets for emergency managers.

- Explore how skill sets are acquired through training.

- Discuss the differences between training and education.

☑ Summary

☑ Discussion Questions

☑ References

Introduction

Tactical operations and emergency management are not the same. Though both are involved in emergency response, their skill sets differ greatly. Those involved in tactical operations are on scene to "fix the problem." They use technical skills related to their specialties such as firefighting, law enforcement, emergency medical services, hazardous materials response, or others. They are the "hands on" first responders.

Emergency management personnel have skill sets for addressing managerial tasks. They act in support of tactical operations by handling issues of coordination, facilitation, safety, public information, liaison, planning, logistics, finance, administration, information, and intelligence. Emergency management personnel often engage in prevention, preparedness, recovery, and restoration, in addition to response. They handle these aspects during response so that those involved in tactical operations have the resources and support necessary to fix the problem. In today's world, emergency mangers are also more directly involved in seeking funding, either through grant writing or formal requests for assistance following a Presidential declaration. In such cases, their jobs are administrative and often require administrative training and education to acquire the necessary skill sets.

Skill Sets for Tactical Operations

For the purposes of this discussion, "tactical operations" refers to all activities conducted in direct response to an emergency or incident that directly impact the resolution of the disruption or interruption of "business as usual." FEMA defines "tactics" as, "Deploying and directing resources on an incident to accomplish incident strategy and objectives."[1] Tactical operations refers to those resources that can solve the immediate problem. For example, when a pipe leaks in a basement, a plumber uses a wrench and other tools to stop the leak. The plumber is engaged in tactical operations, using tools and other resources that can be applied directly to the problem. In the case of a power failure, a line mechanic can use a hot stick to reset a fuse on a utility pole, or operate a bucket truck to access the equipment in need of repair. Both the plumber and the line mechanic are directly involved in fixing the problem. Both may be supported by dispatchers, regional controllers, billing personnel, and communicators, but only those directly involved in tactical operations can actually fix the problem. In short, they turn the wrench.

Specialized skill sets are required for adequate response and restoration. Fire, law enforcement, and emergency medical response personnel have skill sets required in their lines of work. There are many examples, and one that is realized every day would be the act of a firefighter entering a burning building prepared to put water on a fire. Layman's terms are used by this author to describe examples of tactical operations, because there is no attempt to suggest the author has practical or technical knowledge of firefighting, law enforcement, or other specialties outside of management. Nonetheless, a closer analysis would require the very expertise that tactical operations personnel bring to each and every emergency. We cannot minimize the degree of technical expertise and practice first responders possess whether they be firefighters, EMT's, IT analysts, HazMat specialists, hostage negotiators, or other technically proficient responders. In order for these highly-trained first responders to do their jobs, they may need support. The support they may require is often management support.

As technicians performing duties in tactical operations, the skill sets required are vast if viewed as a whole, but quite detailed and sophisticated when viewed in each specialty. Firefighting, for example, is not spraying water on a bonfire using a garden hose. The operation of modern firefighting apparatus and equipment, including personal protective equipment, is more like science. Dealing with high-pressure hoses, pumps, toxic smoke, extraordinarily high heat, and related conditions requires specialized training. Dealing with criminal behaviors, weapons, crime scenes, hostage situations, and active shooters requires specialized training. Dealing with a heart attack, a puncture wound, a blocked airway, shock, and extensive bleeding requires specialized training. The same is true for a number of first responder specialties, for example computer failures, power outages, dam failures, bomb threats, and school shootings. The point is that those involved in tactical operations have very specific skill sets, learned and practiced over a considerable period of time. For example, the list below from the State of Indiana lists the estimated time requirements and topics included in a basic firefighter training curriculum.

Mandatory and Basic Firefighter Training Curriculum

Estimate of Time Requirements

Module 1a	Orientation	1.5 hours
Module 1b	National Incident Management System	1 hour
Module 2	Personal Safety/Special Hazards	2.5 hours
Module 3	Self-Contained Breathing Apparatus	2.5 hours
Module 4a	Search and Rescue	2 hours
Module 4b	Extrication	2 hours
Module 5	Hose Loads	4 hours
Module 6	Fire Streams	4 hours
Module 7	Forcible Entry	2 hours
Module 8	Ladders	4 hours
Module 9	Ventilation	3 hours
Module 10a	Apparatus Familiarization	1 hour
Module 10b	Driver Awareness Level	2 hours
Module 11	Hazardous Materials – Awareness	8 hours *Basic
Module 12	Hazardous Materials – Operations	16 hours *Basic
Module 13	EMS Awareness	2 hours *Basic
Mandatory Curriculum Hours		31.5 hours
Basic Curriculum Hours**		26 hours
**Does not include CPR training[2]		

Similarly, the specialized training for law enforcement personnel contains highly technical skills required for their work in tactical operations. The example below is from the State of Michigan, one 262-hour section in a basic training curriculum requiring 562 hours to complete.

IV. Police Skills
[262 hours of a 562-hour course]

Functional Area *Subject Area* Module Title	Functional Area Hours *Subject Area* Module	*Hours* Hours
A. First Aid		*37*
1. Introduction to First Aid	IV-A-1	3
2. Bandaging Wounds and Controlling Bleeding	IV-A-2	3
3. Treating Fractures	IV-A-3	4
4. Administering CPR	IV-A-4	12
5. Treating Environmental First Aid Emergencies	IV-A-5	2
6. Treating Medical Emergencies	IV-A-6	3
7. Extricating and Transporting Injured Victims	IV-A-7	2
8. Practical First Aid Exercises	IV-A-8	8
B. Firearms		*84*
1. Laws and Knowledge Related to Firearms Use	IV-B-1	16
2. Firearm Skills	IV-B-2	48
3. Firearms Range Assessment	IV-B-3	8
4. Patrol Rifle	IV-B-4	12
C. Police Physical Skills		*77*
1. Mechanics of Arrest and Search	IV-C-1	8
2. Police Tactical Techniques	IV-C-2	5

Continued

3. Application of Subject Control	IV-C-3	4
4. Subject Control	IV-C-4	60
D. Emergency Vehicle Operation		*32*
1. Emergency Vehicle Operation: Legalities, Policies and Procedures	IV-D-1	8
2. Emergency Vehicle Operation Techniques	IV-D-2	24
E. Fitness and Wellness		*44*
1. Physical Fitness	IV-E-1	36
2. Health and Wellness	IV-E-2	8[3]

As we can see, the skill sets required for first responders involved in tactical operations are demanding and highly specialized. When an emergency occurs, the personnel trained in these disciplines are exactly the people we want to focus on "fixing the problem." The examples above are only topical lists from tables of contents. The skill sets listed in the objectives of any of the above course modules are far more detailed and specific. In the next section, one aspect of the Michigan basic training curriculum for law enforcement is presented as an example.

Specialized Skill Sets for Tactical Operations: An Example

In the description of the training module below, law enforcement trainees are presented a scenario in which the decision to use a patrol rifle is discussed (Section IV.B.4.1). The following module presents the common characteristics, types, models, components, and operation of various patrol rifles. The example is offered to provide a basis for identifying the types of skill sets that must be mastered by first responders, in this case Michigan law enforcement officers, as they engage in tactical operations. The example also is presented to contrast the training required for tactical response operations as opposed to the education recommended for emergency management.

Example:

IV.B.4.1 Participate in a Classroom Facilitated Discussion of a Critical Situation that Includes the Decision to Use the Patrol Rifle

a. Using a table-top scenario (see session I of the Facilitator Guide), actively participates in a facilitated discussion of a reality-based critical situation, by discussing:

- the nature of the problem;

- the skills or knowledge necessary to handle the situation;

- various possible responses to the situation; and

- how effective the selected responses are in handling the situation.

IV.B.4.2 Identify Common Characteristics of Patrol Rifles

a. Defines patrol rifle, or carbine, as used by many law enforcement agencies, as a weapon with the following common characteristics:

- semi-automatic;

- magazine-fed (usually external);

- gas operated;

- intermediate power;

- .223 or .30 caliber (on average);

- 18–24 in. barrel length (on average).

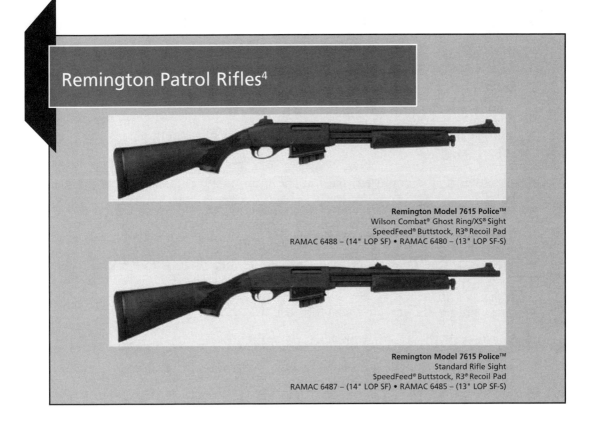

Remington Patrol Rifles[4]

Remington Model 7615 Police™
Wilson Combat® Ghost Ring/XS® Sight
SpeedFeed® Buttstock, R3® Recoil Pad
RAMAC 6488 – (14" LOP SF) • RAMAC 6480 – (13" LOP SF-S)

Remington Model 7615 Police™
Standard Rifle Sight
SpeedFeed® Buttstock, R3® Recoil Pad
RAMAC 6487 – (14" LOP SF) • RAMAC 6485 – (13" LOP SF-S)

b. Identifies the common types of rifles:

- semi-automatic;

- bolt action, where the shooter manually chambers a round;

- pump action, where a hand-grip pump chambers a round;

- lever operated, where a lever located under the trigger guard chambers a round;

- selective fire, including the ability to shoot auto and semi-auto;

- pistol caliber v. rifle caliber.

c. Recognizes the common models of semi-automatic rifles used by law enforcement agencies, including:

- Colt AR-15;

- Remington .223;

- Ruger Mini-14 .223;

- Heckler-Koch G36; and

- other common types of patrol rifles.

d. Identifies the major components of a typical patrol rifle and the functions of each:

- barrel, as the metal, cylindrical part of the firearm through which the bullet travels;

- butt, as the larger end of the rifle that enables placement against the shoulder when shooting;

- chamber, as the enclosed space at the bore of the rifle that holds the round;

- charging handle, as the device that withdraws the bolt to chamber a round;

- extractor, as the mechanism that pulls spent round from the chamber;

- ejector, as the mechanism that causes an empty shell or live round to be expelled from the rifle;

- magazine, as the device that holds the live rounds;

- safety, as the device that prevents the rifle from firing;

- sights, as the devices used to aim the rifle (front and rear);

- trigger, as a lever, when pulled manually by the finger, will fire the weapon; and

- trigger guard, as the part of the rifle that protects the trigger.

e. Describes the basic operations of the patrol rifle, including:

- administrative loading/unloading;

- emergency reloading;

- tactical reloading;

- adjusting sights; and

- use of sling.[5]

The example above involves only one of hundreds of aspects of a law enforcement officer's interactions with "tools of the trade," decisions, identifications, and operations that might be implemented in the act of responding to an incident. An analysis of the skills for tactical response operations presented above is useful in contrasting them to the emergency management skills that follow.

Skill Sets for Emergency Management

The skill sets for emergency management differ from those of personnel in tactical operations. The Commonwealth of Virginia lists skills, knowledge, abilities, and tasks as general occupational qualifications for Emergency Management Specialists commonly recognized by employers. The example below contains such a list.

Skills, Knowledge, Abilities and Tasks

(Technical and Functional Expertise)
Skills
Note: The technical and functional skills listed below are based on general occupational qualifications for Emergency Management Specialists commonly recognized by most employers. Typically, you will not be required to have all of

Continued

the skills listed to be a successful performer. Recruitment and selection standards for an individual state job must be based on the specific knowledge, skills, and abilities for that job as indicated in the job announcement and job description in the Employee Work Profile.

1. Understanding written sentences and paragraphs in work related documents.
2. Talking to others to convey information effectively.
3. Using logic and reasoning to identify the strengths and weaknesses of alternative solutions, conclusions or approaches to problems.
4. Understanding the implications of new information for both current and future problem-solving and decision-making.
5. Monitoring/assessing performance of yourself, other individuals, or organizations to make improvements or take corrective action.
6. Adjusting actions in relation to others' actions.
7. Persuading others to change their minds or behavior.
8. Actively looking for ways to help people.
9. Identifying complex problems and reviewing related information to develop and evaluate options and implement solutions.
10. Determining the kind of tools and equipment needed to do a job.
11. Conducting tests and inspections of products, services, or processes to evaluate quality or performance.
12. Determining how a system should work and how changes in conditions, operations, and the environment will affect outcomes.
13. Identifying measures or indicators of system performance and the actions needed to improve or correct performance, relative to the goals of the system.
14. Managing one's own time and the time of others.
15. Obtaining and seeing to the appropriate use of equipment, facilities, and materials needed to do certain work.
16. Motivating, developing, and directing people as they work.

Knowledge

Note: The technical and functional knowledge statements listed below are based on general occupational qualifications for Emergency Management Specialists commonly recognized by most employers. Typically, you will not be required to have all of the knowledge listed to be a successful performer.

Recruitment and selection standards for an individual state job must be based on the specific knowledge, skills, and abilities for that job as indicated in the job announcement and job description in the Employee Work Profile.

1. Relevant equipment, policies, procedures, and strategies to promote effective local, state, or national emergency management operations for the protection of people, data, property, and institutions.

2. Principles of situational analysis and planning.

3. Principles and methods for curriculum and training design, teaching, and instruction for individuals and groups.

4. Business and management principles involved in strategic planning, resource allocation, human resources modeling, leadership technique, production methods, and coordination of people and resources.

5. Principles and methods for moving people or goods by air, rail, sea, or road, including the relative costs and benefits.

6. Materials, methods, and the tools involved in the construction or repair of houses, buildings, or other structures such as highways and roads.

7. The structure and content of the English language including the meaning and spelling of words, rules of composition, and grammar.

Abilities

Note: The technical and functional abilities listed below are based on general occupational qualifications for Emergency Management Specialists commonly recognized by most employers. Typically, you will not be required to have all of the abilities listed to be a successful performer. Recruitment and selection standards for an individual state job must be based on the specific knowledge, skills, and abilities for that job as indicated in the job announcement and job description in the Employee Work Profile.

1. Communicate information and ideas in speaking so others will understand.

2. Respond to a wide range of issues under stress.

3. Tell when something is wrong or is likely to go wrong. It does not involve solving the problem, only recognizing there is a problem.

4. See details at a distance.

Continued

gender?

? gender?

5. Speak clearly so others can understand you.

6. Quickly analyze, make sense of, combine, and organize information into meaningful patterns.

7. Shift back and forth between two or more activities or sources of information (such as speech, sounds, touch, or other sources) without being distracted.

8. Know your location in relation to the environment or to know where other objects are in relation to you.

9. Identify or detect a known pattern (a figure, object, word, or sound) that is hidden in other distracting material.

10. Listen to and understand information and ideas presented through spoken words and sentences.

11. Focus on a single source of sound in the presence of other distracting sounds.

12. Read and understand information and ideas presented in writing.

13. Communicate information and ideas in writing so others will understand.

14. See details at close range (within a few feet of the observer).

Tasks

*Note: The following is a list of sample tasks typically performed by **Emergency Management Specialists**. Employees in this occupation will not necessarily perform all of the tasks listed.*

1. Collaborate with other officials in order to prepare and analyze damage assessments following disasters or emergencies.

2. Conduct surveys to determine the types of emergency-related needs that will need to be addressed in disaster planning, or provide technical support to others conducting such surveys.

3. Consult with officials of local and area governments, schools, hospitals, and other institutions in order to determine their needs and capabilities in the event of a natural disaster or other emergency.

4. Coordinate disaster response or crisis management activities such as ordering evacuations, opening public shelters, and implementing special needs plans and programs.

5. Direct emergency response teams and provides on-site investigations.

6. Design and administer emergency/disaster preparedness training courses that teach people how to effectively respond to major emergencies and disasters.

7. Develop and maintain liaisons with municipalities, county departments, and similar entities in order to facilitate plan development, response effort coordination, and exchanges of personnel and equipment.

8. Develop and perform tests and evaluations of emergency management plans in accordance with state and federal regulations.

9. Inspect facilities and equipment such as emergency management centers and communications equipment in order to determine their operational and functional capabilities in emergency situations.

10. Keep informed of activities or changes that could affect the likelihood of an emergency, as well as those that could affect response efforts and details of plan implementation.

11. Keep informed of federal, state, and local regulations affecting emergency plans, and ensure that plans adhere to these regulations.

12. Administers public emergency recovery assistance programs.[6]

The example from Virginia was chosen because it comes from the employer, not from trainers or educators of emergency managers. When seeking to prepare individuals for career positions, it is a common practice to examine the workplace requirements, the knowledge, skill sets, abilities, and tasks one must be able to perform on the job. This is not to say that all preparatory programs teach only these things, as some individuals prefer a more broad-based liberal arts curriculum when preparing for their chosen profession. In emergency management, as you can see from the Virginia example, desired capabilities are those pertaining directly to the duties that might be assigned and ultimately mastered by an emergency manager.

There is little similarity between the requirements of the emergency management specialist and those listed earlier for either a firefighter or a law enforcement officer. Though many emergency managers have prior service as first responders, they will clearly describe their emergency manager's duties as very different from the duties they performed as first responders. If the skill sets required of emergency managers are so different from those of first responders, why should time as a first responder be necessary to perform management duties? Like business, industry, the military, and hospital administrators, one need not be proficient in the technical areas in order to be successful in management. The specific competencies recommended for emergency managers will be discussed in detail in Chapters 5 and 6.

Acquisition of Skill Sets

The means by which first responders and emergency managers acquire knowledge and skills are different. Training for tactical response operations involves practice with things such as apparatus, tools, weapons, medical supplies, search and rescue dogs, and personal protective equipment. Preparation for emergency management involves applying regulations, adhering to Presidential Directives, coordination, project management tools, planning, and finance. The instructional strategies differ due to the contrasts in the nature of the skills and knowledge to be acquired.

Tactical Response Operations Training

Skill sets for tactical operations or emergency management are developed in different ways. Typically, tactical operations specialists undergo extensive training, some of which is in the classroom, but much of which is "hands on." Since many tactical operations activities involve tools, equipment, weapons, and difficult environments, training is often combined with ample opportunities for practice. Firefighters, for example, train on apparatus so as to practice their skills in the correct operation of that apparatus. Law enforcement trainees use weapons and live ammunition, high-speed vehicles, and martial arts. Training requirements are often expressed in terms of "hours" to ensure that prescribed, often mandated, training is in compliance with regulations or laws. Safety is a major concern when learning to use equipment for dangerous situations.

Skills are also acquired and developed in the trenches. Experience is an excellent teacher as long as the experience is correct. Coaching by qualified, experienced personnel is also effective. Practice does not make perfect unless such practice is performed correctly or with coaching to ensure proper procedures are applied. Traditionally, time in service has been a trusted measure of training and competence. Veteran or highly experienced firefighters and law enforcement officers have been used as trainers both in the classroom and in the field.

The lack of time these experienced personnel or seasoned veterans are available to be trainers is a serious concern. Ask any firefighter or emergency medical technician how many hours they spend in training, and they will tell you that the schedule is very demanding. Maintaining certification takes many hours. The problem is serious in both volunteer and paid professional fire departments. The volunteers have limited time due to the demands of their regular, full time employment, and paid, professionals have limited budgets for training. Shortages of trained personnel in both cases are a concern.

As an alternative to "on-the-job" training, fire and police academies have assumed greater roles in training pre-service and in-service firefighters and law enforcement officers. Where departments have been involved in training their own personnel, academies have supplemented or replaced department-based training. State Fire Academies and the National Fire Academy in Emmitsburg, Maryland, have provided training opportunities for firefighters. Police academies operated by states, counties, and colleges have provided training for law enforcement. First aid and CPR training has traditionally been provided by the Red Cross.

For tactical operations, the tradition of training has been well established, whether it be done locally, within a department by seasoned veterans, or provided by fire schools, academies, or State and Federal agencies. For some disciplines, training is highly specialized and not easily accessible. Examples are HazMat training, weapons of mass destruction training, National Disaster Medical Services (NDMS) training, search and rescue training, and underwater rescue training. These specialists are provided training more commonly on a regional basis.

Emergency Management Training and Education

For emergency management, preparation is quite different. Emergency managers have traditionally come up through the ranks of first responder organizations. They often have prior training in their respective disciplines. Many have availed themselves of FEMA online or independent study, correspondence courses, taking and passing the examinations to receive course completion certificates. Some have completed the entire suite of management courses and have been recognized by their state emergency management office for their achievement. Emergency management course content is not as easily accessed in the field as tactical operations content might be. Much of the content in emergency management has been learned through classroom instruction. For example, in recent years, FEMA has offered ICS 100, ICS 200, and Independent Study courses such as IS-700 and IS-800 online. For example, see http://www.training.fema.gov/EMIWeb/IS/is200.asp. Higher level ICS courses (300–400) are recommended to be taught in the classroom by state emergency management trainers or proprietary ICS training providers. Emergency management skills are more administrative than the applied skills used in tactical operations. Course objectives in emergency management are often presented in lectures, in Power Point presentations, in tabletop simulations, and in classroom discussions. Assessments or tests are normally written, requiring either multiple-choice or short-answer responses. They are not often similar to the practical skills demonstrations of proficiency associated with learning skills in tactical operations. Educators might say that emergency management training is more cognitive and affective than psychomotor, whereas tactical operations training focuses on the ability to operate equipment and perform physical tasks which are more psychomotor in nature.

Training vs. Education

The mention of the cognitive, affective, and psychomotor domains of learning introduces the topic of training vs. education. Are they different? This is an age-old discussion amongst both trainers and educators. Some say simplistically, "We train a person to operate, and we educate a person to think." Not so! It would be drastic to say that trained firefighters do not think. Thinking skills are a part of problem solving, and firefighters solve problems every day. It would further be shameful to separate training from education by the difficulty of the material to be mastered. Personally, I find the work of a law enforcement officer riding a motorcycle on freeway traffic patrol extremely complex, especially when one considers the inherent dangers of the motorcycle, the traffic, and the exposure to potential criminals. Yet, we say we train firefighters and law enforcement officers on traffic patrol, but we educate emergency managers. Again, not so. Both are offered training and education. I prefer the term "professional development," which includes both training and education. The term speaks to the development of the individual rather than to the mode of instruction or difficulty of the material to be learned. When one is trained to perform new tasks, one is developing new skills. When one is educated to new ways of thinking and doing, one is developing new ideas and skills. When the training or education is in preparation for enhanced performance on the job, or preparation for job advancement, the term "professional" applies to that individual's career development.

Those in tactical operations may seek training to develop all sorts of skills, not just those physical or mechanical skills associated with the performance of a physical task or the operation of a piece of emergency response apparatus. They might also engage in training to develop communication skills, supervisory skills, problem-solving skills or technical skills related to the handling of hazardous materials. Similarly, those in emergency management may seek training or education to learn about laws and regulations, applications for disaster public assistance, crisis communications, leadership, mitigation planning, or conducting after-action meetings. They might also seek skills training in radio operation, computer-based GIS operation, conducting WebEx sessions, entering a code into a rapid notification system, or operating early warning or Emergency Alert System (EAS) equipment. Both tactical operations personnel and emergency management personnel often benefit from training and education.

There are numerous ways to develop new skills or to acquire knowledge. Emergency response and emergency management are presented regularly with new avenues for learning, career preparation, and development. Traditional modes of instruction (fire schools, police academies, on-the-job training, and classroom instruction) are being enhanced by new instructional technologies that make access to lessons easier. Finding the time to attend upon instruction is a major concern for career first responders. Requirements for maintaining certification demand many hours in training. Degree programs demand an extensive commitment of time. New instructional technologies are making access easier.

At last count, there are approximately 142 colleges and universities offering programs in emergency management and related fields in the United States alone. There is a growing number in other countries. Though all are not online, the number and the geographical distribution of campuses offering such programs makes access far more convenient than in the past. In Chapter 5, the attributes of college certificate and degree programs will be discussed in detail. For now, it is important to note that technology has made many college degree programs accessible through distance or online learning. Outstanding examples can be found at American Public University System at http://www.apus.edu/index.htm, Boston University's graduate degree in emergency management and organizational continuity at http://www.bu.edu/online/online_programs/certificate_programs/emergency_management.html, the Empire State College on-line degree in emergency management, homeland security, and fire administration at http://www.esc.edu/ESConline/Across_ESC/cdl/cdl.nsf/byid/5C234B87ADB4C5A08525705E0050AB94.

Summary

The skill sets required for tactical operations differ from those required for emergency management. Tactical operations skills tend to be technical and specialized, involving the safe and effective use of specialized equipment. The training is often "hands on" in settings where the equipment can be demonstrated and actually used by the learners. The physical implementation of the equipment is critical. Relevant examples include fire apparatus, personal protective equipment, weapons, Hazmat gear, underwater rescue equipment, intravenous lines, and so forth. Training in specialties seldom overlaps into other specialties. For example, EMT's are not often trained in the use of weapons. When several specialists are dispatched to a single incident, which is often the case, coordination and communication can become a crucial problem demanding the important role of the emergency manager.

Emergency managers may acquire their skill sets through training and education. The content does not involve as much technical information as is required for tactical operations. Skill sets are included from management, finance, communications, strategic planning, grant administration, public crisis communications, supervision, and delegation. Specialized knowledge included in emergency management professional development might include emergency operations center concepts and skills, emergency planning, exercise program design, facilitation of exercises, exercise evaluation, business case preparation for budget approval, disaster recovery laws and regulations, writing standard operating procedures, telecommunications or rapid notification systems. Many of these skills, concepts and practices can be acquired in the classroom. Classroom instruction, when combined with exercises, role plays, simulations, and internships is highly desirable. Though much of emergency management training is available online and on-the-job, Chapter 5 will discuss what colleges have to offer.

In conclusion, the skill sets of those in tactical operations differ significantly from those in emergency management. The acquisition of skills may be characteristically more practical, "hands on," for tactical operations and possibly more classroom instruction for emergency management. Though different topics apply, both emergency management and tactical response operations require training and education. There are, increasingly, new ways to deliver these topics to both groups.

Discussion Questions

1. Describe training that may be required for firefighters, law enforcement officers or EMT's.
2. List the areas in which emergency managers should be able to demonstrate proficiency.
3. Why is it more likely that those involved in tactical operations would receive more "hands on" training than classroom instruction?
4. Who requires more "hands on" practice through drills or exercises—tactical operations personnel or emergency managers?
5. How would drills and exercises differ for both groups?
6. What types of drills or exercises would be suitable for both groups at the same time?
7. If the skill sets differ, should the training or instructional settings or methods differ?
8. Why is it unrealistic to separate training and education?

References

1. http://training.fema.gov/emiweb/IS/ICSResource/ICSResCntr_Glossary.htm #T retrieved 9/1/2007.
2. Indiana Department of Homeland Security, State Fire Marshall, Division of Training, Mandatory and Basic Firefighter Training Curriculum, http://www.in.gov/dhs/files/currintro.pdf retrieved 9/1/2007
3. Michigan Commission on Law Enforcement Standards Basic Training Curriculum and Training Objectives, http://www.michigan.gov/documents/Basic_Training_Manual_166396_7.pdf retrieved 9/1/2007
4. Remington Law Enforcement and Federal Agencies catalog, http://www.remingtonle.com/rifles/7615.htm retrieved 9/2/2007.
5. Michigan Commission on Law Enforcement Standards Basic Training Curriculum and Training Objectives, Patrol Rifle, IV-B-4, http://www.michigan.gov/documents/Basic_Training_Manual_166396_7.pdf retrieved 9/2/2007.
6. Career Guide for Emergency Management Specialists, Commonwealth of Virginia, http://jobs.state.va.us/careerguides/emergencymgmtspec.pdf retrieved 9/1/2007.

Chapter 3

The Demands of Managing According to the Incident Command System (ICS)

Objectives of this chapter:

- List the Incident Command System command and general staff positions.

- Describe the role of the Operations Section Chief.

- Discuss how the Operation Section Chief is supported by the command and other general staff.

- Describe the roles, responsibilities and skill sets for the command and general staff positions.

☑ Summary

☑ Discussion Questions

☑ References

Introduction

Whereas many incident command system (ICS) courses stress the importance of the Incident Commander's role, the approach here will discuss how the Incident Commander and all other command and general staff positions support the Operations Section Chief, the person who can actually "fix" the problem. For the purpose of examining the gap between tactical operations and emergency management, the discussion of the ICS will be limited to the positions in the command and general staff. The ways in which these positions interact in support of "fixing the problem" will be our focus, not the specific or technical duties of each position. These positions, with the exception of the Operations Section Chief are engaged in management, not command and control.

ICS Command Staff

The ICS originated in the fire service and has become the standard for incident command nationwide. Excellent instructional materials for ICS are widely available from FEMA, State Emergency Management Offices, local emergency response organizations, or proprietary training providers. For purposes of this book, the discussion of ICS will focus on the management skills and how those skills of the command and general staff positions support tactical operations.

NIMS ICS

The Incident Command System (ICS) is the combination of facilities, equipment, personnel, procedures, and communications operating within a common organizational structure, designed to aid in domestic incident management activities. It is used for a broad spectrum of emergencies, from small to complex incidents, both natural and manmade, including acts of catastrophic terrorism. ICS is used by all levels of government—Federal, State, local, and tribal, as well as by many private-sector and nongovernmental organizations. ICS is usually organized around five major functional areas: command, operations, planning, logistics, and finance and administration. A sixth functional area, Intelligence, may be established if deemed necessary by the Incident Commander, depending on the requirements of the situation at hand.[1]

In each ICS course I have attended, all of which have been in the public sector and taught by first responders, the management system has been presented as a "command and control" system. In most cases, material is presented "top down," starting with the Incident Commander. The term "commander" is at the root of the problem in understanding the management function of the position. The positions on the organizational chart in Figure 3.1 depict the structure of ICS command and general staff positions that are managed by the Incident Commander. Since the publishing of the National Incident Management System (NIMS) in 2004, I have chosen to add the Information/Intelligence Function on the line with Section Chiefs, though it may be placed elsewhere at the discretion of the Incident Commander. It is added here as a reminder of how important the function has become since September 11.

The ICS is a "management by objectives" system. This is a term very familiar to managers in the private sector. Of importance is noting from where the objectives originate, from the needs of Operations. They are the stepping stones to "fixing the problem." Start with the Operations Section Chief, where I choose to begin a discussion, presentation or training class on ICS.

Figure 3.1 The ICS model

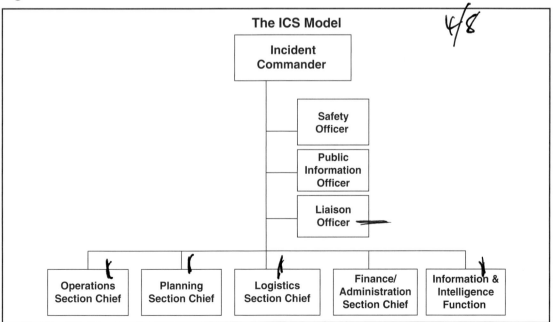

In many incidents, crises, or emergencies, the goal is to correct the situation and restore normal conditions (pre-incident conditions) as safely and soon as possible. There are combinations of resources required to do this. Those resources are the personnel and apparatus in the Operations Section. In the case of a fire, it is the resource that can extinguish the fire; in a blackout, the power utility personnel; in an IT failure, the IT personnel; in a school shooting, law enforcement. Commanding the resources that can accomplish the safe response and do the work of tactical operations is the responsibility of the Operations Section Chief. In my opinion, everyone else on the ICS chart is there to support the Operations Section Chief.

With this in mind, the duties of each other position on the chart become clearer. It is not a "command and control" model as much as it is a model for coordinating all those whose service is in support of Operations.

The Operations Section Chief

Regardless of the nature of the emergency, the person who fills the Operations Section Chief's position will need to have special expertise related to the type of incident. In any case, the goal of ICS is to support the Operations Section Chief by tackling some or all of these responsibilities so the Operations Section Chief can remain focused on solving the problem.

If the incident is a fire, the Operations Section Chief (usually a fire chief) is responsible for putting out the fire. Sounds simple? It is not. If the incident involves an active shooter, the Operations Section Chief might be a police chief or the juris-diction's chief law enforcement officer. Operations Section Chiefs are skilled responders with the knowledge and the tools to handle the emergency. If they need anything, other than the resources to which they have immediate access, they often need someone to support them. Communications systems are in place, in most jurisdictions, to permit a fire chief or chief law enforcement officer to request assistance when needed. It is usually a matter of a radio message to a central dispatcher. In more complex incidents, the need for additional resources might require planning, communicating, sourcing, transporting, funding, and a review of the safety of the on-going situation. It may require responding to the media or working with volunteer organizations such as the Red Cross.

What is critical is that incident command be established, when deemed necessary, after the initial assessment of the emergency or as needed thereafter. In order to support Operations, the ICS must be in place. A quality of ICS that supports all sizes of incidents is that the system is scalable, adjustable to any size incident. Once command has been established, decisions can be made to expand the support system as needed. If ICS is to be supportive of the Operations Section, those in Command and General Staff positions must understand their roles and responsibilities. One objective of ICS training is to instruct responders and emergency operations center personnel in these roles. Readers who may be unfamiliar with the ICS might be well served by accessing the FEMA online training available as an introduction. See http://training.fema.gov/EMIWeb/Is/is100.asp the FEMA Independent Study Program: IS-100 Introduction to Incident Command System, ICS-100 and http://training.fema.gov/EMIWeb/IS/is700.asp for the FEMA Independent Study Program: IS-700 National Incident Management System (NIMS), An Introduction. These are both excellent places to start.

The Role of the Operations Section Chief

The Operations Section Chief is the person best equipped to "fix the problem." He or she has the technical skills, the capabilities, and command of the resources most likely to respond to, contain, or restore to normal, the emergency situation. The specific role of the Operations Section Chief may depend on the nature of the incident. There are many ways to determine the appropriate person for the job. The type of emergency, disaster, or incident, in some places, invokes laws that grant statutory power to certain department chiefs, for example, the fire chief in a Home Rule state at the scene of a structure fire. Law enforcement may be the lead agency at a bank robbery involving hostages, so the logical Operations Section Chief might be a high level law enforcement officer from that jurisdiction. In the case of an IT failure in small city, the right person for the job might be the city's chief information officer. At the scene of a mass casualty incident involving a toxic poisoning, the appropriate person might be the chief medical examiner.

The "Field Operations Guide" (ICS 420-1) from Firescope California (June, 2004) describes the Operations Section Chief as follows:

> The Operations Section Chief, a member of the General Staff, is responsible for the management of all operations directly applicable to the primary mission and ensuring the overall safety and welfare of all Section personnel. The Operations Chief activates and supervises organization elements in accordance with the Incident Action Plan and directs its execution. The Operations Chief also directs the preparation of unit operational plans, requests or releases resources, makes expedient changes to the Incident Action Plan as necessary, and reports such to the Incident Commander.[2]

An item for consideration in the above position description, is, "Which came first, the Incident Action Plan (IAP), or the Operations Section Chief's request for resources and input into the IAP?" An IAP is the plan for the next operational period. It comes about when information from the Operations Section is presented possibly in an initial briefing meeting, even prior to the establishment of the first set of objectives in an IAP. In short, no one really knows the needs, resources, tactics, or strategies to be involved in "fixing the problem" until input is received from Operations. Operations gains its insights into the IAP through initial on-scene assessment of the situation. Sometimes that assessment begins even before arriving on scene, using information provided from those at the scene at the time of the incident, or from prior knowledge of the scene, its proximity to other structures, or knowledge of hazardous materials stored on site. No matter how the information is obtained by the first responders, either they or their Operations Section Chief will relay the description of the incident and the resources needed prior to the creation of an IAP.

Some incidents are considered to be too small in nature to require the establishment of an ICS response organization. A single resource, a fire chief, for example, may respond and direct all resources on scene. This happens thousands of times daily in the United States. In larger, more complex incidents, establishment of an ICS command and general staff is warranted. The main reason for expanding to the ICS model is that the on-scene commanding officer identifies the need for additional support. If that is the case, then all members of the ICS command and general staff should see their roles as supporting the Operations Section Chief, the person whose people can "fix the problem."

As the distance grows between "fixing the problem" with specialized, technical skills to the roles and responsibilities of other members of the command staff or general staff, there will be an observed shift from the need for technical skills to management skills.

The Severe Windstorm Response example (see the boxed text) illustrates, an Operations Section Chief has the personnel to directly respond to the incident and actively engage in the primary mission—safely clean up the debris from fallen trees after the storm to restore the public roadways, drainage systems, and other critical infrastructure. The personnel know how to clear trees from roadways. What they did not have was the equipment to complete the job. In a case such as this, one does not want the Operations Section Chief distracted by having to contract for the lease of the required equipment. There are support personnel skilled in lease contracting who work in the Finance/Administration Section. They have the required management skills to see that the Operations Section Chief can get what is needed to "fix the problem."

Severe Windstorm Response

Following a severe wind storm during which an estimated 30,000 trees fell in Syracuse, New York, the Director of the Department of Public Works served as the Operations Section Chief. He was attempting to direct resources to remove debris from streets, drainage systems, and certain critical infrastructure. He assembled Strike Teams and Task Forces to work together in designated geographical areas. Teams included power utility line crews to determine that downed power lines were safe, National Guard personnel to use chainsaws to cut up the trees, heavy equipment operators to load the debris into dump trucks, and DPW personnel to haul the debris to designated areas where the debris could be ground up in large tub grinders. In short, four different agencies were providing personnel to work together on debris removal.

The Problem: None of the agencies involved had a tub grinder, much less a dozen of them.

The Solution: The Operations Section Chief, acting on the IAP Objective to clear the streets and drainage systems by removing the debris, could call upon first the Planning Section Chief to include 12 tub grinders as required resources in the IAP, and could rely upon the Finance/Administration Section Chief to source and lease the tub grinders. The Logistics Section Chief would then deliver the equipment to the designated sites as per the Operations Section Chief's directions.

Result: The debris removed was ground into wood chips that the local DPW could handle.

What about the Incident Commander's role? When two diverse resources with varied skill sets are asked to work together (DPW and lease contract personnel) their efforts must be coordinated, starting with approval of the plan to use tub grinders to solve the problem. The Incident Commander is responsible for both the approval and the coordination. Other ICS personnel might also be involved in supporting Operations. For example, the Safety Officer might want to know if DPW personnel have been trained in the safe and appropriate operation of tub grinders. The terms of the lease might include trained staff to operate the equipment. There may be a regulation that the lease of such equipment be competitively bid rather than sole sourced. The Finance/Administration Section may have personnel knowledgeable in such matters. The Liaison Office may have to meet with four vendors, all of whom want information about the lease because they all lease, sell, or service such equipment. These issues should be handled by management personnel, because those involved in tactical operations are busy clearing the trees from the streets.

How the Operations Section Chief is Supported by Command Staff

Each Command Staff position has a special, managerial function to perform in support of Operations. If we accept the premise that the Operations Section Chief has the personnel and capability to "fix the problem," then we certainly want to provide support. One critical support function is safety. The Operations Section needs to work safely for the benefit of its own personnel and for the benefit of the public, particularly those most directly affected by the emergency or disaster. Although safety is everyone's responsibility, there may be issues affecting safety that are not as evident as others. The Safety Officer, a direct report to the Incident Commander, performs the following function:

> The Safety Officer's function is to develop and recommend measures for assuring personnel safety, and to assess and/or anticipate hazardous and unsafe situations. Having full authority of the Incident Commander, the Safety Officer can exercise emergency authority to stop or prevent unsafe acts.[3]

The Safety Officer supports the Operation Section by overseeing the safety of all operations, particularly in instances where individuals may be placed in harm's way unknowingly. For example, Operations personnel may be engaged in fighting a fire using aerial ladders and not be aware of an approaching electrical storm where lightening strikes could endanger them. Law enforcement officers could respond to a bank robbery and be unaware of the release of a toxic gas by the suspects to stall law enforcement response. During a sustained response and recovery, safety audits might be performed to ensure that proper safety gear and safety measures are being observed by all responding personnel. In some incidents, dozens of safety audits might be performed over a period of several days. With the Safety Officer conducting such audits, the Operations Section Chief is assured of safe working conditions while directing attention to "fixing the problem."

Whenever an incident occurs, there is almost immediately an information gap. Otto Lerbinger states, "Because every crisis creates an information gap, an organization has a better chance of affecting news coverage when it speedily fills the void."[4] For this and other reasons, someone close to the incident needs to address the media and other stakeholders. If an Operations Section Chief is to remain focused on fixing the problem, a Public Information Officer should be charged with the responsibility for communicating with stakeholders. The Public Information Officer (PIO), like the Safety Officer, is a member of the command staff and reports directly to the Incident Commander.

The Information Officer is responsible for developing and releasing information about the incident to the news media, to incident personnel, and to other appropriate agencies and organizations.[5]

The PIO can protect the Operations Section Chief (police chief, fire chief, and so forth) from interruptions by information seekers, be they from the media or other stakeholder groups. One way the PIO supports Operations is by establishing a location where official releases will be posted or news briefings held, which is a safe distance away from the incident site. When reporters, camera crews, and agency representatives know that the best information will be available at such a location, they are more apt to show up there than to continue to gain access to the chief directing tactical operations. In short, the Public Information Officer supports tactical operations by handling the release of accurate and timely information about the incident.

In addition to the news media and incident response personnel, there may be others who need information about an incident. Examples are labor union officials, volunteer organizations, investor relations entities (stock brokers, bankers, and shareholders), suppliers, customers, family members, and neighboring businesses. Collectively they are called "Agency Representatives," and they are addressed by a Liaison Officer. The Liaison Officer, a member of the Command Staff, "… is the point of contact for the Agency Representatives assigned to the incident by assisting or cooperating agencies."[6]

Sometimes, the Liaison Officer communicates with informal agency representatives, those with a stake in the outcome of the incident, but not necessarily assigned to the incident. An example might be an administrator or officer from a neighboring school or business. Agency Representatives may be interested in a number of concerns regarding the incident. Vincent Covello lists the following: human health, trust, safety, environmental, information, ethics, economics, responsibility, legal, process, pets/livestock, religious, and fairness.[7] These concerns, though often addressed by the PIO in news or employee briefings, should also be addressed by the Liaison Officer with Agency Representatives, family members, or others. Once again, by performing this function, the Liaison Officer is supporting those in tactical operations.

Last but not least, the Incident Commander supports tactical operations in a number of ways. First, the Incident Commander (IC) has the authority to provide overall management of the incident. Management is not the same thing as tactical operations. The IC is responsible for coordinating the efforts and activities of the Command Staff and the General Staff in support of "fixing the problem." The position checklist for an Incident Commander includes such behavioral terms as assess, determine, establish, consider, ensure, approve, coordinate, inform, authorize, and order. These refer to the general management activities required to coordinate the activities necessary to support operations. For example, the Incident Commander approves the IAP crafted by the Planning Section Chief with input from all aspects of the incident response. The IC approves media releases crafted by the Public Information Officer. "The Incident Commander's responsibility is the overall management of the incident."[8]

Some might ask why list the Incident Commander last when discussing the Command Staff. The reason is a justification of the case that all members of the ICS Command and General Staff are there to support the Operations Section Chief. Whether one is a specialist in safety, public information, liaison, planning, logistics or finance/administration, one is only assigned to help the tactical, first responders to "fix the problem."

Role Clarification and Skill Sets for Command Staff

The skill sets for Command Staff are as highly specialized as those of first responders in tactical operations. They are just in different fields. No one would want a Public Information Officer without experience responding to the media or excellent writing skills for crafting official news releases. On the other hand, no one would expect an interior firefighter to have to come away from putting out the fire to appear in an on-scene television interview while the fire was burning. The PIO supports the firefighter by taking care of communications with the media.

Similarly, a Planning Section Chief should have skills in organizing resources, reports, and information to adequately put together an IAP. Planning skills are not the skills of a law enforcement officer establishing a perimeter to limit access to a crime scene. In the same way, one would not expect to find an Emergency Medical Technician signing a memorandum of agreement for ten ALS teams and vehicles when there is a Finance/Administration Section available.

Some first responders have expressed a concern about the use of the term "command" when referring to the ICS command and general staff in response to an incident. This is especially the case with the Incident Commander position. In a large incident, where a Command Post or an Emergency Operations Center (EOC) has been activated, first responders are often hesitant about the command structure, particularly when their Chief is not the Incident Commander. There is a long and well established history of firefighters being led by firefighters, law enforcement officers led by law enforcement officers and so forth. There is also an expectation, valid or not, that the person in command will be an individual with sufficient experience on the ground, in the trenches, however you state it, such as a seasoned firefighter who earned the right to "command" firefighters on scene.

If the roles and responsibilities of all Command Staff or General Staff positions involved commanding the responders, it would be a normal expectation that they had earned the right to command by having served in the respective units. But Command and General Staff personnel in the Command Post or EOC are not there to command the first responders. They are there to support them. Yes, they do exercise supervisory responsibilities for their own staff, but not for first responders in tactical operations, unless they are serving as the Operations Section Chief. What about the Incident Commander? As the position title implies, the Incident Commander is responsible for the "overall management of the incident."[8] Managing the incident is not the same as commanding the first responders in tactical operations. That is a responsibility of the Operations Section Chief. Each member of the Command and General Staff has a specific set of functions to supervise and perform. Each is a specialty.

First responders need to see the Command and General Staff as those using special knowledge, ability, and skill to support Operations. If the support is in the form of managing resources for planning, logistics, finance/administration, safety, pubic information, and liaison, then the Section Chiefs and Officers are not "commanding" or issuing orders to first responders. If this is the case, they may not need years of experience "on the ground" as first responders, but rather experience in management, particularly in their specific functions. As stated earlier, this book is not a course in ICS, but a partial listing of skill sets for Command and General Staff might prove helpful in understanding their roles.

An Incident Commander is responsible several duties, some of which follow:

- Assess the situation
- Determine Incident Objectives

- Establish the immediate priorities
- Establish an Incident Command Post
- Consider the need for Unified Command
- Establish an appropriate organization
- Ensure planning meetings are scheduled as required
- Approve and authorize the implementation of the IAP
- Ensure that adequate safety and personnel accountability measures are in place
- Coordinate activity for al Command and General Staff
- Coordinate with key people and officials
- Keep agency administrator informed of incident status
- Other administrative or managerial functions.

As you can see from this partial list of responsibilities, the duties are by nature managerial. They only direct support of operations through the Operations Section Chief.

A Public Information Officer is responsible for several tasks, some of which follow:

- Determine from the Incident Commander if there are any limits on information release
- Develop material for use in media briefings
- Obtain Incident Commander's approval of media releases
- Inform media and conduct media briefings
- Arrange for tours and other interviews or briefings that may be required
- Obtain media information that may be useful to incident planning
- Maintain current information summaries and/or displays on the incident and provide information on status of incident to assigned personnel
- Other duties as may be assigned regarding information.

Again, the list of responsibilities for the Public Information Officer indicates the degree to which such duties are supportive of operations. The same would be true if the responsibilities of the remaining Command and General Staff were examined. There are a number of specialized training courses available for each position (see www.training.fema.gov/EMIWeb/IS/crslist.asp).

Summary

The ICS was designed initially and in its latest edition as part of the National Incident Management System (NIMS) to provide maximum and efficient coordination and support to first responders through the use of a common management structure available to all jurisdictions. The focus was on incident management, not tactical operations, even though ICS includes the organizational framework for the Operations Section. There should be a clear differentiation between the role of the Operations Section Chief and the role of the Incident Commander. The "Ops Chief" commands the responders who deal directly with "fixing the problem." (His) personnel are highly trained and skilled technicians in the appropriate disciplines for each incident (firefighters, law enforcement officers, IT analysts, HazMat, or EMS personnel). Personnel in the Command and General Staff are engaged primarily in management, having skill sets related to safety, public information, liaison, planning, logistics, finance/administration, and intelligence. Command and General Staff personnel are more often located in a Command Post or Emergency Operations Center rather than much closer to the source of the emergency—a burning structure, forest, or chemical tank, for example. Command and General Staff serve in supportive roles, providing managerial assistance to the Operations Section. They manage by objectives determined in concert with all Command and General Staff positions and collected and distributed each operational period in the IAP. The application of management skills in this manner is critical to the success of first responders.

Discussion Questions

1. Describe how each of the members of the Command and General Staff support the Operations Section as they "fix the problem."

2. How are the requirements from an Operations Section Chief communicated to the Command and General Staff, and where are they recorded?

3. Explain how the responsibilities of Command and General Staff are considered to be managerial rather than tactical.

4. Describe the role of the Safety Officer; the Public Information Officer; the Liaison Officer.

5. List three ways in which the Finance/Administration Section can support Operations, and describe one managerial skill set that would be used to do so.

References

1. *National Incident Management System.* March 1, 2004. Department of Homeland Security, Appendix A, p. 63.
2. Firescope California. June, 2004. *Field Operations Guide, ICS 420–1.* p. 7-3.
3. Firescope California. 2004. *Field Operations Guide,* ICS 420-1, p. 5-7.
4. Lerbinger, Otto. 1997. *The Crisis Manager, Facing Risk and Responsibility.* Mahwah, New Jersey, Lawrence Erlbaum Associates. p. xi.
5. Firescope California. 2004. *Field Operations Guide,* ICS 420-1, p. 5-4.
6. Firescope California. 2004. *Field Operations Guide,* ICS 420-1, p. 5-5.
7. Covello, Vincent T. (2006). "Rick communication and message mapping: A new tool for communicating effectively in public health emergencies and disasters." *Journal of Emergency Management,* Vol. 4, No. 3, May/June 2006, p. 39.
8. Firescope California. 2004. *Field Operations Guide,* ICS 420-1, p. 5-3.

Chapter 4

The Incident Commander: A Chief or a Manager?

Objectives of this chapter:

- Describe the traditional roles of chiefs in emergency response organizations.

- Identify the skill sets required of fire and police chiefs.

- Define the role of incident commander.

- Define the role of an emergency manager.

- Identify the skill sets required of an emergency manager.

- Compare and contrast the skills sets of chiefs or tactical response operations units to those of emergency managers.

☑ Summary

☑ Discussion Questions

☑ References

Introduction

The role of the emergency manager is changing and has been for some time. The active roles of the past when emergency managers wore two or more hats have changed to roles requiring a focus on management skills and little or no involvement in tactical response operations. There were times when experienced firefighters or law enforcement officers became the local emergency manager, but did not abandon their former roles as first responders. In fact, they did both. Many still do. Nevertheless, the demands placed on emergency managers have increased, requiring greater focus, time, and effort on the management aspects of the job. Today, emergency managers should not be wearing multiple hats. They certainly should not be performing the duties of a first responder during an incident. In this chapter, we will examine the specific duties of an emergency manager and contrast that role to the roles of a fire or police chief, and an Operations Section Chief. We will explore how experience, education, and training contribute to the competencies required of emergency managers. The case for "management by objectives" as the model to be followed by emergency managers will also be examined.

Traditional Roles for the Chief

The role of the emergency manager is not the only role that requires management knowledge, skill, and ability. In firefighting and law enforcement, for example, the administrative and management duties of a chief are ever increasing. In a small town, the chief may be required to perform the duties of an interior firefighter, for example. The number of trained personnel is too low for the chief not to engage in the first responder's role of firefighter. The chief may be forced to perform both the roles of tactical responder as well as that of the incident commander. In larger jurisdictions, where the number of firefighters is sufficient, the chief may be able to devote full attention to incident commander responsibilities. It is becoming more common for fire chiefs to be managerial positions, with little or no on-scene responsibilities for tactical response operations. In the example below, from the City of Phoenix, Arizona, the fire chief's job description is largely administrative and managerial. It illustrates how the job has become something other than tactical response operations.

> Administrative duties include planning, directing, and controlling departmental activities including recruitment of personnel, purchase of equipment, control of expenditures, preparation of budget estimates, and the assignment of personnel and equipment.[1]

Planning, directing, controlling, recruiting, purchasing, controlling expenses, budgeting, assigning personnel and equipment are essential duties, but not tactical response operations. These duties are supportive, preparatory, and required if adequate tactical response is to be provided. Though these managerial skills are required, there is much to be said for the chief's need to thoroughly understand the nature of tactical response operations as noted in the experiential requirements of the job description.

> The principles, practices, methods, and equipment employed in modern fire fighting. Responds to alarms and directs activities at the scene of larger fires or incidents; Five years of supervisory fire fighting experience at a level which has afforded the opportunity to become familiar with all phases of departmental operations...[1]

The requirements related to tactical response operations are customarily gained through experience as a firefighter and progressive experience as a department officer. Such experience has also, over the years, contributed to gaining the respect of firefighters under your command, an essential, traditional requirement. Examination of the job description printed below will demonstrate just how much of the chief's job is managerial or administrative, and not involvement in tactical response operations. One should also note the requirement for a Bachelor's degree. Chapter 5 will address the college degree requirement more fully.

Job Description

FIRE CHIEF
(Nonclassified)
JOB CODE 61590
Effective date: 12/92A

DISTINGUISHING FEATURES OF THE CLASS:

The fundamental reason this classification exists is to direct and manage all fire fighting, fire prevention, and fire service activities of the City. The Fire Chief is responsible, through study and consultation with City officials, for developing recommendations for the protection of life and property in the City. Administrative duties include planning, directing, and controlling departmental activities including recruitment of personnel, purchase of equipment, control of expenditures, preparation of budget estimates, and the assignment of personnel and equipment. The Fire Chief consults with the City Manager on problems of policy and planning, but works independently in supervising technical operations.

ESSENTIAL FUNCTIONS:

- Directs and oversees the activities of the Fire Department;
- Plans, implements, and reviews departmental short- and long-range goals;
- Develops general policies for the administration of the department;
- Evaluates needs and makes recommendations for construction of fire stations and the purchase of apparatus and equipment;
- Prepares annual budgets and controls expenditures;
- Establishes operational standards for the department;
- Attends conferences and seminars on fire administration to keep abreast of developments in the field;

- Responds to alarms and directs activities at the scene of larger fires or incidents;

- Develops recommendations for the protection of life and property in the City;

- Consults with the City Manager, the City Manager's staff, and department heads on problems relating to fire fighting, emergency medical services, and other related services;

- Directs administrative functions including planning, personnel administration, equipment purchasing, and the allocation of resources;

- Demonstrates continuous effort to improve operations, decrease turnaround times, streamline work processes, and work cooperatively and jointly to provide quality seamless customer service.

Required Knowledge, Skills, and Abilities:

Knowledge of:

- The principles, practices, methods, and equipment employed in modern fire fighting.

- Fire hazards and fire prevention techniques.

- The use of fire records and their application to fire prevention and fire protection administration.

- The rules and regulations of the department and City laws and ordinances pertaining to fire prevention.

Ability to:

- Direct and coordinate a multidisciplinary staff in fire fighting, fire prevention, and fire service activities.

- Perform a broad range of supervisory responsibilities over others.

- Maintain discipline and respect of employees.

- Communicate orally with customers, clients, or the public in face-to-face one-on-one settings, in group settings, or using a telephone.

- Comprehend and make inferences from written material in the English language.

- Observe, monitor, or compare data to determine compliance with prescribed operating standards.

Continued

- Establish relationships and work cooperatively with City officials, employees, and the public.
- Lead and command effectively in emergency situations.
- Produce written documents with clearly organized thoughts using proper English sentence construction, punctuation, and grammar.
- Review or check the work products of others for conformance to standards.
- Work safely without presenting a direct threat to self or others.

Additional Requirements:

- This position requires the use of personal or City vehicles on City business. The individual must be physically capable of operating the vehicles safely, possess a valid driver's license and have an acceptable driving record. Use of a personal vehicle for City business will be prohibited if the employee is not authorized to drive a City vehicle or if the employee does not have personal insurance coverage.
- Performs other marginal functions as assigned.

ACCEPTABLE EXPERIENCE AND TRAINING:

Five years of supervisory fire fighting experience at a level which has afforded the opportunity to become familiar with all phases of departmental operations and a bachelor's degree, supplemented by successful completion of supervisory courses in fire department administration and fire prevention and business or public administration. Other combinations of experience and education that meet the minimum requirements may be substituted.[2]

Similarly, the job description for a police chief in a large city focuses on managerial responsibilities. As noted in the example below, again from the City of Phoenix, Arizona, the essential functions of the job are management functions.

- "Plans and directs the implementation of the department's short- and long-term goals, objectives, and strategies;
- Writes reports on departmental activities and supervises others in the preparation of reports to the City Manager and Council;
- Presents budget estimates, controls expenditures of departmental appropriations, and establishes operational standards for the department;

- Directs and participates in police training programs;

- Directly supervises the activities of Assistant Chiefs and Commanders in charge of the Professional Standards Bureau and Office of Administration;

- Represents the Police Department in all significant public relations matters;

- Demonstrates continuous effort to improve operations, decrease turnaround times, streamline work processes, and work cooperatively and jointly to provide quality seamless customer service."[3]

These job requirements demand that a police chief be educated or trained in management skills. In addition, as with the fire chief, on-the-job experience may make the greatest contribution to gaining and maintaining the respect of the law enforcement personnel under the chief's command. There is little to indicate that the police chief will be engaged in tactical response operations. Again, there is the required Bachelor's degree or as stated, "Other combinations of experience and education that meet the minimum qualifications may be substituted."[4]

Job Description

POLICE CHIEF
(Nonclassified)
JOB CODE 62690
Effective Date: 06/92A

DISTINGUISHING FEATURES OF THE CLASS:

The fundamental reason this classification exists is to direct, plan, and manage all functions and operations of the Police Department in the enforcement of laws and ordinances, the prevention of crime, and protection of life and

Continued

property. Work involves organizing and directing the activities of the Police Department's five major divisions of Investigations, Support Services, Management Services, Patrol, and Operational Support. The Police Chief reports to and consults with the City Manager in determining plans and policies to be observed in police operations. Except for general administrative direction, the incumbent works independently with performance evaluated on results achieved.

ESSENTIAL FUNCTIONS:

- Plans and directs the implementation of the department's short- and long-term goals, objectives, and strategies;
- Writes reports on departmental activities and supervises others in the preparation of reports to the City Manager and Council;
- Presents budget estimates, controls expenditures of departmental appropriations, and establishes operational standards for the department;
- Directs and participates in police training programs;
- Directly supervises the activities of Assistant Chiefs and Commanders in charge of the Professional Standards Bureau and Office of Administration;
- Represents the Police Department in all significant public relations matters;
- Demonstrates continuous effort to improve operations, decrease turnaround times, streamline work processes, and work cooperatively and jointly to provide quality seamless customer service.

Required Knowledge, Skills, and Abilities:

Knowledge of:

- Principles, practices, and procedures of police science and modern police administration, organization, and operation.
- Municipal finance, budgeting, personnel, and labor relations.
- Standards by which the quality of police service is evaluated and use of police records and their application to the solution of police problems.

Ability to:

- Maintain discipline and respect of employees and to lead and command a sworn and civilian multidisciplinary staff in law enforcement and crime prevention activities.

Continued

- Perform a broad range of supervisory responsibilities over others.
- Establish and maintain cooperative working relationships with City officials, employees, other law enforcement agencies, boards, commissions, and the general public.
- Produce written documents in English with clearly organized thoughts using proper sentence construction, grammar, and punctuation.
- Communicate with individuals and groups in a face-to-face one-to-one setting or by telephone.
- Understand community and social conditions to determine needs.
- Maintain moral integrity.
- Work safely without presenting a direct threat to self or others.

Additional Requirements:

- Possession of A.L.E.O.A.C. certification.
- This position requires the use of personal or City vehicles on City business. Individuals must be physically capable of operating the vehicles safely, possess a valid driver's license and have an acceptable driving record. Use of a personal vehicle for City business will be prohibited if the employee is not authorized to drive a City vehicle or if the employee does not have personal insurance coverage.
- Appointments to positions in the Police Department are subject to appropriate polygraph and background standards.
- Performs other marginal functions as assigned.

ACCEPTABLE EXPERIENCE AND TRAINING:

Five years of experience in modern police work which has afforded progressively responsible experience in a variety of police functions including major command responsibilities, supplemented by formal training in police administration and scientific methods of crime detection. Bachelor's degree in a job related field is required. Other combinations of experience and education that meet the minimum qualifications may be substituted.[4]

The Shift from Tactical Response Operations to Management

Over time, as departments have grown, a number of factors (personnel management, grant writing, compliance documentation, and so forth) have required a shift from tactical response operations to management functions for chiefs. There is less time to fight the fire, and more time to administer all those components of the department that make firefighting possible. The same is true in police departments. The number of programs, laws, and regulations affecting the provision of personnel, equipment, apparatus, training, insurance, and supervision require the full attention of department chiefs. I once heard a fire chief say that the only fire he would not suppress would be the burning of the paperwork on his desk.

There are not only increasing demands to do management work as a department chief, but there is a demand to acquire management skills of a much different type than those learned through firefighting experience. A chief does not gain proficiency in grant writing or budgeting by using a tool to ventilate a roof, though done hundreds of times as a firefighter. Clearly, the skill sets developed in tactical response operations are not those required for fulfilling the duties of a chief. How effective is it then, to continue the tradition of promoting (or electing) the most experienced firefighter to the position of chief? It is common practice to advance through the ranks, even though experience in the ranks alone doesn't adequately prepare one for the management position of chief. Hence, the traditional career path leading to chief may no longer be appropriate without additional training or education in management.

Management Roles of the Incident Commander

The position title, "Incident Commander," has special significance in the Incident Command System. Oddly, the term "emergency manager" does not appear in ICS documents. In fact, it only appears as a footnote in the *National Incident Management System* (NIMS) document,[5] and more recently is mentioned once in the text of the *National Strategy for Homeland Security*.[6]

It is important to differentiate between the Incident Commander and the emergency manager. The Incident Commander has specific roles and responsibilities identified in

Incident Command System documents, of which there are several. The role pertains to the period of incident response, not a permanent position outside of emergency or disaster response. By one definition, "Emergency management is the managerial function charged with creating the framework within which communities reduce vulnerabilities and cope with disasters."[7] The role of the emergency manager pertains to duties and responsibilities that are on-going in all phases of emergency management—mitigation, preparedness, response, recovery, and restoration. The work of the emergency manager is largely managerial and administrative. In recent years, emergency managers and academic professors of emergency management have produced descriptions of the competencies and characteristics deemed essential for professional emergency management. The descriptions have been discussed, explored, and refined by college professors in emergency management degree programs and members of the International Association of Emergency Management (IAEM). The written products of such discussions have been *Blanchard 2005* collected by B. Wayne Blanchard as part of the Higher Education Project at the FEMA Emergency Management Institute in Emmitsburg, Maryland.

In October 2005, the list of Ten Competencies of Professional Emergency Management was written as follows: *DEM Competencies*

1. Comprehensive Emergency Management Framework or Philosophy
2. Leadership and Team-Building
3. Management
4. Networking and Coordination
5. Integrated Emergency Management
6. Emergency Management Functions
7. Political, Bureaucratic, Social Contexts
8. Technical Systems and Standards
9. Social Vulnerability Reduction Approach
10. Experience[8]

The document continued to describe each of the ten competencies in greater detail. In preparing his paper in 2005, Blanchard noted that an earlier 2003 document had presented competencies for emergency managers, but that the events since then such as Hurricane Katrina had prompted the revision of those competencies. Early in the document, Blanchard states in a footnote cited in Chapter 1:

> One would think it apparent by now that emergency managers at all levels of government need to have emergency management competencies when obtaining their positions. It should no longer be accepted that anyone, at any level of government, be put into a lead emergency management position without having such competencies as those described herein.[8]

The competencies have been reviewed and revised, for example, following the Higher Education Conference at Emmitsburg in 2007. They were defined in a work by David Etkin, Coordinator, Emergency Management Program, Atkinson Faculty of Liberal and Applied Studies, School of Administrative Studies at York University, in a paper entitled, "Emergency Management Core Competencies." Etkin defined core competencies as "The fundamental knowledge and basic skill set needed for practitioners to perform competently."[9] More recently, in July 2007, eight core principles of emergency management were described by Michael D. Selves, CEM, and President of the International Association of Emergency Management (IAEM) and published by the IAEM, as follows:

1. Comprehensive
2. Progressive
3. Risk-Driven
4. Collaborative
5. Integrated
6. Coordinated
7. Flexible
8. Professional[10]

In an earlier document (2003) addressing the same topic, emergency management competencies, management skills were more specifically listed.

> Administrative, Management, Public Policy Knowledge, Skills, and Principles
>
> Personnel Management—Recruiting, Retaining, Managing People (staff/volunteers), Teams
>
> Program Management—Developing and Managing Programs
>
> Fiscal Management—Acquiring and Managing Funding (Budgets)

Resource Management—Technical and physical

Information Management—Gather, analyze, interpret, sort, act upon

Organizational Management (normal and crisis)

Creating Public Value Skills—Getting others to value and promote disaster reduction[10]

The documents cited above contain more complete descriptions and discussions of the competencies and principles. Of note is the emphasis on management skills, not on tactical response operations.

There is attention to the leadership competency of emergency managers. Blanchard speaks of the need for leadership,

> Especially, but not just, in the immediate pre-impact and early response phases, leadership is needed – not just an ability to provide a command presence, but the demonstration of vision, compassion, flexibility, imagination, resolve, and courage. Without leadership, bureaucratic organizations and their personnel will tend to stay within more or less business as usual bureaucratic systems and methods of operation. It takes a leader to break down these barriers to expeditiously move people and resources to where they are needed.[11]

According to Patrick W. Carlton, Professor of Educational Leadership at the University of Las Vegas, Nevada (UNLV),

> Emergency Managers are among those who not only observe, but also participate, in important acts of leadership on a daily basis. Their challenge is that of adopting a leadership model—or models, which will allow for effective participation in this "growth industry," one that is dedicated to the management of natural, technical, and manmade catastrophes.[12]

Such a model has not been adopted, not clearly defined or widely accepted with the exception of noting that it is *not* a tactical response operations model.

An examination of the job description for an Emergency Management Coordinator (Emergency Manager), again from the City of Phoenix, demonstrates the emphasis on management skill sets required of those in emergency management. Of note, also, is the requirement for a Master's degree and the Certified Emergency Manager (CEM) credential.

Job Description

EMERGENCY MANAGEMENT COORDINATOR
JOB CODE 06190
Effective Date: Rev. 03/07N

DISTINGUISHING FEATURES OF THE CLASS:

The fundamental reason this classification exists is to serve as the City's liaison on emergency preparedness issues, coordinate training programs and emergency operations drills, assist departments with their emergency and mitigation plans, grant application and administration, and administer the submittal process for Federal and State reimbursement claims for the City's costs during emergency operations. The Emergency Management Coordinator reports to the Public Safety Manager and works only under the most general supervision. Work is evaluated primarily on the basis of results achieved.

ESSENTIAL FUNCTIONS:

- Provides staff support to the Public Safety Manager and the City Manager's Office to coordinate actual or potential emergency preparedness or response efforts;

- Serves as the City's liaison on emergency preparedness issues with the United States Federal Emergency Management Agency, the State of Arizona Division of Emergency Management, Maricopa County Department of Emergency Management, and other local municipalities;

- Coordinates training programs and emergency operations drills to prepare City department staff to respond quickly and effectively to emergencies;

- Develops cost estimates and makes budget projections;

- Writes memos, City Council Reports, Damage Reports, and other administrative reports;

- Advises departments on their emergency plans and coordinates interdepartmental activities;

Continued

- Applies for and administers federal and state grants;
- Administers the process for submitting federal and state reimbursement claims for City's costs during and after emergency operations;
- Serves as the City's Radiological Defense Officer;
- Represents the City on various internal and external task forces and committees;
- Directs and supervises the Emergency Preparedness volunteer program;
- Reviews state and federal proposed legislation and provides recommendations;
- Demonstrates continuous effort to improve operations, decrease turnaround times, streamline work processes, and work cooperatively and jointly to provide quality seamless customer service.

Required Knowledge, Skills, and Abilities:

Knowledge of:

- The principles and practices of public administration and government organization.
- Research techniques, methods, and procedures.
- The principles, methods, and practices of municipal budgeting and finance.
- Federal and state grant application processes and sound fiscal administration of grants.
- Principles and practices of local emergency management.

Ability to:

- Integrate and apply the concepts of comprehensive emergency management (mitigation, preparedness, response, and recovery) into the City's disaster programs.
- Identify and analyze the effects of hazards that threaten the City.
- Secure technical and financial assistance available through state and federal programs and grants.
- Develop and maintain working relationships with private, military, local, state, and federal officials in order to keep up-to-date on current issues facing the emergency management community.

Continued

- Interpret federal and state funding regulations as they impact the City.
- Gather pertinent facts, make thorough analyses, and arrive at sound conclusions.
- Comprehend and make inferences from written material in the English language.
- Work cooperatively with other City employees, representatives from state and local governments, and the public.
- Produce written documents with clearly organized thoughts using proper English sentence construction, punctuation, and grammar.
- Communicate orally in a face-to-face one-on-one setting, in group settings, or using a telephone.
- Remain in a sitting position for long periods of time.
- Observe, compare, or monitor data included in management reports to determine compliance with procedures.
- Work safely without presenting a direct threat to self or others.

Additional Requirements:

- This position requires the performance of other essential and marginal functions.
- This position requires the use of personal or City vehicles on City business. Individuals must be physically capable of operating the vehicles safely, possess a valid driver's license, and have an acceptable driving record. Use of a personal vehicle for City business will be prohibited if the employee is not authorized to drive a City vehicle or if the employee does not have personal insurance coverage.
- Must complete the Certified Emergency Manager (CEM) program through the National Coordinating Council on Emergency Management by the end of the probationary period.

ACCEPTABLE EXPERIENCE AND TRAINING:

Five years of responsible experience in public administration, research, and finance, grants application and administration, including three years of emergency management experience and a master's degree in public or business administration, government management, industrial engineering, or a related field. Other combinations of experience and education that meet the minimum requirements may be substituted.[13]

Experience, Education, and Training: How They Contribute to Competency

Experience, education and training all contribute to the competencies of emergency managers. Certainly, portions of all three are gained on the job and in the classroom. The position descriptions cited earlier list required experience as follows:

- **Fire Chief:** Five years of supervisory fire fighting experience at a level which has afforded the opportunity to become familiar with all phases of departmental operations…

- **Police Chief:** Five years of experience in modern police work which has afforded progressively responsible experience in a variety of police functions…

- **Emergency Management Coordinator:** Five years of responsible experience in public administration, research, and finance, grants application and administration, including three years of emergency management experience…

It is important to note that the emergency management coordinator position does not require experience in tactical response operations. The focus is on administrative functions, and only three years of emergency management experience is required, as opposed to five years for both fire and police chief positions. When education requirements are listed, the fire chief and police chief positions require an undergraduate or Bachelor's degree, whereas the emergency management position requires a graduate or Master's degree. Why, you ask? The crux of the matter is that management, supervisory, and administrative skills are traditionally taught and learned in the classroom and performed in an office or emergency operations center. They do not require the same level of psychomotor skills and physical conditioning as might be used in fire and police work.

One way to look at the functions performed by emergency managers is to look at the program elements of a community comprehensive emergency plan. Emergency managers are often responsible for writing, updating, and training employees on such plans. According to NFPA 1600, the National Fire Protection Association, "Standard on Disaster/Emergency Management and Business Continuity Programs, 2007 Edition," there are 16 program elements, all of which are recommended to be included in a disaster/emergency management or business continuity program. They are as follows:

1. General

2. Laws and Authority

3. Risk Assessment

4. Incident Prevention

5. Mitigation

6. Resource Management and Logistics

7. Mutual Aid/Assistance

8. Planning

9. Incident Management

10. Communications and Warning

11. Operational Procedures

12. Facilities

13. Training

14. Exercises, Evaluations, and Corrective Actions

15. Crisis Communication and Public Information

16. Finance and Administration.[14]

In creating, editing, updating, or seeking approval for such a plan, an emergency manager may use a number of managerial and administrative skills. The skills of tactical response operations are not used. Many tasks performed by emergency managers are similar to working with such a plan and various aspects of the sixteen program elements. Moreover, the work involved with such a planning activity occurs before, during, and after an emergency, crisis, or business interruption. Creating such a plan spans the functions of mitigation, preparedness, response, recovery, and restoration. The work of an emergency manager starts before an incident and continues long after.

Management by Objectives

One similarity between the Incident Commander in the ICS structure and the work of an emergency manager is the application of the concept of "management by objectives," (MBO).

Management by objectives (MBO) is a systematic and organized approach that allows management to focus on achievable goals and to attain the best possible results from available resources. It aims to increase organizational performance by aligning goals and subordinate objectives throughout the organization. Ideally, employees get strong input to identify their objectives, time lines for completion, etc. MBO includes ongoing tracking and feedback in the process to reach objectives.

Management by Objectives (MBO) was first outlined by Peter Drucker in 1954 in his book *The Practice of Management*. In the 90s, Peter Drucker himself decreased the significance of this organization management method, when he said: "It's just another tool. It is not the great cure for management inefficiency… Management by Objectives works if you know the objectives; 90% of the time you don't."[15]

In emergency management, knowing the objectives is critical. Whether engaging in mitigation, preparedness, response, or recovery, an emergency manager must know what needs to be accomplished, what resources are required to accomplish it, and by when it is to be accomplished. Using ICS, these items are collected in an Incident Action Plan (IAP) for each operational period of an emergency or disaster response. The IAP is compiled from the combined input from command and general staff. It is written, documented, and distributed by the Planning Section and approved by the Incident Commander as one of the IC's managerial responsibilities. An emergency manager may use Management by Objectives for any of several duties performed in an emergency management office, before, during, and after a disaster. The objectives may be part of a mitigation plan, a business plan, a preparedness plan, an evacuation plan, a shelter-in-place plan, a communications plan, or another plan, all of which an emergency manager may be tasked to complete.

During a response to an incident, tracking of objectives is often accomplished on a status board, or through the use of a computer-based emergency operations application. Such tasks as tracking progress on an objective, communicating, planning, finance, intelligence, information, and administration are management skills. They are the responsibilities of the command and general staff, but not necessarily the work of an Operations Section Chief. The Operations Section Chief, though often more supervisory than operational, directs the section that performs tactical response operations. All of the objectives in the Incident Action Plan are there to support the operations required to stabilize the incident and move toward recovery or business as it was before the incident occurred – normal operations as opposed to emergency operations.

Management by objectives helps to maintain focus on the goals of the emergency response team rather than on any one specific activity. At times, a response organization could lose sight of the principle objectives only to expend entirely too many resources on a secondary objective.

Case Study: The Super Bowl and the Ice Storm

In January 1998, a major ice storm occurred in the Northeast downing power transmission lines and distribution lines to customers in several states and Canadian provinces. In upstate New York, over 3000 electric utility workers were deployed from over 25 companies from as far south as Tennessee and as far west as Detroit. Hundreds of utility workers were billeted on cots in university field houses with little or no heat. The response was difficult, lasting 31 days, but utility workers, emergency responders, the military and emergency management officials endured the disaster, returning communities to seasonally normal conditions. As tasks were undertaken in the county Emergency Operations Centers (EOC's) across northern New York, one college partnered with the emergency responders to stage a Super Bowl party, complete with a large screen, projection television broadcast of the game, pizza, wings, and beverages. The intention was to create some rest and relaxation to enhance the morale of the workers. Though several hours and multiple resources went into planning this event, one conscientious, regional manager pulled the plug and refused to grant the workers the time to attend the event. The viewing of the Super Bowl did not meet the criteria for an essential function according to the Incident Action Plan. Customers were still in danger and without power. The Incident Commander could not justify such a morale-boosting activity to take precedence over the continued work required to restore power. Though very well intended, the Super Bowl activity did not address critical objectives. The regional manager placed a higher priority on restoring power than did those who planned the morale-boosting party.

The Super Bowl example doesn't mean that morale is unimportant. On the contrary, morale is extremely important as a component of practicing good mental health during a response to a disaster. Perhaps another example will illustrate a morale activity that did not conflict with management by objectives.

Case Study: 9/11 and the New York Mets Game

In the response to the 9/11 attack on the World Trade Center in New York City, I served as a temporary mental health unit leader (sometimes as Chaplain) in the Disaster Mortuary Operational Response Team (DMORT). Dispatched on 9/11/2001, I joined our unit first at Stewart Air Force base near Newburgh, NY, and later at Ground Zero. For a time, we were billeted at the LaGuardia Marriott Hotel across from LaGuardia International Airport. We worked two shifts per day, twelve hours each. As things progressed, word came that the first baseball game following 9/11 was going to be played at Shea Stadium, home of the New York Mets. I was offered fifty free tickets to the game for our personnel, and our National Commander, Tom Shepardson, since deceased, was given the honor to be one of the responders to throw out the first pitch. What an opportunity to boost morale by joining with thousands of New Yorkers and millions across the world to celebrate the resiliency of New York through the continuance of the baseball season. Two things had to happen. One, we could issue tickets only to off-duty personnel, the night shift. Two, DMORT is not a first responder unit. We don't save lives or property; we identify the remains of the victims bringing accurate information to their survivors. We were able to boost morale without interfering with the management by objectives of the Incident Commander housed at Pier 92.

Management by objectives, as a concept and as a practice, is taught in many venues, from business management, to the military, to emergency response. It provides for organization, clarity of purpose, and direction for deployment of resources. In the application of the Incident Command System, it is the result of teamwork, bringing information and expertise together from the command staff and general staff, usually during a briefing meeting where the Incident Action Plan is developed for each operational period. MBO unifies all aspects of emergency response. It combines vision, direction, purpose, and action. It also provides a basis for performance measurement and post–incident evaluation. It is clearly a management activity that supports tactical response operations.

Summary

The role of an Incident Commander will vary with the size of the emergency. In smaller incidents, a fire or police officer on scene may both act as an Incident Commander and provide tactical operations response. As incidents become more complex, the Incident Commander must focus on the management aspects of the response, not on tactical response operations. Unlike the firefighter or law enforcement officer on scene, fire and police chiefs are more involved in the application of management skills, not tactical operations skills. In larger incidents, multiple responders from multiple response organizations require coordination, direction, command, control, and other support components. When these multiple entities respond to a single incident, management is required. The application of management skills to a complex emergency incident is the role of an emergency manager – providing resources, communication, public information, planning, logistics, finance, administration, information, and intelligence. The Incident Commander must be dedicated to these functions and not involved in tactical response operations. Using the principles of management by objectives allows for a focused emergency response.

In Chapter 5, we will explore what colleges have to offer emergency managers, both pre- and in-service, to enhance one's ability to provide professional management skills to support tactical response operations.

Discussion Questions

1. How does the job description of a Fire Chief or a Police Chief indicate a focus on management rather than tactical response operations?

2. What is the significance of the requirement for a chief to have a Bachelor's degree?

3. How does management by objectives indicate a need for Incident Commanders or emergency managers to have management skills?

4. What are the functions coordinated by emergency managers that support tactical response operations, but do not require training in tactical response operations?

5. Are there management skills that might be better taught in a classroom than learned from on-the-job experience?

References

1. City of Phoenix Job Spec—Fire Chief, http://phoenix.gov/JOBSPECS/61590.html retrieved October 15, 2007.

2. Job Description—Fire Chief, http://phoenix.gov/JOBSPECS/61590.html retrieved October 15, 2007.

3. City of Phoenix, Job Spec—Police Chief, http://phoenix.gov/JOBSPECS/62690.html retrieved October 15, 2007.

4. Job Description—Police Chief, http://phoenix.gov/JOBSPECS/62690.html retrieved October 15, 2007.

5. *National Incident Management System*, Draft Upgrade Revision Version 1, February 1, 2007, p. 20.

6. Homeland Security Council, *National Strategy for Homeland Security*, October 2007, p. 5.

7. Selves, Michael D. "Update on the Emergency Management Roundtable Project," IAEM Bulletin, July 2007, p. 2. Retrieved October 18, 2007, from http://www.iaem.com/membersonly/bulletin/documents/200707bulletinonline.pdf

8. B. Wayne Blanchard, "Top Ten Competencies of Professional Emergency Management," Emergency Management Institute, October 7, 2005, p. 1.

9. Etkin, David. 2006. "Emergency Management Core Competencies (DRAFT)," Toronto, York University, p. 3.

10. Blanchard, B. Wayne. 2003. "Outlines of Competencies to develop successful 21st Century Hazard or Disaster or Emergency or Hazard Risk Managers," Emergency Management Institute, printed in Blanchard, Op. Cit. p. 8.

11. Blanchard, B. Wayne. 2003. "Outlines of Competencies to develop successful 21st Century Hazard or Disaster or Emergency or Hazard Risk Managers," Emergency Management Institute, printed in Blanchard, Op. Cit. p. 2.

12. Carlton, Patrick W. 2007. "Leadership: The 'Constant Variable' in Emergency Management," UNLV Executive Master of Science in Crisis and Emergency Management September 2007 News, p. 1.

13. City of Phoenix, Job Spec—Emergency Management Coordinator, http://phoenix.gov/JOBSPECS/06190.html retrieved October 15, 2007.

14. NFPA 1600 Standard, 2007 Edition. This edition of NFPA 1600, *Standard on Disaster/Emergency Management and Business Continuity Programs*, was prepared by the Technical Committee on Emergency Management and Business Continuity. It was issued by the Standards Council on December 1, 2006, with an effective date of December 20, 2006, and supersedes all previous editions. This edition of NFPA 1600 was approved as an American National Standard on December 20, 2006.

15. Management by Objectives. http://www.1000ventures.com/business_guide/mgmt_mbo_main.html retrieved October 18, 2007.

Chapter 5

What Colleges Have to Offer

Objectives of this chapter:

- Discover the added value that college degree programs bring to emergency management.

- Explore the wide variety of college degree and certificate programs available.

- Identify the accessibility of online degree programs in emergency management.

- Examine the curriculum in degree programs.

- Identify the prerequisite skills and practices that enhance success in college programs.

- Determine how education differs from training.

- Discover what research by colleges and universities contributes to emergency management.

☑ Summary

☑ Discussion Questions

☑ References

Introduction

College courses, degrees, and certificate programs in emergency management and homeland security are growing in number in the United States from 1 in 1983 to 142 in 2007. Additional programs are under development. They exist at all levels from Associate Degree programs to Doctoral Degree programs. They are becoming increasingly more accessible due to online instructional technology, flexible scheduling, and geographic proximity. Students are largely adult learners, but many are entering community colleges directly from high school and entering graduate degree programs directly following graduation from undergraduate degree programs. Many adult students are entering from emergency services agencies, from fire departments to FEMA. A large percentage of students are currently working in some aspect of emergency services. Several of my students have indicated a desire to earn a college degree to qualify for promotions into emergency management or department management positions. Students who have years of experience in emergency response operations bring that experience to their college learning projects. Their participation in classes with lesser experienced students has been invaluable. There are also a large number of degree candidates who are currently serving in the armed forces, looking to transfer their military skills to civilian emergency management careers. What is most impressive is the wide range of age, experience, and technical skills these students bring to college classrooms or online learning leading to a college degree. It is this mix of student experience and instructor experience that adds value to the college degree offerings.

College professors and their students engage in research that is highly valuable to emergency management. Studies of new technologies, geological factors, weather, communications, incident management systems, interpersonal communication and negotiation have all contributed to enhanced emergency services and emergency management practices. College students in emergency management learn research methods to seek answers to significant questions, while those in tactical response operations benefit from the results of such research. Research is not putting out a fire, but researchers may discover a new tool or technique for fire suppression. There is a time to research and a time to respond; a time to learn and a time to apply learning; a time to study and a time to practice. There are emergency management and tactical response operations, and a time for both to work together.

The Growth of Emergency Management College Programs

The rapidly increasing number of emergency management college degree programs in the United States and Canada expands the opportunity for students of varied ages and backgrounds to learn about the principles, practices, research studies, and their application to all aspects of emergency management. Resources for tracking and exploring these programs are provided by the FEMA Emergency Management Higher Education Project, directed by B. Wayne Blanchard at the Emergency Management Institute (EMI) in Emmitsburg, Maryland. The principal goal of the FEMA/EMI Project is to enhance the professionalism and abilities of the next generation of hazard and emergency managers through solid college-based emergency management education programs (http://www.fema.gov/institution/university.shtm).

One goal of FEMA is to encourage and support the dissemination of hazard, disaster, and emergency management-related information in colleges and universities across the United States. We believe that in the future more and more emergency managers in government as well as in business and industry will come to the job with a college education that includes a degree in emergency management. We also believe that in order to build disaster resistant and resilient communities, a broad range of college students and professionals need courses that introduce them to hazards, disasters, and how to manage them (http://www.training.fema.gov/emiweb/edu/).

More Time to Study and Learn

In my experience, the college classroom and online discussions are quite different from training programs and discussions with colleagues in emergency management forums. Much has been gained through participation in local gatherings of representatives from fire, police, EMS, government, humanitarian agencies, education, and specialty response groups, such as K-9 Search and Rescue or Amateur Radio Groups. There have also been valuable weekend to week-long training courses offered by proprietary organizations, especially at large conferences such as the semi-annual Disaster Recovery Journal Conferences and the World Conference on Disaster Management held annually in Toronto. Certification organizations also offer excellent training programs, e.g. Disaster Recovery Institute International (DRII).

The college model is somewhat different. First, there is more time devoted to a single course than is normally available in a training or certification course. Training courses range from one day to usually not more than 5 days, whereas college courses are spread out over a 13–14 week semester. The additional time provides for discussions, presentations, and guest lectures. There is also more time between sessions allowing for student reading, research, and reflection upon material presented. The additional time may also provide for students to prepare written assignments in the form of short papers, term papers, class presentations, and work-related projects. There just is not time for these activities in most training programs. The additional time allows for greater depth of study and learning.

The classroom offers opportunities for in-depth reading. There is a growing textbook and journal inventory wherein students can access the work of scholars and veteran practitioners who have begun to write for textbook publishers and journals. The information they contribute is invaluable to students seeking knowledge about all aspects of emergency management. College degree programs traditionally have included the reading of textbooks and scholarly journal articles as a foundation. Students will gain a broader background for acquiring knowledge and skill in emergency management, especially the management skills, from exposure to in-depth writings and research reports.

Another added value of the increased time devoted to college courses is interdisciplinary discussion. In most of my classes, from associate degrees to master's degrees, the cross section of learner backgrounds makes for rich discussions. For example, in one online graduate course on emergency planning, students are enrolled from the military, currently serving in Iraq and Afghanistan, from state emergency management offices, from volunteer fire and EMS departments, and, in one case, an emergency room physician. There is a "real world" tone to every discussion. In an instructor-led graduate course, my students participated in a one-hour phone conversation with Ed Devlin, author of one of several required texts on crisis management planning.[1] The discussions provide the opportunity to include current emergencies and disasters in progress. For example, this fall (2007), classroom and online discussions drew from the California wildfire response, the Minneapolis bridge collapse, the FEMA ill-advised press conference, and the drought situation in Atlanta. In college courses, the time is available to include these real life events in addition to reading textbooks and research studies that may include incidents and examples from history.

My students, in many cases, lack a fundamental background in the history of emergencies and disasters. In the college setting, there is time to read about the history of emergency response and significant natural disasters. Knowing the history is foundational to managing mitigation and preparedness projects. FEMA guidelines for preparing all-hazard mitigation plans require a thorough analysis of disasters that have impacted communities in the past. Understanding past disasters and lessons learned from responders and emergency managers is extremely valuable. College students are encouraged to read historical accounts from incidents of tidal waves, floods, fires, earthquakes, tsunamis, ice storms, and other incidents to build the background for applying the lessons learned from such incidents.[2]

Finally, the increased time devoted by students to college courses allows for the writing of term papers, wherein students can do an in-depth analysis of an emergency management issue. Often the students can choose the issue to be explored and analyzed. They are motivated to read and write when the topic is of their own choosing. The term paper experience prepares a student to combine original thinking with support from the literature. It strengthens a student's ideas by providing evidence to support those ideas. It provides an opportunity to sharpen writing skills. In my classes, students receive feedback on their written work, not only about the content of the paper, but also about writing skills, grammar, spelling, and proper citation format. These skills are transferable to the work emergency managers are doing in preparing grant proposals, press releases, business cases for the budget, and improvement plans following exercises or real incident debrief sessions. Good writing skills are valuable assets for emergency managers.

Curriculum for Emergency Management

Each college or university has its own curriculum for emergency management degree programs. Specific information is best obtained by contacting the admissions office or the department responsible for emergency management at each college of interest. The most comprehensive list of emergency management degree programs is maintained by B. Wayne Blanchard at the Emergency Management Institute (see the College List at http://www.training.fema.gov/EMIWeb/edu/collegelist/). Using this site, one can access degree programs sorted by Emergency Management or Homeland Security. Levels of study are categorized by degree or certificate ranging from courses offered to Doctoral Programs. In many cases, one can download the syllabus for specific courses. There are curricular threads that focus on emergency management, homeland security, fire protection, law enforcement, hazardous materials, geophysical natural disasters, health emergencies, and emergency management policy, amongst others.

Selecting an appropriate institution or degree program is a matter of personal preference. It is often determined by the school's location, hours of course offerings, online capabilities, and tuition costs.

An excellent presentation of current issues in emergency management education is available at http://www.training.fema.gov/EMIWeb/edu/docs/HighEd Slide Presentation.ppt.[3] In this Power Point presentation, professors from several leading college programs offer statements about the benefits colleges are bringing to the field of emergency management. The presentation offers commentary on emergency management courses, research, professional qualifications, and statistics on program growth at U.S. colleges and universities. It is a testament to the growing interest in such programs and the added value they bring to the practice of emergency management.

Twelve Important Questions About External Quality Review

If you are considering enrolling in a course of study or program at a higher education institution, you may find it useful to inquire about the external quality review of the course, program, or institution.

- Is the course, program, or institution accredited?
- What are the standards of quality? Is there an available summary of the last review?
- If the course, program, or institution is not accredited, is it certified for quality by another organization?
- What external quality review is performed by this other organization and what are the standards?
- Is there a summary of the last review?

How can the organization that accredits or provides other types of external quality reviews be contacted?
    You may address these and similar questions to:

- The institution or provider under consideration for enrollment
- Certifying organization, if necessary

If you are considering enrolling in an initial course of study or program at one institution and may want to enroll in a further course of study or program at another higher education institution in the future, you may find it useful to inquire about transferability of credits and courses.

- Will other institutions accept the credits and courses earned?
- Will other institutions count the credits and courses toward a degree?
- Will graduate schools accept the credits and courses for admission?
- Who decides toward what the credits or courses count? How can they be contacted?

You may address these and similar questions to:

- The institution or provider under consideration for enrollment
- The institution or provider under consideration for transfer

If you intend to use a course of study or program for employment purposes or would like your employer to provide tuition assistance, you may find it useful to inquire about acceptance of credits and courses by employers.

- Will employers accept the credits and courses earned?
- Will employers acknowledge the credits and courses for upgrading, retraining, and additional compensation?
- Who should be contacted to learn what courses and credits an employer may accept?

You may address these and similar questions to:

- The employer or likely future employer[4]

Curriculum can focus on management skills or on practical skills in emergency management. It can focus on theory or practice. It can focus on research or case studies or both. A typical course of study will include the following core courses:

- Introduction to Emergency Management
- Emergency Response Planning
- Exercise Program Management
- NIMS and ICS

- Public Information in Disaster Response
- Mental Health Issues in Disaster Response
- Mitigation Planning
- Hazardous Materials Incident Management
- Weapons of Mass Destruction
- Public Health Emergency Management
- Homeland Security.

In addition to core courses, several related courses are more specialized. Some address social and cultural aspects of disaster response. Some explore public perceptions of emergency and disaster management. At the certificate or associate degree levels, there is often a concentration on practical application. Courses are offered based on FEMA, Department of Justice, or FBI curriculum for specific duties of emergency management personnel. Examples are courses in ICS specializations—Planning Section & Logistics Section; Public Information Officer; Emergency Response to Terrorism; Environmental Health in Emergencies and Disasters. There are college courses based on ICS training—ICS 100, 200, 300, and 400.

At the four-year degree level, courses are a bit more managerial or theoretical at some colleges. Examples are as follows:

- Emergency Communications;
- Risk Management;
- Public Health Emergency Management;
- Emergency Response and Management in Film;
- Public Law in Emergency Management;
- Business Continuity;
- Humanitarian Aid in Disasters; and
- Mitigation Planning.

Most colleges require core courses in liberal arts and sciences in addition to the courses of the emergency management concentration. Emergency managers will benefit greatly from core courses in writing skills, accounting, chemistry (due to HazMat issues), adult literacy, communication, government, and computer technology.

Graduate schools build upon the education of undergraduate programs. A goal of some graduate programs in emergency management is to attract students with varied undergraduate majors—public administration, business, chemistry, biology, environmental science, engineering, and health services. These students may have interest in research that can add value to the field of emergency management. Some graduate programs require as few as 15 graduate credits or 5 courses in the emergency management concentration. They prefer graduate students also study such areas as human resource management, information systems, finance, planning and project management, leadership, and research skills. They might also require a capstone course, bringing together students from multiple disciplines. At Elmira College, for example, the Master of Science Degree Program in Management offers four concentrations— information technology management, health services management, general management, and emergency and disaster preparedness management. A student in any of the four concentrations may cross-register in another concentration, but will be required to take the capstone course that involves students from all four concentrations in the same course. The interdisciplinary aspects of the capstone course encourage the very cooperative efforts emergency managers apply in unified command or community response support systems such as EMAC, the Emergency Management Assistance Compact. Emergency mangers are often required to interact with diverse organizations during planning, response, or recovery efforts.

Prerequisite Skills and Practice

Students in college emergency management degree programs enter at all stages of life and career. Some colleges attract students currently serving in emergency response services—fire, law enforcement, emergency medical services, search and rescue, 9-1-1 centers, hospitals, and psychiatric clinics, and others. Those with special skills in tactical response operations seek to learn about the management aspects of safety, security, and disaster prevention and response. Often, they are seeking career advancement in departments and agencies where college degrees are required for key leadership, promotional positions. Many of the larger municipalities are requiring college degrees for police and fire chiefs. When those with experience in tactical response operations enter college emergency management degree programs, they bring invaluable, transferable skills. There is no question that fire ground, law enforcement patrol, or investigative experience is a benefit to an emergency management student. What is sometimes overstated is the notion that all emergency managers need to have this experience.

Though it is highly valuable, it is not a requirement for success in an emergency management position. As detailed in Chapter 2, this is largely due to the differences in skill sets.

The prerequisite skills most applicable to college study of emergency management are reading, writing, speaking, analytical, and computer skills. Even in introductory emergency management courses reading is essential. We are enriched by the volume of scholarly writing and current practices presented in textbooks and journal articles. The reading can become overwhelming if a college student lacks reading skills. In practice, emergency managers spend hours reading instructions for grant proposals, new laws and regulations, after-action reports, news articles, research findings, and association publications. Reading is so essential in practice, it would benefit any college degree applicant to assess and improve one's reading ability. It is also important to recognize the amount of time one will spend reading as a college student of emergency management and to plan for time to devote to reading.

Writing skills are required for the college assignments of reports, discussion boards, and research papers. Emergency managers will be required to write grant proposals, budget justifications, emergency communications, memos, after-action reports, and press releases. In addition to the fundamentals of proper grammatical structure and spelling, most college-level writing requires proper documentation. Emergency managers must support their ideas with evidence from scholarly sources, articles, legal documents, Presidential directives, and historical facts. Colleges will require students to follow a style guide such as the Publication Manual of the American Psychological Association which is updated regularly. Using consistent form for documenting sources, regardless of the style guide required or selected, is a basic requirement of college writing. Why is this important to emergency managers? The field of emergency management frequently involves conversations, discussions, arguments, and other forms of informal communication. Learning is often acquired from such interactions. In order for opinions, facts, lessons learned, comments, and criticisms to be widely understood and valuable, they must be captured in writing, so there will be less misunderstanding of what was stated or accomplished. It is just as important in the field of emergency management to write clearly and document correctly as it is in any other professional endeavor. By using highly recognized, acceptable writing standards, we distinguish ourselves as professionals.

Speaking skills are equally important to emergency managers. Presentations are common in public arenas. We speak to present a budget, to inform the public, to conduct a briefing session, or to issue on scene instructions. Our speaking skills need to be effective. Colleges offer courses in public speaking, conflict mediation, and group facilitation. There are proprietary courses, some of which are acceptable for college credit. High on my list are the Dale Carnegie® Course and their course in High Impact Presentations. Both are excellent and highly respected sources of presentation and speaking skills. Today, my graduate students in emergency and risk communications pose questions on presentation skills that clearly indicate the need for acquiring speaking skills. One aspect of speaking in public that emergency managers learn in college courses is audience analysis. Knowing the needs of multiple audiences before, during, and after a crisis is critical to crafting appropriate emergency communication. Responding to the media also requires speaking skill. An excellent source for research-based advice on audience analysis and message generation is the work of Vincent T. Covello, Director of the Center for Risk Communication.[5] Dr. Covello's work on message mapping and his analysis of questions asked by the media have provided invaluable insight to college students in emergency management programs.

Analytical and computer skills are growing in importance as required tools for success in emergency management. Mitigation plans involve use of geographic information systems (GIS); preparedness and early warning systems are enhanced by a number of commercially available computer applications; weather information is largely computer based; incident management systems such as E-Team[6] and WebEOC[7] are widely used by municipal emergency management offices; and 9-1-1 centers across the nation are employing sophisticated computerized telephone technologies. For emergency managers, basic understanding and application of computer skills have become daily essentials. Colleges offer countless opportunities from courses to help desks for students of emergency management to acquire such skills.

Analyzing data of all sorts is helpful in emergency planning. Hazard identification, population densities and demographics, evacuation routes, communications plans, weather data, resource allocation, and personnel accountability all require analytical skills. Emergency managers are required to make informed decisions that may save lives. The ability to analyze or assess a situation is critical to emergency communication and the activation of emergency plans.

The prerequisite skills discussed above are essential to success in emergency management. Though they are part of college curricula in emergency management, they can also be acquired before entering a college degree program. Practitioners in emergency response organizations often have job requirements that provide opportunities to practice all of the skill sets mentioned above. Students in high school have more than adequate opportunities to learn reading, writing, speaking, analytical, and computer skills. Those involved in tactical response operations may find time to enroll in proprietary or community adult education courses where these basic skills are taught and practiced. One thing is clear, in today's world of emergency management, perhaps more than ever before, these basic skills are required—all of them.

Education vs. Training

What is the difference between education and training? Do emergency managers need more of one and less of the other? Is one or the other more applicable to tactical response operations than emergency management? The first question, education vs. training has been a matter of discussion and debate for some time, especially amongst those in the academic ranks of colleges and universities. In modern college and university settings, Rensselaer Polytechnic Institute (RPI) is credited with breaking "… the classical barrier in 1824 to become the first college of engineering."[8] At that time, engineering was regarded as a skill, unlike the liberal arts more frequently associated with college study—English, literature, history, science, mathematics, rhetoric, art, music, and so forth. The introduction of specific skills training into educational settings increased during the industrial development periods in history due to the needs for people to learn to operate specific equipment as opposed to the broader learning associated with education. Training is often characterized by being practical, field-dependent (trained to do something specific to a content area), narrow-based, hard skills, specific amount of time allotted, and tangible. In contrast, education is characterized by being theoretical, field-independent, broad-based, soft skills, lifelong, and abstract.[9]

For emergency management college degree programs, both education and training should both be considered "learning." It is common for college courses to include reading and discussion that consider the connections of one discipline to another, for example early warning systems and communication models and theories. In the same course, students might craft messages and deliver them using communications technology such as computerized callout systems, Emergency Alert System activation software, or radios. The study of communication models from Aristotle to Berlo to Monroe would be considered education, whereas the sending of the messages via a computerized callout system would be considered training.

Emergency managers must often see the relationships among multiple disciplines. College courses could provide an opportunity for students to study the Incident Command System (ICS) and then write a term paper on its application to a specific site or an entire municipality. Students in my graduate classes at American Public University frequently apply studies of systems such as ICS to job-related assignments such as preparing a site-specific response plan for a mass casualty incident. They become involved in examining the relationship between one system and another. For example, students study the need for an incident management system in an organization which may not be familiar with ICS. They may additionally receive ICS training. In their college course, they might be required to examine ways to make ICS applicable to a business setting, where management is totally unfamiliar with ICS. They use learning from organizational behavior, management by objectives, communication, and ICS training to construct a paper on how to diffuse the innovation of an emergency response management system into a traditional business organization. The study of multiple disciplines is part of the college experience.

On the other hand, those involved in tactical response operations need to operate equipment, apparatus, and highly specialized tools in situations where time and life safety are paramount. Training in the application of such equipment, apparatus, and tools is critical to the success of their mission—protecting life, property, and the environment. The ability to operate, to perform, to execute is in the forefront; not the ability to plan, strategize, analyze, or synthesize. Training requires a focused effort on a limited spectrum of activity.

Colleges make excellent use of training tools and methods. One example in emergency management courses is the use of simulations. Emergency managers need to learn how to design and manage exercise programs. An excellent tool for teaching students about exercises is the simulation board. The board is a model community sometimes similar in scale to an HO model railroad set (in HO scale, 3.5 mm represents 1 real foot; HO is half of O scale which preceded it in model railroading).[10] When such a board is planned, careful attention is given to the inclusion of critical infrastructure, emergency response facilities (fire houses, police stations, EMS facilities, hospitals), businesses, and industries that may utilize hazardous materials, places of assembly (churches, schools, arenas, parks, movie theaters), significant geophysical features (rivers, lakes, swamps), and weather indicators. When used to simulate critical incidents, model trains, Matchbox-sized emergency response vehicles, school buses, commercial and passenger vehicles are deployed as dispatched or otherwise indicated in an exercise scenario. Students participate in decision making and communications using hand-held radios for sending and receiving messages from remote dispatchers. Facilitators manipulate the model vehicles as directed by students role playing fire, law enforcement, EMS, government, and emergency management personnel.

Figure 5.1 Photo by Tom Fritsch

Roles often also include personnel from business, industry, humanitarian organizations, and schools. In the photograph in Figure 5.1, Elmira College graduate students in emergency management are using a simulation board to practice decision making and communication skills. The board is a replication of the many features of the Elmira community.

In summary, both education and training are forms of learning. There is a place for both in college and university programs. Generally, the practical focus on operating equipment, apparatus, and tools utilized in tactical response operations is categorized as training. The study of various disciplines such as management, communication, planning, history, government, and economics are categorized as education. The debate over their similarities and differences will not end here. Colleges, depending on their mission, will continue to provide both.

Research

Colleges and universities have traditionally been the centers of scholarly and scientific research. In emergency management this is growing as the number of programs in emergency management increases. Particularly at the graduate level, significant research in emergency management and geophysical hazards has been ongoing for years. The Natural Hazards Center at the University of Colorado at Boulder has served since 1976 as a national and international clearinghouse of knowledge concerning the social science and policy aspects of disasters. The Center collects and shares research and experience related to preparedness for, response to, recovery from, and mitigation of disasters, emphasizing the link between hazards mitigation and sustainability to both producers and users of research and knowledge on extreme events.[11]

Similarly, the George Washington University Institute for Crisis, Disaster and Risk Management has provided graduate level studies and research support through their Department of Engineering Management and Systems Engineering since 1994. George Washington's graduate students frequently publish their research findings in the *Journal of Emergency Management*.[12]

Significant research has been conducted and published by many colleges and universities. Research is helping to advance emergency management as a profession.

> Introducing university-level knowledge-based programs is encouraging a more systematic introduction and treatment of risk, hazard, emergency, and organizational management theory. It has enabled research findings to directly aid practice. This development has enabled [EM] to be taken as a university/college subject in its own right. Many [EM] agencies are realizing that there are distinct advantages from linking operational effectiveness with empirical research. Moreover, many decision-makers are seeing the benefit of recruiting people who are academically trained and familiar with the research literature that underpins risk, hazard, and emergency management.[13]

Brenda Phillips in DRC Disaster Research Handbook (2006) wrote of the important contribution research can make to the emergency management profession.

> If disaster research is helping to spawn a new discipline as some suggest…then its work remains incomplete. For a new discipline to emerge, take shape, and become recognized as a substantive field of knowledge, research must infuse the writings and materials used in the classroom. The presumed benefits of doing so include legitimacy and acceptance within the academy; professionalization that generates promotions, higher salaries, and social prestige; and more effective emergency management practice.[14]

Creating connections between research and practice in emergency management is a major goal of college degree programs. With increased funding and recognition of the scholarship of emergency managers prepared through college education, the impact of research may well save lives, property, and the environment by reducing the impact of disasters and improving the methods and tools available to first responders and emergency managers alike.

Summary

In summary, colleges and universities have much to offer the field of emergency management. The complexity of our world requires a different approach. Future emergency managers will be educated in college classrooms as opposed to the more traditional preparation through years of emergency service as emergency responders. The basis for education vs. training is in the list of skills required of emergency managers when compared to those required of tactical responders. Today's emergency managers need to learn the management skills associated with grant writing, plan development, vulnerability assessment, incident management, resource management, budgeting, accounting, systems technology, and other processes commonly learned through classroom instruction. More time is required to acquire this knowledge than is typically provided in training programs. Learning from multiple disciplines will provide emergency managers with the ability to comprehend, analyze, synthesize, and judge emergency planning and management issues before, during, and after disasters and other critical incidents. College programs will continue to conduct research that is invaluable in all phases of emergencies and disasters. The professional emergency manager will be one who makes the best use of research and multidisciplinary studies when practicing emergency management.

Discussion Questions

1. Why earn a college degree in addition to or instead of obtaining certifications?

2. What are the prerequisite skills required for success in a college emergency management degree program and in the practice of emergency management?

3. Where can you learn about college and university programs in emergency management?

4. What is learned from research in emergency management?

5. What is the difference between education and training?

6. How is education beneficial to an emergency manager?

7. If an emergency manager is educated in college, might training also be necessary?

References

1. See Devlin, Edward S. (2007). *Crisis management planning and execution.* Boca Raton: Auerbach, Taylor & Francis Group.
2. See Rubin, Claire B., editor. (2007). *Emergency management: The American experience 1900–2005.* Fairfax, VA: Public Entity Risk Institute.
3. http://www.training.fema.gov/EMIWeb/edu/docs/HighEd Slide Presentation.ppt retrieved November 14, 2007.
4. Council for Higher Education Accreditation, Fact Sheet #3, September 2001, http://www.chea.org/pdf/fact_sheet_3_12ques_01.pdf retrieved October 24, 2007.
5. www.centerforriskcommunication.com
6. www.eteam.com
7. www.marc.org/emergency/weeoc
8. Miller, V.T. "The history of training," in Craig, R.L., ed. (1987). *Training and development handbook: A guide to human resource development,* third edition. New York: McGraw-Hill. p. 6.
9. Ogle, Gwen. (1997). "Education vs. training." www.edtech.vt.edu/Gwen/Training/EducVsTraining.pdf retrieved December 26, 2007.
10. "HO scale." Wikipedia. http://En.wikipedia.org/wiki/HO_scale retrieved December 26, 2007.
11. http://www.colorado.edu/hazards/about/ retrieved December 26, 2007.
12. The *Journal of Emergency Management* may be contacted at www.emergencymanagement-journal.com.
13. Neil Britton and John Lindsey, "Designing Educational Opportunities for the [EM] Professional of the 21st Century…, May 2005 quoted in Blanchard, B. Wayne. (2007). Higher Education Slide Presentation.
14. Phillips, Brenda in Rodriquez, H. et al., Ed. (2006). *Disaster Research Handbook.* Berkeley: Springer, p. 456.

Chapter 6

The Career Path in Emergency Management

Objectives of this chapter:

- Explore the opportunities for service in emergency management.

- Discover the difference between entry-level and promotional positions.

- Learn the difference between civil service and appointed positions.

- Examine the impact of volunteering on career advancement.

- List the types of positions at local, state, regional, and national levels.

- Learn about career development skills applicable to emergency management.

☑ Summary

☑ Discussion Questions

☑ References

Introduction

Many of us, as we come through the traditional education system, learn about careers in only the most general terms—doctor, lawyer, firefighter, nurse, professional athlete. When one explores the organization chart of even a small corporation, it is amazing how many positions or job titles there are. For example, when I worked as a career development professional at a mid-size, investor-owned power utility company (gas and electric), there were 1,450 job titles. In discussions with high school guidance counselors, who were advising talented students about college and career options, I found that many of them were totally unaware of the multitude of position titles. In emergency management, the list of possible positions is smaller on the local level, but grows as the area of responsibility increases in size, from local to state, regional, and national levels. Exploring the job titles, knowledge, skills, and abilities required for each is an excellent way to plan one's preparation for entry and advancement in a career field, including emergency management.

In some career fields there are multiple levels of positions. The term "career ladder" often applies. The position titles, for example, indicate a promotional series from entry-level to the highest position of leadership. We see this in the ranks used in the fire service and in law enforcement. Ranking is very well defined in the military. In business and industry the hierarchy is more complex when the concepts of line positions and staff positions are present. There is also the term "individual contributor" identifying an employee who does a job that does not involve any form of supervision, direction, or management of others. The career ladder often appears as an organizational chart listing the head of the organization and all those reporting up the chain of command to that individual. In emergency management, we are most familiar with such a chart in the Incident Command System (ICS) where the Incident Commander is at the top of the chart and the direct reports are shown below with lines showing their reporting structure. Such charts are common in government, especially in complex organizations. The organization chart for the Department of Homeland Security is large, even when it only lists the names of the agencies. When the personnel positions are listed, the chart is huge.

Entry-Level Positions

Where and how one enters a career is as often a matter of circumstance and networking or "who you know" as much as it is a matter of preparation and planning. Ideally, entering the world of work is following your dream. In career development workshops I conducted in the 1990s, participants often spoke of how their "dream" had been interrupted by changes in plans, some seemingly beyond their control. Many took entry-level positions to get "a foot in the door" to a company that was known for good salaries and excellent benefits. Some followed in the footsteps of their parents, taking entry-level positions in the company where a parent had a position of rank and influence. Some had come in through the "front door," applying for advertised positions through the human resource department where skills, abilities, education, and experience were considered first. A closer look at the skills and strategies of career development follows later in this chapter.

In emergency management, the "farm team," to use a professional baseball analogy, has traditionally been emergency services—fire, law enforcement, and EMS. More recently, much attention has been given to political appointments of high-level leaders who lack emergency services experience. The leadership, for example, of FEMA has been a matter of widespread discussion. Former FEMA Director James Lee Witt's emergency management experience has been compared to the lack of similar experience of those who have directed FEMA since. Whether at the national level or the local level, political appointments are common in emergency management. Public officials across the nation are becoming aware of the number of experienced and educated men and women who can bring their skills and abilities to emergency management. With more and more individuals becoming educated in emergency management, government leaders should have less trouble finding qualified individuals to appoint to positions in emergency management.

Entry-level positions in emergency management are as much a matter of funding as they are a matter of need and preparation. Often, an emergency manager applies for Federal funding for a municipal program which, when approved, provides funding for a temporary addition to staff for the duration of the funded project. Examples would be funding for mitigation planning under the Disaster Mitigation Act (DMA) of 2000, or the Homeland Security Exercise and Evaluation Program (HSEEP). When grant funds are obtained, local departments may open temporary positions to accomplish the work associated with the grant. To accomplish the goals of the grant, emergency managers or municipal chief executives seek persons with excellent research skills, writing skills, communication skills, and public relations skills. The entry-level employee will be involved in researching such things as past disasters impacting the area, identifying hazards and vulnerabilities, compiling and updating contact lists, collecting maps and documentation of past disasters and incidents, and assisting with planning task force and public meetings. Excellent organization skills are required. In local emergency management offices, entry-level personnel may be required to work on their own, without a great deal of supervision, so self-directed individuals are most valuable.

In today's emergency management offices, there are new technologies such as geographic information systems (GIS), computer-based emergency operations systems, weather and early warning systems. Computer and technical skills are highly desirable in entry-level positions. It is often the case that local emergency managers are unfamiliar with the new technologies and rely on newly-hired, college educated, entry-level personnel to utilize the new systems. Recently, my work has taken me to extremely rural county emergency management offices where newly hired college graduates with degrees in computer science or geology have been hired to implement the GIS system, which is also a newly acquired resource.

Frequently, entry-level personnel in emergency management are new to their positions, but widely experienced in one or more aspects of emergency response. Many of the emergency management personnel in city, county, or state emergency management departments came with years of experience in volunteer fire departments, law enforcement, the Red Cross, the military, the Forest Service, or other emergency services. In most cases, in addition to their on scene experience, these positions required a college degree. Education, particularly in emergency management, is highly desirable.

In some college programs in emergency management, administrators and professors state that their students are being hired either before graduation or before they have the opportunity to pursue an advanced degree. In a graduate class I taught of ten students at Elmira College, two of the ten were hired in private sector positions before completing their degrees in emergency management. They were attractive candidates due to their prior work experience and the fact that they were studying for a master's degree in emergency management. As explained by Greg Shaw,

> One of our problems is that some of our graduate students are being hired out from under us—by merely being enrolled in the Crisis and Emergency Management Program.[1]

Emergency management positions are becoming more common in the private sector. Business continuity planning has been a part of corporate culture for many years. Since the attacks of September 11, there is an increased emphasis on security and crisis management in the private sector, particularly privately owned critical infrastructure, banking, heath care, pharmaceuticals, and manufacturing. According to the 9/11 Commission Report, "…the private sector controls 85 percent of the critical infrastructure in the nation."[2] Those interested in entry-level positions should be encouraged to explore private sector opportunities as well as public sector.

There are many similarities between private sector business continuity planning positions and public sector emergency management positions. It is not at all unusual to find former law enforcement officers and firefighters in private sector safety and business continuity positions. Many public sector emergency responders engage in college degree programs while on the job because they are aware of degrees being required in many private sector positions which they are interested in pursuing as second careers. As for the career ladder, an informal study I conducted at a Disaster Recovery Journal conference in San Diego in 2002 revealed 104 job titles in business continuity or emergency management from amongst 300 responders who provided a business card bearing their title.[3]

Finding an entry-level position in management differs from entry-level positions in general. It is not starting at the bottom of the rank and file, but rather at the lower end of the leadership area. Therefore, one can expect to find that the credentials required of an entry-level candidate in emergency management may include the following:

- A college degree;
- Prior successful work experience;
- NIMS training;
- Field experience in disaster or critical incident response;
- Excellent writing and speaking skills;
- Computer skills;
- Excellent references.

In the past, most job postings provided for the substitution of years of experience for a college degree. This is changing rapidly as noted in Chapter 2. Experience in volunteer work in response to a disaster is highly valued and readily available as noted in the next section.

Gaining Experience as a Volunteer

The director of an information technology (IT) department, responsible for disaster recovery (DR), once asked me how his employees could gain experience in disaster response. He was concerned that their only exposure was in one or two DR exercises each year. They performed well in those exercises, but they also demonstrated heightened interest in disaster response, communications, incident command, logistics, and other aspects of emergency response and management. He wanted them to become skilled in these areas, but didn't have the opportunity nor the budget to give them greater exposure and practice. My response was based on my experience as a volunteer with the Red Cross.

Though large scale disasters appear to be occurring more frequently than in the past, they fortunately are far less frequent than smaller ones at the local level. We know about hurricane season, tornadoes, winter storms, draughts, and earthquakes. These devastating natural disasters, as often as we see them on the news, are not daily occurrences. Fires and floods, however, occur far more frequently, and are usually local issues. As a Red Cross volunteer in disaster services, one could be called upon to respond to local residential fires on a daily basis. The Red Cross provides training for its Disaster Services volunteers. A corporate employee, with a heightened interest in disaster recovery, could receive Red Cross training and be called upon frequently to assist on scene at local residential fires. Important skills in communication, documentation, damage assessment, resource allocation, stress management, and logistics are all taught and applied in Red Cross Disaster Services work.[4]

Red Cross Disaster Services

Each year, the American Red Cross responds immediately to more than 70,000 disasters, including house or apartment fires (the majority of disaster responses), hurricanes, floods, earthquakes, tornadoes, hazardous materials spills, transportation accidents, explosions, and other natural and man-made disasters. Red Cross disaster relief focuses on meeting people's immediate emergency disaster-caused needs. When a disaster threatens or strikes, the Red Cross provides shelter, food, and health and mental health services to address basic human needs. In addition to these services, the core of Red Cross disaster relief is the assistance given to individuals and families affected by disaster to enable them to resume their normal daily activities independently.

The Red Cross also feeds emergency workers, handles inquiries from concerned family members outside the disaster area, provides blood and blood products to disaster victims, and helps those affected by disaster to access other available resources.

See http://www.redcross.org/services/disaster/ for an on line video-based introduction to Disaster Services volunteering.

Volunteering provides ample opportunity to learn, practice, and apply disaster recovery skills that are transferable, in many cases, to private sector work in disaster recovery or business continuity. There are other volunteer opportunities that also provide an excellent basis for emergency management careers.

The Community Emergency Response Team Program (CERT) is another community-based opportunity for volunteers to learn valuable, transferable skills in emergency response and management. CERT volunteers from banking, finance, business continuity, and many other businesses have been impressed by what they have learned in the CERT program.

Community Emergency Response Teams (CERT)

The Community Emergency Response Team (CERT) Program educates people about disaster preparedness for hazards that may impact their area and trains them in basic disaster response skills, such as fire safety, light search and rescue, team organization, and disaster medical operations. Using the training learned in the classroom and during exercises, CERT members can assist others in their neighborhood or workplace following an event when professional responders are not immediately available to help. CERT members also are encouraged to support emergency response agencies by taking a more active role in emergency preparedness projects in their community.

The CERT course will benefit any citizen who takes it. This individual will be better prepared to respond to and cope with the aftermath of a disaster. Additionally, if a community wants to supplement its response capability after a disaster, civilians can be recruited and trained as neighborhood, business,

Continued

and government teams that, in essence, will be auxiliary responders. These groups can provide immediate assistance to victims in their area, organize spontaneous volunteers who have not had the training, and collect disaster intelligence that will assist professional responders with prioritization and allocation of resources following a disaster. Since 1993 when this training was made available nationally by FEMA, communities in 28 States and Puerto Rico have conducted CERT training.[5]

There is no more widely known or rooted volunteer opportunity than the local volunteer fire department. A part of American and world culture for generations, volunteer fire departments have been leaders in tactical response operations. They have also been the pioneers of much of what we know today as the Incident Command System (ICS) which has major implications in emergency management as discussed earlier in Chapter 3. Serving in a volunteer fire department gives a person on scene experience in both operations and management. Fire department service is an opportunity to see ICS in practice, to witness the principles of incident command, communication, resource deployment, safety, public information, and victim issues on a far more frequent basis than the annual IT disaster recovery exercise. Volunteering is also an opportunity to save lives, property, and the environment; to provide service to your neighbors; and to reduce insurance and local property taxes. Volunteer fire department experience is excellent training for future emergency management personnel. Many of our nation's emergency managers have served or currently are serving in volunteer fire departments.

There are many other opportunities to acquire transferable skills from volunteering and professional organizations. Faith-based organizations involved in humanitarian relief, corporate disaster relief programs, non-governmental organizations focused on disaster assistance, the Association of Contingency Planners (ACP),[6] and student chapters of such organization are among the many opportunities. Volunteering provides a chance to test one's interest in emergency management while providing a valuable service to the community. There are countless transferable skills to be acquired.

Local, State, Regional, and National Positions

As emergency management departments, offices, and agencies grow in size, the number of positions increase. In many local, usually county, emergency management offices, there may be only one or two employees—the manager and one clerical person or an assistant manager. The size of the office and the staff depends on the population and nature of the county. Location is also a factor. Counties have larger emergency management departments when located closer to natural hazards such as earthquake sites, coasts, flood-prone areas, and a history of damaging hurricanes and tornados. The presence of man-made potential hazards such as large dams, nuclear power plants, international airports, commercial ports, and chemical plants also tends to increase the personnel required in local emergency management departments. For example, a somewhat rural, sparsely-populated county might have a considerable responsibility for emergency management if that county is the site of one or more nuclear power plants (For example, Oswego County, New York is home to three nuclear power plants.).

Cities with large populations and business centers nevertheless operate as local governments with local emergency management offices. Yet the nature of emergency management, when hundreds of thousands of people are collected in a few square miles, requires far more personnel than a less densely populated area. Cities are well known for their emergency management initiatives. We have seen cities in action, coordinating disaster responses in Oklahoma City, New York, Los Angeles, Minneapolis, and New Orleans, to name but a few. Some have been highly successful, while others have been overwhelmed with massive disasters. Cities tend to employ several specialists in their office of emergency management (OEM). Jobs in large city OEMs vary from city to city.

The table below is from the New York City OEM Job Opportunities listing.[7]

Title	Unit	Date Posted
Program Manager	Planning and Preparedness	12/17/07
Senior Project Manager	Planning and Preparedness	12/17/07
Hazard Impact Modeler	Geographic Information Systems (GIS)	12/10/07
Geographic Information Specialist	Geographic Information Systems (GIS)	12/10/07
Emergency Preparedness Specialist	Human Services	11/27/07

Continued

Title	Unit	Date Posted
Special Needs Outreach Coordinator	Human Services	11/27/07
Planning Specialist	Human Services	11/27/07
Interagency Training Coordinator	Training & Exercise	11/20/07
Desktop Support Technician	Technology	10/16/07
Director of Health & Medical	Health & Medical	05/14/07
Logistics Planner	Logistics	05/14/07
Transportation & Infrastructure Planner	Transportation & Infrastructure	04/11/07

In Chicago, The Office of Emergency Management & Communications (OEMC) manages and operates the City's public safety communications systems that coordinate the response of police, fire, and Emergency Medical Services (EMS) resources to 911 calls. The OEMC operates a world-class voice and data radio system, giving police and fire personnel on the street valuable information to help them respond quickly to emergency situations.

The OEMC's Emergency Management Team acts as the coordinator for the City's efforts to develop, plan, analyze, implement, and maintain programs for disaster mitigation, preparedness, response, and recovery. The Emergency Management Team is also responsible for directing the activities of City departments and other agencies at disaster scenes.[8]

In Washington, DC, The Homeland Security and Emergency Management Agency (HSEMA) provides coordination and support of the city's response to emergencies and disasters of all types, both natural and manmade.

The mission of the Homeland Security and Emergency Management Agency is to reduce the loss of life and property and protect citizens and institutions from all hazards by operating and maintaining a comprehensive all-hazard community-based, state-of-the-art emergency management infrastructure. This is accomplished by:

- Developing plans and procedures to ensure emergency response and recovery capabilities for all emergencies and disasters;
- Coordinating emergency resources for emergencies and disaster incidents;

- Providing training for all emergency first responders, city employees, and the public;

- Conducting exercises; and

- Coordinating all major special events and street closings.

In addition, in furtherance of its mission, HSEMA also:

- Serves as the central communications point during regional emergencies;

- Conducts an assessment of resources and capabilities for emergencies;

- Provides public awareness and outreach programs, and

- Provides 24-hour emergency operations center capabilities.

In carrying out its mission the agency works closely with other emergency response agencies, including the Metropolitan Police Department, the District of Columbia Department of Fire and Emergency Medical Services, the District of Columbia Department of Health and other District and federal agencies, as well as with the major utility companies and non-profit and volunteer organizations such as the Red Cross and the Salvation Army.[9]

As you can see from the scope of the department job postings, missions, and responsibilities in New York, Chicago, and Washington, DC, there are much larger departments and career positions in cities, though they are still local emergency management offices.

At the state level, offices of emergency management also have a larger territory and responsibility and therefore more positions within their OEM organizations. Since state organizations offer support to localities, they are expected to have greater expertise in certain areas. Specialist positions exist in areas such as planning, mitigation, telecommunications, GIS, resource management, geology, hazardous materials, forest management, flood control, public alert systems, training, and disaster legislation. State Offices of Emergency Management desire individuals with undergraduate majors in the sciences, especially geology and chemistry, who have graduate degrees in emergency management, to become state-level emergency management specialists. Computer science majors, familiar with GIS and telecommunications systems are in demand, especially with the new focus on interoperability. State offices of emergency management often cooperate with other state agencies when developing disaster preparedness plans or when responding to a disaster. The connections between state emergency management offices and state departments of corrections, health, mental health, forensics, education, transportation, technology, and regulatory agencies such as the public service commission are highly important. They all play significant roles in disaster preparedness and response. Positions related to emergency planning and management also exist in these other departments. For example, in New York State, the Department of Education employs specialists at the state and regional levels in health and safety who have the responsibility for overseeing the emergency plans of schools and colleges. The Department of Corrections has personnel responsible for emergency planning in correctional facilities, and the department responsible for mental health facilities has similar personnel. At the state level, emergency management positions exist in departments other than the state office of emergency management.

On the national level, there are many opportunities in the public sector. There are the Federal agencies responsible for emergency situations of all types. The list below is one of seven pages of job vacancies posted on the Department of Homeland Security site on one day in December, 2007.[10]

Closing	Job Title	Agency	Location	Salary
12/31/2007	Emergency Management Program Specialist	Homeland Security, Federal Emergency Management Agency (FEMA)	US-PA-Philadelphia Metro area	66,914.00+
1/4/2008	Emergency Management Program Officer	Homeland Security, Federal Emergency Management Agency (FEMA)	US-PA-Philadelphia	94,028.00+
12/31/2007	Hazard Mitigation Grant Program Group Supervisor	Homeland Security, Federal Emergency Management Agency (FEMA)	US-FL-Orlando	63,417.00+
12/31/2007	Contract Specialist	Homeland Security, Federal Emergency Management Agency (FEMA)	US-IL-Chicago Metro area	68,569.00+
12/31/2007	Deputy Director, Legislative Affairs	Homeland Security, Federal Emergency Management Agency (FEMA)	US-DC-Washington	110,363.00+
12/31/2007	Program Support Assistant	Homeland Security, Federal Emergency Management Agency (FEMA)	US-DC-Washington	30,386.00+

Continued

Closing	Job Title	Agency	Location	Salary
12/31/2007	Electric Power Controller	Homeland Security, Federal Emergency Management Agency (FEMA)	US-MA-Maynard	21.27+ /hr
1/2/2008	Human Services Specialist	Homeland Security, Federal Emergency Management Agency (FEMA)	US-VA-Winchester	37,640.00+
1/3/2008	Training Specialist	Homeland Security, Federal Emergency Management Agency (FEMA)	US-MD-Emmitsburg	55,706.00+
1/4/2008	Program Analyst (Auditing)	Homeland Security, Office of the Inspector General	US-DC-Washington, DC	46,041.00+
1/4/2008	Electric Power Controller	Homeland Security, Federal Emergency Management Agency (FEMA)	US-GA-Thomasville, Georgia	21.92+ /hr
1/4/2008	Supervisory Program Specialist	Homeland Security, Federal Emergency Management Agency (FEMA)	US-DC-Washington	93,822.00+
1/7/2008	Program Specialist	Homeland Security, Federal Emergency Management Agency (FEMA)	US-DC-Washington	66,767.00+

Continued

Closing	Job Title	Agency	Location	Salary
1/7/2008	Deputy External Affairs Officer	Homeland Security, Federal Emergency Management Agency (FEMA)	US-LA-New Orleans Metro area	75,414.00+
1/10/2008	Supervisory Program Manager	Homeland Security, Federal Emergency Management Agency (FEMA)	US-DC-Washington	93,822.00+
1/14/2008	Civil Engineer	Homeland Security, Federal Emergency Management Agency (FEMA)	US-DC-Washington	79,397.00+
1/14/2008	Public Affairs Specialist (Internal Communications)	Homeland Security, Federal Emergency Management Agency (FEMA)	US-DC-Washington	82,165.00+
1/14/2008	Lead Public Affairs Specialist	Homeland Security, Federal Emergency Management Agency (FEMA)	US-LA-New Orleans Metro area	77,484.00+
1/31/2008	Contract Specialist	Homeland Security, Federal Emergency Management Agency (FEMA)	US-DC-Washington	46,041.00+

Continued

Closing	Job Title	Agency	Location	Salary
1/31/2008	Contract Specialist	Homeland Security, Federal Emergency Management Agency (FEMA)	US-MD-Emmitsburg	46,041.00+
1/31/2008	Contract Specialist	Homeland Security, Federal Emergency Management Agency (FEMA)	US-VA-Round Hill	46,041.00+
1/31/2008	Contract Specialist	Homeland Security, Federal Emergency Management Agency (FEMA)	US-DC-Washington	79,397.00+
1/31/2008	Contract Specialist	Homeland Security, Federal Emergency Management Agency (FEMA)	US-MD-Emmitsburg	79,397.00+
1/31/2008	Contract Specialist	Homeland Security, Federal Emergency Management Agency (FEMA)	US-DC-Washington	46,041.00+
3/31/2008	Procurement Analyst	Homeland Security, Federal Emergency Management Agency (FEMA)	US-DC-Washington	79,397.00+

Continued

Closing	Job Title	Agency	Location	Salary
12/31/2007	Inventory Management Specialist	Homeland Security, Federal Emergency Management Agency (FEMA)	US-DC-Washington	55,706.00+
1/3/2008	Logistics Management Specialist (Documentation Unit Lead)	Homeland Security, Federal Emergency Management Agency (FEMA)	US-FL-Orlando	54,364.00+
1/9/2008	Supervisory Management & Program Analyst	Homeland Security, Federal Emergency Management Agency (FEMA)	US-DC-Washington	79,397.00+
1/11/2008	Management Analyst	Homeland Security, Federal Emergency Management Agency (FEMA)	US-TX-Denton	78,560.00+
1/18/2008	DIRECTOR, OFFICE OF ACQUISITION MANAGEMENT	Homeland Security, Federal Emergency Management Agency (FEMA)	US-DC-Washington	111,676.00+
1/31/2008	Contract Specialist, GS-1102-9/11/12	DHS Headquarters	US-DC-Washington,	46,041.00+
1/31/2008	Contract Specialist, GS-1102-12/13	DHS Headquarters	US-DC-Washington, DC	66,767.00+
1/31/2008	Contract Specialist, GS-1102-13/14	DHS Headquarters	US-DC-Washington, DC	79,397.00+

Continued

Closing	Job Title	Agency	Location	Salary
1/31/2008	Contract Specialist, GS-1102-14/15	DHS Headquarters	US-DC-Washington, DC	93,822.00+
1/2/2008	Management and Program Analyst	Homeland Security, Transportation Security Administration	US-VA-Arlington	53,180.00+
1/4/2008	Logistics Management Specialist	Homeland Security, Transportation Security Administration	US-VA-Arlington	79,052.00+
1/10/2008	Financial Management Specialist	Homeland Security, Transportation Security Administration	US-VA-Arlington	79,052.00+
1/11/2008	Property Management Specialist	Homeland Security, US Secret Service	US-DC-Office of Administration, Administrative Operation	46,041.00+
1/9/2008	Training Specialist	Homeland Security, Federal Emergency Management Agency (FEMA)	US-DC-Washington	55,706.00+
12/31/2007	Budget Analyst	Homeland Security, Transportation Security Administration	US-VA-Arlington	53,180.00+
1/8/2008	Program Analyst	Homeland Security, Transportation Security Administration	US-VA-Arlington	53,180.00+

Continued

Closing	Job Title	Agency	Location	Salary
1/15/2008	Program Manager	Homeland Security, Transportation Security Administration	US-VA-Arlington	79,052.00+
1/18/2008	Director, Administration	DHS Headquarters	US-DC-Washington	111,676.00+
1/21/2008	Transportation Security Specialist Principle Security Inspector (PSI)	Homeland Security, Transportation Security Administration	US-VA-Arlington	64,799.00+
1/21/2008	Transportation Security Specialist Principle Security Inspector (PSI)	Homeland Security, Transportation Security Administration	US-DC-Washington	64,799.00+
1/28/2008	Lead Program Analyst—Maritime	Homeland Security, Transportation Security Administration	US-DC-Washington, DC and Arlington	64,799.00+
1/2/2008	Sector Enforcement Specialist	Homeland Security, Customs, and Border Protection	US-AZ-Yuma, AZ	29,655.00+
1/2/2008	Disaster Recovery & Operations Specialist	Homeland Security, Federal Emergency Management Agency (FEMA)	US-TX-Dallas-Ft Worth Metro area	55,119.00+
1/2/2008	Program Specialist	Homeland Security, Federal Emergency Management Agency (FEMA)	US-DC-Washington	67,767.00+
1/2/2008	Sector Enforcement Specialist	Homeland Security, Customs, and Border Protection	US-TX-El Paso, TX	29,655.00+

As one can see, the degree of specialization at the Federal level is far greater than at the local or state levels. On this one day, 309 jobs were listed in the category of emergency management.

Selected excerpts from the job postings indicating the degree to which managerial skills are required.[10]

Emergency Management Program Specialist

The Mitigation Division, Hazard Mitigation Branch is located in Region 3 where the division oversees implementation of the FEMA mitigation grant programs to include technical assistance, analysis, monitoring, and policy interpretation to support Federal and state grants management processes. The management processes include project scoping through application development, review, award, implementation, and close-out.

FEMA is looking for an individual to serve as an Emergency Management Program Specialist with strong analytical skills and the ability to interpret policies covering a myriad of constantly changing topics often under stressful situations.

Deputy Director—Legislative Affairs

FEMA is looking for an individual with exceptional strategic thinking, writing, and oral communication, problem solving and interpersonal skills to serve as a Deputy Director, Legislative Affairs.

Human Services Specialist

1. Knowledge of disaster assistance programs with respect to legislation, policies, and regulations concerning human services, housing assistance, and grant programs to affect an eligibility determination.

2. Knowledge of the Agency's NEMIS computer database or other databases to research, verify, and analyze information to make decisions regarding casework.

3. Skill in applying analytical and evaluative techniques to the identification, consideration, and resolution of complex issues or problems.

4. Ability to communicate both orally and in writing to collect and verify information from a variety of people due to the effects of a disaster and to provide customer service.

Training Specialist

The Emergency Management Institute (EMI) provides a nationwide training program of resident and nonresident instruction in emergency management to participants from state, local, and tribal governments, FEMA, DHS, and other Federal agencies, private sector, and non-governmental partners. The incumbent of this position plans, develops, monitors, evaluates, and manages one or more curricula areas and exercise programs, specifically in the curriculum and courses supporting the Incident Command System (ICS)/National Incident Management System (NIMS).

- Knowledge and application of the theories, principles, and techniques of adult education and performance-based training and exercise programs.
- Ability to plan adult training course delivery requirements including administrative and logistical arrangements using internal and external resources.
- Ability to determine job performance requirements and provide training and exercise solutions for federal, state, local and/or tribal audiences involved in providing emergency management services in accordance with the National Incident Management System (NIMS)/ Incident Command System (ICS) and/or the National Response Framework (NRF).
- Ability to effectively communicate orally with top-level officials in Federal, state, local and/or tribal government.
- Ability to effectively communicate in writing with top-level officials in Federal, state, local and/or tribal government.

Descriptions of the positions listed above all require management skills. Few, if any, references are made to skills associated with tactical response operations. Rarely, at the national level, is attention given to prior service in emergency response operations. What we see in the above representative sample are analytical skills, strategic thinking, writing, oral communication, problem solving, interpersonal skills, identification, and resolution of complex issues or problems. In addition, the job applicant must display proficiency in the application of theories, principles, and techniques of adult education and performance-based training and exercise programs. As discussed in Chapter 1, these are management skills, most of which are taught in college degree programs.

Career Development Skills for Emergency Managers

Given the job descriptions presented above, one might ask what career development skills are applicable to emergency managers at the local, state, and national levels? Some of the strategies and skills applied in business, industry, education, and public service will serve emergency managers well. The basics are preparation, presentation, and identification of transferable skills, networking, resume writing, and interview skills.

There is no substitute for preparation. We often hear successful people say they knew nothing about how to do their current job, when, in fact, they are succeeding at it. The truth is they were prepared by prior experience, or the transferability of knowledge from prior learning. Preparation for your next position should not have stopped when you got your current position. Lifelong learners continue to study, learn, and develop skills even as they perform in their present job. If your present position required a high school diploma, start work on an Associate's Degree. If you had a Bachelor's Degree when you were last hired, look for a graduate certificate or Master's Degree program. After I was hired as manager of emergency planning and employee communications in a power utility company, I completed a dozen or more training classes in ICS, weapons of mass destruction, emergency response to terrorism, OSHA HAZWOPER certification, Red Cross CPR, and a Doctoral Degree in education, to name a few. There is great joy associated with learning new things. Emergency managers must continually prepare for management of a new universe of threats. Just as we prepare for emergencies and disasters, we should prepare ourselves for the next step in our career.

Emergency managers are leaders who often must be convincing in their presentations, either to supervisors who control the budget or to citizens whose lives may be in jeopardy from an approaching storm. In either case, an emergency manager with excellent presentation skills is a valued asset. By improving one's presentation skills, the emergency manager presents a professional image and enhances the delivery of an important message. Not all emergency management messages are delivered via radio or the Internet. Many are delivered in face-to-face presentations.

Presentation skills are often overlooked in the greater scheme of career development. Effective speaking is not the only presentation skill. In today's world, messages are often enhanced with visuals. It is important for emergency managers to be able to craft visual aids using computer technology such as Power Point or to communicate at a distance using WebEx.

Identifying one's transferable skills is an exciting endeavor. Transferable skills are those acquired in one position or life experience that may be applicable to another position or experience. Many adults simply do not realize how many skills they possess. There are career development tools that can help. Whether you use methods prescribed by Studs Terkel, Howard Figler, William Bridges, Richard Bolles or any of the other career development authors, completing a skills inventory is bound to assist you in your career. The results of a skills inventory will provide language for your resume, recollection of past accomplishments, training, or educational gaps you can fill through additional study, and an improved sense of self worth. I strongly recommend Richard Nelson Bolles annually updated *What Color is Your Parachute?*[11] Many have read and completed the exercises for completing a skills inventory with great satisfaction.

Networking is highly valued by emergency managers. It is part of building working relationships amongst response agencies that must work together in disasters. It should also be a career development tool. One way to meet your next boss is to have a discussion at an emergency management association conference such as the annul conference of the International Association of Emergency Managers (IAEM);[12] the World Conference on Disaster Management (WCDM)[13] held annually in Toronto; the Disaster Recovery Journal[14] conferences held twice each year (March in Orlando, and September in San Diego); or one of the numerous association or privately sponsored conferences held regularly. Many states have statewide emergency manager's associations that conduct regular meetings or annual conferences. In some counties, bimonthly meetings are held for multiple emergency response agencies. All of these gatherings of emergency response, business continuity professionals and emergency management personnel provide excellent networking opportunities. When you attend, do not just sit there. Get up and introduce yourself; volunteer to help with the next program, or make a presentation about your program. Get out of the office as networking is done best face to face.[15]

Help with resume writing is readily available in most communities. The local small business development agency may assist; there are private career services; and the Department of Labor employment services units may all provide assistance.

The job of the resume is to get you the interview. Research shows that those who review resumes for posted positions may only read the first eight lines below your name and address. In those eight lines, they want to answer the question, "What can this person do for me?" So, use the first eight lines to identify your most valuable assets—skills, abilities, proven accomplishments. Don't waste lines writing about your career aspirations. Work experience, education, publications, and community service can follow, once the reader becomes interested in you by reading the first eight lines.

Your resume helps you get the interview and ultimately the job. With word processing widely available, there is no reason for a resume to be outdated. Update your resume every time you complete a training course, a college course, or attend a conference. It is easy to forget what you have done and where you have been, especially if a major disaster occurred on your watch.

Summary

In this chapter we have explored the career path in emergency management by looking at issues of entry-level positions, gaining experience as a volunteer, exploring positions at local, state, and national levels, and listing career development skills for emergency managers. Throughout the chapter, there have been opportunities to once again focus on the managerial aspects of careers in emergency management.

These are not careers in tactical response operations. In fact, there is little evidence in emergency management position titles, job requirements, or skills that match the titles, requirements, or skills required for success in tactical response operations. There is little to support the notion that experience as a first responder is essential for a career position in emergency management. In the three case studies that follow in Chapters 7, 8, and 9, an on scene look at emergency management in practice will be offered—at Ground Zero following the September 11 Attack, in Sri Lanka following the Indian Ocean tsunami, and in Louisiana and Mississippi in response to Hurricane Katrina.

Discussion Questions

1. How are entry-level positions in emergency management announced?

2. Where might one find a list of open positions?

3. What transferable skills can one develop as a volunteer?

4. What does volunteering have to offer business continuity professionals in business careers?

5. Why are emergency management positions at the state and national level more specialized than at the local level?

6. Are career development strategies and tools of any use to a person who already has a position in emergency management?

7. What are the associations and organizations that sponsor some of the largest conferences and networking opportunities in North America?

8. How can you learn more about the International Association of Emergency Managers (IAEM)?

References

1. Greg Shaw, in Blanchard, B. Wayne. (June 28, 2007). FEMA EMI Higher Education Presentation, Emmitsburg, Maryland.

2. *The 9/11 Commission Report: The final report of the national commission on terrorist attacks upon the United States.* (n.d.). New York: Norton. p. 398.

3. Phelan, T.D. (2001, Winter). *What's in a name? What do position titles tell us about the development of our profession?* Disaster Recovery Journal, P. 100.

4. http://www.redcross.org/services/disaster/ retrieved December 29, 2007.

5. https://www.citizencorps.gov/cert/about.shtm retrieved December 29, 2007.

6. http://www.acp-international.com/ retrieved December 29, 2007.

7. http://nyc.gov/html/oem/html/about/job.shtml retrieved December 29, 2007.

8. http://egov.cityofchicago.org/city/webportal/portalEntityHomeAction.do?entityName=Emergency+Communications&entityNameEnumValue=12 retrieved December 29, 2007.

9. http://dcema.dc.gov/dcema/cwp/view,a,3,q,531996,dcemaNav_GID,1531,dcemaNav,%7C31868%7C.asp retrieved December 29, 2007.

10. http://jobsearch.usajobs.opm.gov/jobsearch.asp?q=emergency+management&re=0&sort=rv&vw=b&jbf574=HS*&FedEmp=N&ss=0&brd=3876&FedPub=Y&caller=%2Fagency_search.asp&tm=&rad=&zip=&x=42&y=13 retrieved December 29, 2007.

11. Bolles, R.N. (2008*). What Color is Your Parachute? 2008: A Practical Manual for Job-hunters and Career-Changers.* Berkeley: Ten Speed Press.

12. See www.iaem.com

13. See www.wcdm.org

14. See www.drj.com

15. Phelan, T.D. (2005, November). "Get out of your office: networking is best face to face." *IAEM Bulletin.* p. 4.

Chapter 7

Case Study:
Ground Zero

Objectives of this chapter:

- Describe the complexity of tactical response operations.
- Describe the role of emergency management in a terrorist attack.
- Explain how widespread knowledge of ICS was an asset to the September 11 response.
- Describe the role of the Emergency Operations Center (EOC) at Pier 92.
- List the ways in which a Family Reception Center demonstrates a basic difference between tactical response operations and emergency management.
- List the matters that emergency management must handle long after tactical response operations are completed.

☑ Summary

☑ Discussion Questions

☑ References

Introduction

Much has been written about the September 11 Attack on the World Trade Center in 2001. At a minimum, emergency managers should have read *The 9/11 Commission Report: Final Report of the National Commission on Terrorist Attacks Upon the United States*.[1] After my deployment on September 11, 2001, with the Disaster Mortuary Operational Response Team (DMORT), I returned and contacted Congressman James Walsh (R) of New York to request a thorough after-action report conducted by a special commission. The commission needed, in my opinion, to be started immediately following the incident, to capture the rough notes of those on scene. My request was said to be premature, that there was something else underway in Washington that might include an effort led by Governor Tom Ridge of Pennsylvania. This was before the Department of Homeland Security had been established. My point was to capture the "real story" of first responders and emergency managers who were doing their jobs, and not thinking about saving their notes and recollections for recorded history. Since then, many of the first person accounts have been published, largely from the recollections of those who were involved. Though my notes are contained in a folder I carried from Ground Zero to the two temporary morgues on either side of it, to Piers 92 and 94, to the Medical Examiner's Office at First and 30th Streets, and to DMORT's command post near La Guardia International Airport, they are as close to being there as I can recall. They will serve as the background, however sketchy, for this case study.

The intent of this chapter is to compare and contrast the respective roles of tactical response operations and emergency management personnel. They both played important parts in responding to the attack. How they worked together and supported each other is of greater interest than how they differed. The purpose here is to show from one incident how the gap between emergency management and tactical response operations was bridged, if only for this one, highly documented moment in history.

Tactical Operations

First responders live to save lives. They save property and the environment in the process. The actions of the first responders—fire, police, EMS, search, and rescue teams—and a multitude of others, including valiant civilians, are now a matter of historical record. Following the first responders, there were others with special skills and abilities whose tireless efforts supported not only the first responders, but the victims and their families. Tactical response operations were conducted to rescue, recover, and restore those at Ground Zero as well as an entire nation. The 14,000 informant reports collected by the detectives of the New York City Police Department (NYPD) listed the cause of death as "homicide." How could so much physical destruction, fire, building collapses, debris, dust, odor, and thousands of responders be dealing with a mass homicide? Let us not forget that there were also two airliners, each with passengers and crews. Though focusing on New York, we must also remember the two other flights in Virginia and Pennsylvania.

Our culture, prior to September 11 dictated that when a fire is reported, fire-fighters respond and suppress it. They assess the scene as best they can, rescue anyone in harm's way, and put out the fire. It is our practice to run toward the building on fire. Tom Creamer once reported after September 11 that firefighters he encountered on a trip to Eastern Europe asked him, "Why do the American firefighters run toward a burning or bombed building?" Apparently, in more war-torn cities, fire-fighters are taught to stay away from the buildings under attack until the attack has ended. Then they rush to save those affected. In the United States, we have always done the opposite. Prior to September 11, with few exceptions, firefighters saw the burning building as the place on which to focus their response. The hazardous conditions at Ground Zero on September 11 were not obvious and unprecedented in this country.

An example of the shift in thinking that occurred following September 11 came to my attention on September 18, 2001. While on duty at Ground Zero, I received a call from my backup emergency planner in Syracuse, reporting an evacuation due to a bomb threat. Over 1,200 employees had evacuated the corporate headquarters, a seven-story building at its highest point. The employees had asked if they were far enough away from the building. Prior to September 11, those same employees merely wanted to comply with an evacuation or fire drill by just stepping outside the doors. After having seen the collapse of two 110-story buildings at the World Trade Center, they were now concerned about the building collapsing and the proper safe distance to avoid personal injury. This had never been a concern before.

Tactical response operations, under extremely unfamiliar and difficult conditions, suffered from a number of things. Number one was the tragic loss of life of civilians at work in the World Trade Center, and members of service who responded to save them. There were also the highly documented concerns about radio communication, estab-lishment of unified command, certain problems with messages and directions, and the on-going differences between the fire department (FDNY) and the police (NYPD).

When all is considered, the lives saved greatly outnumber those lost, though any loss of life is a major discouragement to first responders.

What I saw was an operation with over 10,000 workers per shift, and two 12-hour shifts per day. First responders from across the country were working at Ground Zero, together, and in an organized manner. Firefighters continued to contain and suppress fires that hampered search and rescue efforts for days. Teams of firefighters, resembling miners entering a mine shaft, climbed onto the rubble pile to enter paths leading to the depths where victims might still be alive or remains could be recovered. Steel workers partnered with firefighters to clear hot, heavy debris to make continued search and rescue, and recovery operations possible.

From the street along side the 16-acre site, the rubble pile appeared to be about 11 stories high, compressed from 110 stories. There were firefighters everywhere and search and rescue teams with their highly trained dogs. Even the dogs, according to their handlers, were showing signs of fatigue and depression because they were unable find anyone alive. I recall watching a line of firefighters with miner's headlights on their hard hats entering a cave-like opening about six stories up. The rubble pile was still smoldering, and the debris, especially the steel beams, seemed too hot to touch. It was clear that concerns with responder safety had risen to a new height. Signs of shoring, safety gear, and the presence of safety engineers were everywhere.

I worked the night shift, 6:00 p.m. to 6:00 a.m., and spent most of my time that first week at the Medical Examiner's Office uptown. When I visited Ground Zero, it was to make my rounds as the night shift mental health unit leader to each of DMORT's sites—two temporary morgues, one on Trinity Place and one in a tent near West and Vesey Streets, on the northwest corner of the World Trade Center. There were also the DMORT personnel at the Family Reception Center at Pier 94; the Emergency Operations Center (EOC), under development at Pier 92; the Medical Examiner's Office; the DMORT command post at the LaGuardia Marriott Hotel; and a small unit assisting the airlines at the hotel next door.

My observations of first responders were from points adjacent to the rubble pile rather than from being on it. There were many opportunities to observe, first hand, the work of those in tactical response operations. In discussions with some first responders, I became acutely aware of their dedication to their duties and their technical preparation to perform them.

Tactical response operations included the special skills of first responders— firefighters, search and rescue, emergency medical services personnel, and police.

One could see firefighters deploying apparatus around the 16-acre site, using adjacent buildings for strategic placement of fire hoses above the fires, and using every available device to clear debris and search for lost civilians and brother firefighters. Urban search and rescue teams were observed from other cities, including Oklahoma City, whose firefighters came as others had come to them in 1995. Chief John Cowin, from Syracuse was there with his search and rescue team. We had a moment in passing to talk between the fallen towers and the nearby marina on the Hudson River side of the World Trade Center. Fire suppression continued for days, with new challenges presented as the determination to find everyone lost took firefighters deeper into the wreckage of the fallen buildings.

While tactical operations continued, the entire area was designated as a crime scene. Security was tightened, and the NYPD was assisted by the National Guard. Members of the Guard were ever present, especially at night on street corners, when I found myself walking around the World Trade Center to get from Trinity Place to Vesey Street. The entire area had been sealed off. Seldom did I encounter anyone other than the security patrols or food service workers from any number of humanitarian organizations. Outside the morgue, on Vesey Street, there were always one or more clergymen, offering prayers over the remains of victims that arrived sporadically. Firefighters slept on the sidewalks of narrow side streets. They needed rest, but did not want to leave the area. Possibly they were concerned about not being able to get through security or traffic to find their way back if they went home. Chief John Pritchard of Battalion 41, Flatbush, Brooklyn, was quoted as saying,

> We tried to get them to go home and rest. But we had ten thousand guys who wouldn't go home.[2]
>
> …everywhere we turned were sleeping firefighters—they refused to go home because they were afraid they wouldn't get back, and they wanted to be there. So they'd sleep where they dropped.[3]

As first responders, their lives had been dedicated to saving others and putting out fires. They were not about to leave the biggest single incident they had ever seen, and certainly not without uncovering every bit of debris in search of their fellow responders.

The scene was a collection of skill, courage, emotion, and stamina, all directed toward tactical response operations. Like the players in a Broadway show, they were on stage performing their best, hot, under the lights, talented, trained, and ultimately applauded. One major difference—they were risking their lives.

Emergency Management

When first responders are heavily involved in tactical response operations, emergency management personnel are engaged in supporting them. Other than those on scene when the attack occurred, and ultimately involved in either evacuation or the rescue of others, no one in Emergency Management was in a life-threatening situation. As I understand the Incident Command System (ICS), as detailed in Chapter 4, all those on the organization chart are there to support the Operations Section Chief, the person who directs the effort to "put out the fire." In this case, the "fire" was a complex set of objectives including search and rescue, fire suppression, crime scene investigation, identification of hazardous material, debris removal, containing contamination, identification of remains (both civilian's and responder's), communications, logistics, personnel accountability, missing persons, media relations, resource management, politics, and national security.

If we do nothing more than look at the roles identified on the ICS command and general staff chart, we see the emergency management functions supporting operations—safety, public information, liaison, planning, logistics, finance, and administration. At Ground Zero, there were massive initiatives underway from the start involving emergency management support of tactical response operations.

My unit was DMORT. We assist the Medical Examiner's Office in identification of remains in a mass fatality incident. At the time, we were a unit of the U.S. Department of Health and Human Services, led by Secretary Tommy G. Thompson. Our National Commander was Tom Shepardson, of Syracuse, New York, who passed away February 18, 2003. We served in the background, in temporary morgues a block away from the fallen World Trade Center Towers, at the ME's office uptown, at the Family Reception Center at Pier 94, in the EOC at Pier 92, at our command post near La Guardia in East Elmhurst, and at Fresh Kills landfill in Staten Island. At some locations we provided forensic science, at others information to family members, and at still others, mental health support.

Background Information

TOM SHEPARDSON, FATHER OF THE DMORT PROGRAM

Thomas J. Shepardson, known in the disaster response community as father of the Disaster Mortuary Operational Response Team (DMORT) program, died suddenly Tuesday, Feb. 18.

"As a volunteer, Tom's efforts to add mortuary affairs and forensic experts to the National Disaster Medical System brought comfort and peace of minds to thousands of families," said HHS Secretary Tommy G. Thompson. "The identification of victims and proper treatment of their remains is Tom's lasting legacy. He will be truly missed by not only everyone in the DMORT program but also the entire National Disaster Medical System."

Shepardson first became a volunteer with the Department of Health and Human Services' Office of Emergency Preparedness in the late 1980s with a vision and plan to improve our nation's ability to respond to major disasters involving mass fatalities. He proposed volunteer teams be formed of professionals with expertise in not only mortuary affairs but also a variety of forensic sciences.

As a result of his efforts, HHS presented Shepardson's plan to the National Disaster Medical System (NDMS). It was accepted and in 1992 a network of ten DMORT teams, one in each federal region of the country, was established.

Shepardson continued to be a driving force behind the new DMORT program. He was instrumental in the development and procurement of portable morgue systems. As an instructor, he traveled across the country teaching mass fatality incident response at the Emergency Management Institute, the NDMS national conference and for many state governments.

As DMORTs began to carry out missions, Shepardson was there for every major deployment. His first assignment came when a DMORT was sent to assist state and local officials at the Oklahoma City Murrah Building bombing. Shepardson supervised the first use of the portable morgue system for the Korean Air crash in Guam. He also led DMORT response to a series of airline accidents including the 1999 Egypt Air and Alaskan Air crash in 2000.

"Facing the difficult challenges of disaster response with mass fatalities takes an extraordinary individual," said Acting Assistant Secretary for Public

Continued

Health Emergency Preparedness Jerome Hauer. "Tom was someone I knew we could always count on to be there in those trying times. He will be sorely missed."

While working with the National Transportation Safety Board, Shepardson helped develop the family assistance program that is now a key element in our nation's disaster response efforts.

After the September 11, 2001, terrorist attacks, Shepardson helped lead DMORT missions that saw teams deployed to both New York City and the Pennsylvania crash site. Over the course of the following ten months, Shepardson continued to lead DMORT assistance to the New York City Medical Examiner's office, which was critical in helping to identify hundreds of victims from the World Trade Center attack.

Ever the innovator, shortly before his death, Shepardson established a DMORT forensic oversight committee and was leading efforts to add cadaver dogs to the DMORT program.[4]

In the ICS structure, we were a branch under the Operations Section. As we understood it, because of the terrorist act of homicide, the response was under the direction of the NYPD. Unified Command, though not established on Day 1, was set up when the EOC was re-constructed at Pier 92. The Office of Emergency Management had moved its operations center from World Trade Center 7 which ultimately collapsed, to the Police Academy on Church Street and then to Pier 92. From the perspective of a support unit, one could see the structure of emergency management at work.

> The Command Center and the Family Reception Center were models of disaster response that could be applied to other emergencies of different types and sizes anywhere in the world.[5]

Let me list a few examples.

Accountability

There were thousands of personnel on scene at Ground Zero. It was a dangerous site due to the instability of the debris, on-going fires, hazardous dust and fumes, and the potential for accidents because of the array of apparatus, heavy construction equipment, and the possible threat of subsequent attacks. Many precautions were taken by emergency management to protect and account for the on-scene personnel. Once Pier 92 was equipped and staffed, special photo identification cards were issued to authorized personnel. The ID cards displayed icons for each area to which one was granted access. Mine contained a white letter Z in a red square for Ground Zero, the restricted zone around the World Trade Center; boxes with the numbers 92 and 94 for the EOC at Pier 92 and the Family Reception Center at Pier 94; a black letter E in a yellow square for Emergency Services; and a white letter M in a black square for the Morgues. It was a management function to provide proper clearances and identification to all those on scene. Such information was maintained in a database, a responsibility of the Planning Section. "No fewer than seven checkpoints were established along the Emergency Vehicle Access routes to Ground Zero at the World Trade Center."[6] These were along the West Side Highway north from Church Street. "I was always driven by one or two law enforcement officers in their patrol car since security was very tight."[6] At each checkpoint, law enforcement personnel or National Guard personnel would check the ID's of everyone in the vehicle.

Logistics

First responders and emergency management personnel need to be sustained while responding to an incident. Food, lodging, medical care, equipment, supplies, clothing, and sanitation all need to be provided. While those involved in tactical response operations are attending to their duties, emergency management personnel are sourcing the supplies and services required to sustain operations. Initially, everyone pitched in.

> Everybody down there was so willing to help. You couldn't walk 50 yards in any direction and not find a hot meal…meals prepared by chefs from the most famous restaurants in New York, giving you their specialties—and you ate them across the street from the rubble of the World Trade Center.[6]

> Supplies were available everywhere we turned—whatever you needed: knee pads, socks, underwear, gloves.[7]

For our unit, after spending the first night on a cot in a wash hanger at Stewart Air Force Base in Newburgh, we were provided hotel rooms, laundry service, and access to medical and mental health services. The Office of Emergency Management partnered with Verizon to position trailers within a block of the World Trade Center with banks of telephones on them so responders could call home. Partnerships with the Red Cross, the Salvation Army and local churches provided 24/7 food service. The USNS Comfort was docked along the Hudson River with medical facilities and doctors for any responder in need.

Planning and Public Information

At Pier 92, and Emergency Operations Center was quickly set up to provide emergency management support for the ongoing operation. The Command staff were positioned on a raised platform with curtained cubicles set up for each of the administrative units, equipped with computer equipment, phones, and Internet connectivity. Incident Action Plans were developed daily listing each day's objectives, personnel rosters, weather forecasts, resources, and public information releases. Mayor Rudy Giuliani played a major role as the primary spokesperson for the City. He was assisted by a staff of media relations professionals. In accordance with ICS, the Planning Section included the initiatives of each section in the daily Incident Action Plans.

Mutual Aid

At Pier 92, emergency management personnel from across the State of New York were observed staffing critical command and general staff positions. Because so many had been trained in ICS, shift changes were smooth and efficient. New York's emergency services departments—fire, police, and EMS—continue to this day to train in ICS to improve their capability to respond effectively to large-scale emergencies.

At Ground Zero, so many leadership personnel, particularly in the Fire Department of New York (FDNY) had been lost in the initial response, mutual aid services of other departments were critical to safety both at Ground Zero and throughout the other parts of the city.

Family Assistance Center

One exceptional management accomplishment following the September 11 Attack was the establishment of a Family Assistance Center. Staffing, equipping, and activating a large family assistance center is a major project requiring a management plan. It was done so well that it attracted visitors with broad humanitarian relief experience.

> Thereafter, the Secretary-General [Kofi Annan] stopped at the Family Reception Center, where those seeking missing relatives were interviewed in an attempt to locate or identify their loved ones. The Center also offered interpretation in many languages, grief and spiritual counseling in many faiths, child care, food, access to computers and televisions, a rest area with massage, and a sheltering space where grieving families could find all the information and support possible.[8]

The Center came together without prior planning largely due to the managerial efforts of Gino Menchini and Larry Knafo who coordinated the participation of multiple stakeholders. They included those whose offices had been in the Twin Towers, insurance companies, religious organizations, counseling services, the Red Cross, DMORT, and all of the suppliers who delivered and installed the telecommunications to support the Center. They even gathered artwork from the Metropolitan Museum of Art to create a respectful, comfortable atmosphere.

Private Sector Interface

Many private sector enterprises supported the response of both first responders and emergency management. For example, the IBM Crisis Response Team assisted with expertise in developing wireless input systems for use by City building inspectors. This provided for rapid relay of building inspections to the EOC so that confirmation of safe buildings would allow for companies to reopen. The Office of Emergency Management did their best to screen and approve for deployment many of the items and ideas offered by private sector companies. Ironing out the terms and conditions of the services provided continued far into the following years before all accounts were settled. Some things were donated, some leased, some borrowed, and some sold. The City has since developed a process for emergency response that will simplify this issue. This is a finance and administration responsibility under ICS.

Summary

In summary, emergency management functions at Ground Zero following the September 11 Attack involved management skills and strategies in support of the efforts of tactical response operations. Firefighters put out the fires, rescued as many people as possible, and saved lives. Law enforcement personnel investigated the reports of missing people, maintained order and security, and gathered the evidence leading to the determination of responsible parties for the attack. Beyond that, there were multiple demands for managing City personnel, facilities, public information, contractors, resources, communications, support for families, private sector issues, food service, medical service, housing, and liaison with multiple agencies and organizations offering assistance. Restoring the world's financial district was no small matter, even though the bulk of the damage was on a 16-acre site.

The September 11 Attack on the World Trade Center taught us many lessons. We increased our focus on terrorism, interagency cooperation, Unified Command, interoperable communications, family assistance centers, identification of remains, and air travel safety. The job done by those in tactical response operations was exceptional and not without extreme sacrifice. The tasks completed by emergency management personnel were vast and complex, and many continue to this day. There is little similarity, however, in the duties, roles, and responsibilities of on-scene first responders when compared to those of emergency management personnel. The gap between the two at Ground Zero was less evident during the on-scene response than it appears since that time. Anyone there could see the two working hard to meet their common objectives—saving lives, recovering from a vicious attack, and restoring the affected areas of New York's financial district. The Office of Emergency Management, NYPD, and FDNY, along with several other City agencies continue to plan for training and increased cooperation to bridge the gap between emergency management and tactical response operations.

Discussion Questions

1. List five responsibilities of tactical response operations demonstrated at Ground Zero.

2. List five responsibilities of emergency management personnel at Ground Zero.

3. Compare the two lists created in questions 1 and 2.

4. What similarities do you see? What differences?

5. Explain how emergency management supported operations in the response to the September 11 Attack on the World Trade Center.

References

1. *The 9/11 Commission Report: Final Report of the National Commission on Terrorist Attacks Upon the United States.* (n.d.). New York: Norton.
2. Ben Court, Josh Dean, Sean Flynn, Tom Foster, Devin Friedman, Alex Markels, Michael Ray, and David Wiley. (2001, November). "The Fire Fighters." *Men's Journal.* p. 78.
3. Phelan, Thomas D., Ed.D. (2001, October–November). "At Ground Zero." *Niagara Mohawk News.* p. 3.
4. United States Department of Health & Human Services. (2003). http://www.hhs.gov/news/press/2003pres/20030219.html retrieved December 30, 2007.
5. Gillian Martin Sorensen. (2001). A Visit to "Ground Zero," *United Nations Chronicle Online Edition.* XXXVIII: 3. http://www.un.org/Pubs/chronicle/2001/issue3/0103p8.html retrieved December 30, 2007.
6. Phelan, Thomas D., Ed.D. (2001, October–November). "At Ground Zero." *Niagara Mohawk News.* p. 4.
7. Phelan, Thomas D., Ed.D. (2001, October–November). "At Ground Zero." *Niagara Mohawk News.* p. 3.
8. Gillian Martin Sorensen. (2001). A Visit to "Ground Zero," *United Nations Chronicle Online Edition.* XXXVIII: 3. http://www.un.org/Pubs/chronicle/2001/issue3/0103p8.html retrieved December 30, 2007.

Chapter 8

Case Study: The Tsunami Response in Sri Lanka

Objectives of this chapter:

- Appreciate the difficulty of emergency response to an incident that took over 30,000 lives in a single day.

- Become aware of the role of the military in disaster response.

- Explore the challenges of setting up a national EOC, the Centre for National Operations.

- Identify the strategies adopted by the National Government for rescue, recovery, and restoration.

- Clarify the ways in which private sector and non-governmental organizations assisted in the response to the tsunami.

- Identify the new tools developed as a result of private sector involvement in the response.

- ☑ Summary

- ☑ Discussion Questions

- ☑ References

Introduction

In this case study of the Sri Lankan response to the Indian Ocean Tsunami in 2004, we will explore how private sector and nongovernmental organizations played a significant role in emergency management. We will also see an example of a nation where tactical response operations are conducted largely by the military. There was no formal national emergency management agency at that time. The most effective emergency response was provided by neighbors and family members, churches, temples, and humanitarian organizations. Local branches of the national government conducted on-scene response. The damage was almost all sustained along the coastlines, leaving the higher elevations as safe havens for survivors, many of them orphaned children. Unlike most disasters, the Indian Ocean Tsunami affected several countries—India, Indonesia, Sri Lanka, Thailand, Malaysia, Maldives, Myanmar, and Somalia on the coast of Africa. Tactical response operations differed in each country. They have different disaster response resources and cultures. For emergency managers, the immediate issues were recovery and restoration. Several unique challenges came later, assisting families and children to cope with their lost loved ones, post-traumatic stress, and finding permanent shelter. There were and still are the on-going issues of preparedness for future disasters.

This case study is based on perceptions from my role as a member of the IBM Crisis Response Team under the leadership of Brent Woodworth. We were deployed two days after the tsunami on December 28, 2004, as an advance team of four members, arriving first in Chennai, India, and later going on to Colombo, Sri Lanka. There we divided our team with two of us remaining in Colombo and two going on the Indonesia. My perspective is based on our response in Colombo, Sri Lanka in January 2005.

Tactical Operations

In Sri Lanka, the first responders to the tsunami were civilians. Neighbors, friends, churches, temples, and local police departments responded to assist anyone who had survived the enormous tsunami waves. Once survivors were collected on higher ground, recovery operations were conducted along the beaches, roadways, and railroad tracks close to the shores. Many fishing villages were located very close to the water line so as to make launching and drawing up fishing boats convenient. Many of the primitive homes were constructed too close to the water, with fragile building materials. Schools, churches, and temples were built on higher ground since the eastern coast of Sri Lanka along the Indian Ocean is narrow, rising sharply to bluffs above the shores and then on to the mountains in the center of this island nation. For the most part, the capital city, Colombo, the center of the national government, was unaffected except along inlet waterways. Colombo is on the western side of the island, facing India, and away from the Indian Ocean. Tactical response operations were conducted locally and included sheltering, burying the deceased, salvaging building materials and fishing equipment, and preserving religious sites. The immediate response operations dealt with search and rescue, sheltering and feeding survivors, and accounting for those lost.

In Sri Lanka, fishing provides the main source of food and income. With fishing villages washed away, food was in short supply. By government estimates, there were over 500,000 citizens in camps (shelters). Setting up the logistical support for many in camps was an incredible task. To complicate matters, the country was engaged in a struggle between the government and the Tamils in the northern and eastern provinces. Though both had been impacted by the tsunami, both continued to protect their "turf" during the response and recovery periods. The military, responsible to the government, had a twofold job dealing both with tsunami devastation and remaining on guard for possible Tamil attacks. The citizens in the north and east had the same concerns. Though sympathetic to the Tamils, they had to deal with the tsunami while being on guard for government retaliation. The only signs we saw of this in Colombo were the numerous military checkpoints on city streets, tight security at the president's offices, and sketchy reporting of tsunami-related death figures from the Tamils. There was a perception that reporting the actual number of casualties would portray weaknesses in the Tamil forces.

The military assisted in providing tactical support to the distribution of disaster relief supplies and to the collection of data on survivors in the camps. With communications systems damaged along the coasts, the military provided convoys that delivered critical supplies on their trips from Colombo to remote provinces. On their return trips, they brought data on numbers of survivors, their condition, medical, and food needs. They were also in a position to provide protection from opposition forces in civil conflict.

Sri Lanka does not have three levels of government, like in the United States where we have local, state, and Federal governments. The local governments, including the police, are branches of the national government.

Sri Lankan Government Structure

Although Sri Lanka is a unitary state, it is nonetheless divided into nine provinces (out of which 2 have been later amalgamated for the purpose of establishing one provincial council) whose borders follow historic and traditional lines. The key administrative unit has traditionally been the district, into which the provinces are further divided. There are a total of 25 districts under the control of senior civil servants who are district officers responsible to the government in Colombo for ensuring justice, maintaining law and order, collecting revenues, and allocating development funds.

In addition to Sri Lanka's government response efforts, many of the tactical operations were performed by humanitarian organizations, foreign government assistance, and nongovernmental organizations (NGOs). I visited an NGO who provided assistance to orphaned children. Sarvodaya had regional facilities with Internet connectivity in many, if not all, of the provinces. They offered the use of their facilities to help the government gather data from the camps. This could speed the receipt of critical information leading to the rapid distribution of relief equipment and supplies, especially food. The offer was denied by the government, teaching me that NGO assistance can sometimes be held suspect by government officials.

Sarvodaya

The Lanka Jatika Sarvodaya Shramadana Sangamaya (Sarvodaya) is Sri Lanka's largest and most broadly embedded people's organisation, with a network covering: 15,000 villages, 345 divisional units, 34 district offices; 10 specialist Development Education Institutes; over 100,000 youth mobilised for peace building under Shantisena; the country's largest micro-credit organization with a cumulative loan portfolio of over US$1million (through SEEDS, Sarvodaya Economic Enterprise Development Services); a major welfare service organisation serving over 1,000 orphaned and destitute children, underage mothers and elders (Sarvodaya Suwa Setha); and 4,335 pre-schools serving over 98,000 children.

According to Sarvodaya, "Giant Tsunami waves that crashed onto the Sri Lankan coast carried away the lives of 40,983 people on the island and injured 23,189. A total of 4,846 people are still reported missing. The greatest tribute anyone can make to those who were lost to the catastrophe is to help their loved ones recover their lives that were left in shambles. Sarvodaya has indeed been engaged in this work since the day tsunami struck..."[1]

We also saw American military conducting supply missions using helicopters. Air Force units were staying in the Colombo Plaza Hotel and completing several flights per day to deliver food and medical supplies to affected areas along the coast. In addition, we met pilots from Franklin Graham's Samaritan Purse faith-based organization, flying needed supplies on a daily basis. Christian missionary organizations had previously-established relationships with villagers along the coast. Their work, particularly in restoring housing, continues to this day.

There were crews working to clear the rail lines where passenger trains had been upended and derailed by the waves. Telecommunications workers were restoring vital communication systems where poles and wires had been destroyed. Police officials had taken on the responsibility for burying the dead in sandy graves along the coast. Unwarranted fears of contracting disease from the remains prompted hasty burials. The police, however, had photographed each victim for identification purposes. To the extent they could, they collected documents, particularly those that identified foreigners, so as to determine their country of origin. This proved to be vitally important later.

Emergency Management

Emergency management in the hours and days immediately following the tsunami was headed by the military. We met with the Assistant Secretary of Defense on Wednesday, January 5, 2005, who explained the nature of his disaster response efforts. His primary mission was the transport by truck of food, medicine, water, equipment, tents, and building materials from Sri Lanka's only airport in Colombo and from three harbors, Colombo, Trinco, and Galle. Trinco is located in the northeast, where

Tamil rebels were a threat. The port at Galle, in the southeast, had been heavily damaged by the tsunami. Government and private firms operated a tracking system for supplies entering the country at the Colombo airport, with the goal of properly and equally distributing everything received. The system was also to track which agency was responsible for which supplies. He explained that there were three roads for getting supplies to those in need:

1. Ministry of Social Welfare and Women's Affairs and in the northeast, Ministry of Rehabilitation ad Reconstruction;

2. Ministry of Health, Medical Supply Division;

3. NGO and individual donations.

He explained that local donations were very high. The World Food Program had food in storage which was sent. The difficulty was coordinating the efforts of each program with ministries.

We visited the airport to see the distribution system. On the government side, it was chaotic and hampered by regulations. We saw entire shipments remain on aircraft which could not be off-loaded due to customs regulations. The warehouse was in disarray. On the private side, the handling of supplies was managed by a partnership among DHL, FedEx, and UPS. The traffic manager was a retired DHL manager from Ireland. He had a computerized tracking system and a warehouse filled with medical supplies from Italy, blankets from India, rice from China, and countless other donated shipments, organized like a modern warehouse. As material was loaded on trucks, identification data was collected about the truck, the driver, the organization, and the destination. The only missing link was confirming that the supplies were needed, and in what quantities, at the destinations indicated. It became absolutely clear to us that we might best serve by providing emergency management expertise, especially in logistics through computerized applications for managing donated supplies.

We were invited to a meeting in the Parliament chambers at the capitol by President Chandrika Kumaratunga's Secretary of Education, Dr. Tara De Mel. She requested a meeting with all private sector and NGO representatives interested in assisting with the relief efforts. The meeting was very well organized and could serve as a model for other governments responding to a disaster.

Sri Lankan Government's Model for Disaster Response by Businesses and NGOs

In Sri Lanka, following the tsunami, the president appointed Dr. Tara De Mel, secretary of education, to direct the Centre for National Operations (CNO), a national emergency operations center. When the search and rescue operations shifted to recovery and restoration, Dr. De Mel outlined the recovery operations using a three concentric circle diagram showing the progression from the inner circle (humanitarian relief), to the second circle (reconstruction), to the outer circle (economic development).

As the focus shifted from humanitarian relief to reconstruction, Dr. De Mel called a meeting in the Parliament Chamber at the national capital for business and other private sector representatives. The meeting attracted approximately 250 private sector leaders. Dr. De Mel presented the model for rebuilding Sri Lanka and invited businesses to submit a one-page form describing products, services, or donations the private sector wished to bring to the attention of the government for use in the reconstruction. The user-friendly forms were collected at the meeting, and participants were informed of the government plan to review the ideas presented and to contact the private sector starting on or about Feb. 1, 2005. The form contained the following:

We wish to pledge the following toward rebuilding the nation:

- Infrastructure—Housing/Shelter
- Schools—Child Care
- Hospitals—Medicine & Healthcare
- Fisheries
- Transportation
- Other

Our company/organization will undertake to fully/partially construct the above mentioned and pledge the value of rupees for this purpose which will be by way of direct finance/expertise/or handover after completion.

With one brief meeting, the Sri Lankan government had invited the private sector to recommend possible solutions to the complex problems of rebuilding a nation following a serious disaster. The meeting was conducted with the government plan presented clearly, followed by a Q&A period for business and other private sector clarification.[2]

The Centre for National Operations

Sri Lanka did not have a national office for disaster response in December of 2003 when the tsunami hit. Immediately after the disaster, a large room in the capitol was converted into an emergency operations center called the Centre for National Operations (CNO). When I arrived, about 100 people were present, working from tables with telephone and computer cables strung everywhere. The room had beautiful natural wood-covered walls, which, though quite attractive, echoed tremendously. It was a chaotic scene. There were advisors from the United Nations, USAID personnel, government ministry personnel, and our team from IBM. We were the only private sector people in the room. We had come prepared to propose a computer application that could greatly reduce the confusion, especially with logistics.

In the four days following the tsunami, a group of IT professionals, all based in Sri Lanka, had come together to create an application to track people, both survivors and deceased victims, camp registration, requests for supplies, donations, and organization information. The newly created application was called "Sahana." The IBM country manager for Sri Lanka, Kavan Ratnayaka, had introduced us to Dr. Sanjiva Weerawarna of the Lanka Software Foundation, and an IBM employee. The foundation had created Sahana. The IBM Team went to the government to offer Sahana and corporate support for its becoming the principal database for the CNO. This powerful, open source, application could possibly help to organize the disaster relief operations.

Sahana

Sahana is a Free and Open Source Disaster Management system. It is a Web-based collaboration tool that addresses the common coordination problems during a disaster from finding missing people, managing aid, managing volunteers, tracking camps effectively between Government groups, the civil society (NGOs) and the victims themselves.

Sahana is an integrated set of pluggable, web based disaster management applications that provide solutions to large-scale humanitarian problems in the aftermath of a disaster. Our aspirations are as follows:

1. **Primary:** Help alleviate human suffering and help save lives through the efficient use of IT during a disaster

2. Bring together a diverse set of actors from Government, Emergency Management, NGOs, INGOs, spontaneous volunteers and victims themselves in responding effectively to a disaster

3. Empower the victims, responders, volunteer to better enable them to help themselves and others

4. Protect victim data and reduce the opportunity for data abuse

5. Provide a Free and Open Source solution end-to-end available to everyone

With the above aspirations, the main applications built into Sahana and problems they address so far are as follows:

1. **Missing Person Registry** - Helping to reduce trauma by effectively finding missing persons

2. **Organization Registry** - Coordinating and balancing the distribution of relief organizations in the affected areas and connecting relief groups allowing them to operate as one

3. **Request Management System** - Registering and Tracking all incoming requests for support and relief up to fulfillment and helping donors connect to relief requirements

4. **Camp Registry** - Tracking the location and numbers of victims in the various camps and temporary shelters setup all around the affected area

5. **Volunteer Management** - Coordinate the contact info, skills, assignments and availability of volunteers and responders

6. **Inventory Management** - Tracking the location, quantities, expiry of supplies stored for utilization in a disaster

7. **Situation Awareness** - Providing a GIS overview of the situation at hand for the benefit of the decision makers

Current Deployments

Sahana has currently been deployed successfully in the following places:

1. **Tsunami - Sri Lanka 2005** - Officially deployed in the CNO for the Government of Sri Lanka

2. **AsianQuake - Pakistan 2005** - Officially deployed within with NADRA for the Government of Pakistan

Continued

3. **Southern Leyte Mudslide Disaster - Philippines 2006** - Officially deployed with the NDCC and ODC for the Government of Philippines

4. **Sarvodaya - Sri Lanka 2006** - Deployed for Sri Lanka's largest NGO

5. **Terre des Hommes - Sri Lanka 2006** - Deployed with new Child Protection Module

6. **Yogjarkata Earthquake - Indonesia 2006** - Deployed by ACS, urRemote and Indonesian whitewater association and Indonesian Rescue Source

Recognition

Though application of Sahana is the greatest recognition of the value of the Sahana system to help out in disasters, our work also has been recognized in other ways

1. Sahana won the Free Software Foundation Award for Social Benefit in 2006 amongst other contenders such as OLPC, Project Gutenburg and Wikipedia

2. Software 2006, USA - Good Samaritian Award - 2006

3. Network Wold Article 2006 on Top Open Source Companies to Watch: Identified as one of the top 10 Open Source "companies" to watch by Network world

4. Interview of core team in BBC program "code breakers" - 2006

5. One of the three top finalists in the Health category in Stockholm Challenge - 2006

6. Sourceforge Project of the Month for June 2006

7. Sahana inspired the new Free Software Foundation Award for Social Benefit - 2005

8. Redhat User Award - Given to the founder of Lanka Software Foundation Dr Sanjiva Weerawarna - 2005

For a more detailed account of Sahana you can download any of the following

1. More detailed Sahana overview (PDF)

2. UNDP IOSN Case Study on Sahana (PDF)

3. Sahana Brochure (PDF)[3]

The CNO data was ultimately made available on a web site. At one point, a person could log on to the CNO website and sort a database by country, and find information about a person from that country who had been listed as a victim, deceased, or alive. Furthermore, the site contained maps, showing statistical data on tsunami casualties.

The mandate of CNO was to monitor and coordinate all initiatives taken by government ministries, agencies, and other institutions relating to post-tsunami relief efforts. The purpose of CNO was to ensure that each effort fits into the overall objectives of the government relief programme, prevent the duplication of tasks and maximize the efficient utilization of resources.[4]

The CNO benefited from emergency management expertise provided by several nations. The amazing collection of experienced emergency management professionals who gathered in Sri Lanka demonstrated the ability of emergency management principles and practices. As a result of their expertise, they were able to create order out of chaos. The strategic plan developed in the CNO to progress from humanitarian relief to reconstruction to economic development (the three stages outlined in Dr. De Mel's meeting with the private sector), resembled the Incident Action Plan objectives used in the United States today as part of ICS. The plan included specific objectives for each of the three operational periods—(1) Humanitarian Relief, (2) Reconstruction, and (3) Economic Development.

Summary

In Sri Lanka, the military, both Sri Lankan and foreign, assisted by NGOs and faith-based organizations performed tactical response operations. The initial efforts were local, often provided by Sri Lankan citizens assisting their families, friends, and neighbors. Later, heavy logistical operations were assisted by private sector shipping companies. Camps were set up and managed by both the government and NGOs. There were major efforts to distribute critical supplies to those in need. Private sector shipping specialists from DHL, FedEx, and UPS sorted and moved donated supplies from all over the world.

The critical need for supplies, especially food, medicine, water, and building materials, gave rise to the mission of the government's Centre for National Operations. This became the hub of emergency management personnel. United Nations personnel experienced in disaster relief, and private sector members of the IBM Crisis Response Team worked side by side.

The multitude of skill sets utilized in the tsunami relief effort in Sri Lanka clearly demonstrated the differences between tactical response operations and emergency management. The relief effort also showed how they must work together, front line efforts and background management to support them.

The emergency management functions performed in the CNO were necessary to support the work of first responders in the affected provinces along the eastern coast. Strategic planning, financial management, communications, and coordination of multiple agencies were all performed by the management personnel in the CNO. Both management and on-scene relief efforts continue today, and continue to demonstrate ways to bridge the gap between emergency management and tactical response operations.

Discussion Questions

1. List the actions taken by tactical responders, often civilians, following the tsunami in Sri Lanka.

2. What are some of the logistical operations required to support over 500,000 people in camps?

3. What was the significance of the military's role in Sri Lanka?

4. How did the Sri Lankan government enlist the support of the private sector and NGOs?

5. What were some of the management functions of the Centre for National Operations?

6. What are the contributions made by the creation of Sahana?

References

1. http://www.sarvodaya.org/about/ retrieved December 31, 2007.
2. Dr. Thomas D. Phelan. (2006 Winter). "Inviting Businesses to Respond," Disaster Recovery Journal, 19:1. http://www.drj.com/articles/win06/1901-ppbi.html retrieved December 31, 2007.
3. http://www.sahana.lk/overview retrieved December 31, 2007.
4. Centre for National Operations, http://globalhand.org/data/organisation.2006-01-04.9080706205/ retrieved December 31, 2007.

Chapter 9

Case Study: Private and Public Perspectives from Katrina

Objectives of this chapter:

- Identify the roles of tactical response operations and emergency management in a single branch responding to Katrina.

- Explore the potential for private sector involvement in disaster relief.

- Examine how FEMA affected DMORT operations in identification of the deceased.

- List some of the differences between private and public response to Katrina.

- Describe how tactical response operations were supported by emergency management principles and practices at DMORT's Command Post.

- Identify lessons learned from emergency management challenges in one branch.

☑ Summary

☑ Discussion Questions

☑ References

Introduction

There are many ways to view the response to Hurricane Katrina. Volumes have been published on the performance by FEMA, the governors of Louisiana, Mississippi, Alabama, Texas and Florida, communications interoperability, levee construction, evacuation, victim relocation, restoration of New Orleans, and countless related topics. This case study will focus on only one public sector branch, DMORT (Disaster Mortuary Operational Response Team), and how one member's perspective was influenced by responding for both private and public sector units following Katrina.

My first assignment was private sector consultant, assisting colleges and universities in assessing damage and applying for emergency assistance from FEMA. I felt challenged to have spent three weeks on the ground serving as a private, emergency management consultant and then to receive a phone call on the plane going home to respond with DMORT in the public sector for another three weeks. The transition from private sector response to public sector was unique. The dual roles gave me the opportunity to gain two very different perspectives of the same disaster; to compare tactical response operations and emergency management close up. As in the previous two chapters, the observations are personal and solely my own.

Tactical Operations

When I arrived in Baton Rouge, Labor Day weekend, 2005, Hurricane Katrina was history. What remained was the devastation left in her path. My travels took me from Baton Rouge to Bourbon Street, from Louisiana to Long Beach, Mississippi, observing the destruction along the way. My experience with tactical response operations started in St. Gabriel, Louisiana, where DMORT had set up their morgue and command post operations. My arrival was through the Louis Armstrong New Orleans International airport, which had just shut down the temporary medical and evacuation operations. It was strange to arrive at such a large airport and find no one there. It was Saturday,

October 8, 2005. I was part of a third wave of DMORT personnel. The morgue in St. Gabriel was well-established and well-staffed with experts in forensics when I arrived. The City of St. Gabriel had converted a single-story elementary school into a City Hall, complete with a Mayor's Office, the Police Headquarters, and a senior citizen's center. The surrounding grounds looked as though they were used for sports and recreation—one or more ball fields. Adjacent to the school building was a modern, single-story warehouse with loading docks at one end. The Disaster Portable Morgue Unit (DPMU) was set up inside.[1] The school building had been converted to DMORT's Command Post. A medical unit was in one room, and several classrooms were now billeting areas where cots, pillows, and sleeping bags were arranged, about 20 per room. The gym was our supply area at one end, and our daily briefing meeting area on the end with the stage. Outside, there were logistical support units including a tractor trailer housing showers (Birds' Bath); two tractor trailers for the kitchen and food storage along side a mess hall tent and hand washing areas; a laundry service trailer, two hard shell structures called yurts constructed on raised platforms and used for giving massages; a few motor homes; a refueling island; and 35 leased vehicles. The vehicles, our motor pool, became one of my responsibilities as Deputy Logistics Section Chief.[2]

The tactical response operations of DMORT are not first responder operations in the traditional sense. Normally, before our work can begin, first responders have made the site safe, established a perimeter, and rescued and treated any survivors. We respond to mass casualty incidents where the resources of the local medical examiner have been exhausted or exceeded. Recovered remains are brought to our portable morgues nearby. (There was another DMORT morgue in Biloxi, Mississippi for Katrina response.) In St. Gabriel, we worked to support both the Louisiana State Medical Examiner (Dr. Cataldie) and the Orleans Parish Coroner (Dr. Frank Minyard). Both Dr. Cataldie, and Dr. Minyard were on site while I was there. DMORT personnel supported them as they worked tirelessly. They spent many nights in motor homes parked close to the morgue.

What is a Yurt?

Figure 9.1 Photos of the yurts.

The DMORT camp had yurts (Figures 9.1 and 9.2) constructed that were used by Salvation Army massage therapists daily. Yurts are nomadic-style structures that originated in Mongolia thousands of years ago. They doubled as sleeping quarters for the therapists and other personnel.

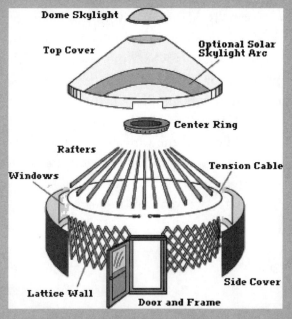

Figure 9.2 Schematic of a yurt. ©2008 Pacific Yurts Inc. – Cottage Grove, OR – www.yurts.com.

DMORT tactical operations in the morgue were supported by a Command Post, organized according to the Incident Command System. Even in such a highly specialized base camp, there are multiple logistical issues. We needed special trailers for forensic dentists, refrigerated trailers for storage of remains, specialized units within the morgue for X-rays, photography, finger printing, DNA sampling, casketing, and documentation. Initially we deployed our WMD unit and set up a decontamination station where remains entered the morgue. This was later deemed unnecessary and demobilized.

DMORT's facility was highly secured by Federal law enforcement units and private contractor security companies. We needed radios for internal communication since the morgue and the refrigerated trucks were at two different sites. Radios were also highly utilized for communication between the various areas within the compound—Command, Planning, Human Resources, Logistics, Security, Supply, Medical, Trailer Management, and the Chaplain. Dozens of cell phones, walkie talkies, and encrypted radios were issued.

In addition to the tactical operations in the morgue, we had strike teams whose job it was to recover remains that had been disrupted in cemeteries, often several hours away. These teams had to encounter flooded bayous where caskets had been washed out of cemeteries. They were constantly on guard for insects, alligators, snakes, and dangerous fallen debris. They were often off site for days at a time, sleeping in churches and communicating with the Command Post periodically, but not always regularly. Seriously damaged caskets required recasketing remains. For this purpose, remains were shipped back to St. Gabriel where identification and recasketing could be properly done. DMORT had gained experience in this process following Hurricane Floyd in North Carolina.

The professional skills of medical examiners, forensic dentists, X-ray technicians, DNA specialists, finger print specialists, and funeral directors are examples of tactical response operations. They all require specialized training, most of which is done in college classrooms and accredited degree programs. The tasks are analogous to what firefighters and law enforcement officers do, but the tasks require more education than training. The dedicated work of DMORT is not emergency management. DMORT has its own staff of emergency management professionals, involved in Command Post operations, planning, logistics, finance, and administration. They are all on scene to support the morgue operations.

Emergency Management

Emergency management skills are required to support DMORT as a single branch, just as they are required for the incident as a whole. DMORT gained a great deal of experience with the Incident Command System at Ground Zero. We had seen active duty before ICS was required, for example at the TWA 800 crash in 1996, and in Guam following the crash of Korean Airlines Flight 801 in 1997. Our National Commander, Tom Shepardson, was from Syracuse where the Public Safety Training Center, under the direction of Rich Flanagan, had been teaching ICS for some time in cooperation with the New York State Emergency Management Office (SEMO). I remember being appointed to a position at Ground Zero where Tom Shepardson had asked me to ensure that our Command Post was adhering to ICS principles and practices. It was not easy to introduce ICS in the field to DMORT seasoned veterans who were not as familiar with ICS as they were with our core mission. Just-in-time field training on ICS is not recommended, from my experience. ICS training should precede active deployment and be on-going. The point is that management skills need to be taught in advance of requirements to use them in the field during a disaster.

The ways in which the emergency management principles and practices supported DMORT Operations following Katrina were countless. We had a Command Staff and each of the four sections comprising the general staff—Operations, Planning, Logistics, and Finance/Administration. The Logistics Section Chief's desk was in the same elementary school classroom as Planning, Transportation, and one FEMA supply advisor. The adjacent offices housed Command, Human Resources, and a unit from the Forest Service, which supplied logistical and facilities support. The Medical Unit was in a separate wing. The storeroom or warehouse was across the building in the gym. All of us were about 50–100 yards from the morgue.

Planning completed a daily Incident Action Plan and spent a great deal of time enlisting support personnel for the next reporting period. DMORT members were contacted all across the country to report to duty in St. Gabriel. Human Resources did double duty keeping track of personnel and assisting with hourly time sheets for payroll, and expense reporting.

Logistics had several areas of responsibility. My responsibilities as Deputy Logistics Section Chief were in transportation, communication, supply chain, and distribution. The section administered the transportation unit, a fleet of 35 rented vehicles.

We distributed and maintained communication equipment. Perhaps our most critical function was procurement of supplies and equipment. For this, we worked with FEMA in Baton Rouge and New Orleans. It was often difficult communicating to veteran FEMA personnel the needs of a mortuary unit. DMORT was new to FEMA, and FEMA procurement personnel were unfamiliar with our supply needs. It was the cause of some tension, partly because of the sensitive nature of mortuary supplies, and partly because of our remote location. We had formerly been a unit of Health and Human Services, and were returned to HHS when DHS was restructured following Katrina.

Health professionals seem to understand the needs of medical examiners better than do the disaster recovery personnel. Oddly, DMORT had to do both, forensics and emergency management. In the former organization, when DMORT was under Health and Human Services, our requests for technical equipment and supplies were not questioned. There was a high degree of professional respect for our medical examiners and mortuary specialists. At the St. Gabriel morgue, we were separated from the FEMA procurement unit in Baton Rouge. Often, Logistics had to supply lengthy rationales for the ordering of supplies. This took additional time and often delayed the ordering and receipt of supplies. The details we had to present were known to DMORT personnel, but not to FEMA personnel who did the purchasing. One example was an order for a set of rolling aluminum stairs for accessing refrigerated trailers where remains were stored. The order was at first rejected because our facility had a loading dock. FEMA procurement could not understand that several trailers were located adjacent to the morgue, but trailer management personnel from DMORT did not need to move the entire trailer to the loading dock. They needed only to load and unload remains in body bags while the trailers were parked. As an alternative, the Forest Service built a set of steps from pressure-treated lumber. The steps were perfect, but too heavy to move from trailer to trailer without a fork lift. The Forest Service personnel on site in St. Gabriel performed many similar tasks to facilitate our work.

DMORT performed well in response to Katrina, bringing expertise from earlier disasters and professional experts from across the nation. Our success was because of the professionals who worked inside the morgue and the trained emergency management personnel who supported them. We were honored to be visited by Admiral Thad Allen when he took command of Katrina Operations. He inspected our site, had dinner with us, and addressed the DMORT unit.

Hurricane Katrina: Dignity, Respect and ICS

(This excerpt is from a 2005 article written for *Disaster Recovery Journal*, closer in time to the actual DMORT response.)

This professional effort was supported by a staff of administrators using the Incident Command System. There was an Incident Commander, PIO, Safety Officer and all of the required Section Chiefs (Operations, Planning, Logistics, and Finance/Administration). They were from DMORT regions all across the country. A daily Incident Action Plan was prepared by Planning, and daily briefing meetings were held each morning. A specially trained WMD task force from DMORT was deployed when signs of contamination were observed due to contaminants in flood waters. DMORT personnel and support personnel were housed on cots in former elementary classrooms and special purpose rooms. Local employees maintained the facility with care given to the provision of bottled water, bedding, laundry services, and even massage. Religious services were held in the camp and at local churches. One local church provided ice cream socials and access to televised football games and the World Series which helped with morale.

The spirit amongst personnel in the camp was excellent. There was singing and playing of folk guitars. One of New Orleans' noted coroners is a jazz trumpeter, and he entertained the troops one morning. Admiral Thad Allen joined us one evening for dinner and a brief message. About 50 media representatives were escorted through the non-morgue areas of the camp one afternoon, after which a press conference was held in the smoking tent. As a PPBI member and a member of DMORT, it was interesting for me to witness the usefulness of the NIMS Incident Command System in practice. PPBI offers a course on the use of NIMS ICS in Business and Industry. It's an excellent way to organize leadership and personnel for response to a crisis. From what I saw in the field, I'd recommend it to anyone in business, government or industry who truly wants to be prepared for managing a disaster.[2]

Private Sector Response

The private sector work, a topic for another book, was intense and eye-opening. My private sector assignment was with the IBM Crisis Response Team, as an Emergency Management Specialist. We were to assist the IBM office in Baton Rouge with providing consulting services to their clients. I worked primarily with the President's Office of the LSU System on the campus of LSU in Baton Rouge. LSU President Bill Jenkins and his staff were directing and assisting several college campuses with response and recovery efforts. Among them were the University of New Orleans, the LSU Health Science Center Medical School, the School of Dentistry, and Charity Hospital. It gave me a chance to see the devastation in New Orleans and in Long Beach, Mississippi, and everywhere along the way. I saw first hand how the intricacies of coping with state issues and dealing with FEMA for public assistance.

Our IBM Team met with high-level college and university leaders, some of whom had vast experience in crisis management. We met with former FEMA Director James Lee Witt, when his consulting firm was contracted to assist Governor Blanco. We stood in line with the Rev. Jesse Jackson to offer our services to the State of Louisiana, particularly the systems IBM has used in Sri Lanka for tracking victims and donations and at Ground Zero for reporting building inspection data.

One advantage of the private sector experience was learning about the larger issues of coordination and cooperation across levels of government and building relationships between government and the private sector. For example, we were escorted into downtown New Orleans by the Louisiana State Police to attend on scene meetings with veterinarians from the U.S. Public Health Service and the LSU Health Science Center Medical School to check on laboratory animals left behind when Katrina struck. Once the animals were found alive, they were transported by vehicles from the Department of Corrections and by the Primate Center at Tulane University. My experience with the Animal and Plant Health Inspection Service (APHIS) under USDA a few years earlier was invaluable to my work on the ground in New Orleans. Coordinating the safe evacuation of laboratory animals to the School of Veterinary Medicine at LSU in Baton Rouge was an effort requiring an understanding of the "big picture" and emergency management.

Summary

From a highly specialized branch and base camp, DMORT provided me an opportunity to see emergency management and tactical response operations in very close proximity. Was there a gap, even within a single unit? Yes, the gap was there, but so was the bridge. Emergency management, as applied to DMORT, provided the support necessary to sustain the efforts of professionals in the morgue. We needed to have managers to coordinate our work with FEMA. Left on our own and provided the appropriate funding mechanisms, we might have done even better. Things just do not work that way when multiple jurisdictions using multiple funding sources were needed to respond to a large disaster. The interdependencies were great; and the required coordination to achieve cooperation was extraordinary.

Our professional forensic personnel were not only good at tactical response operations, they were a close-knit team, similar to the "brotherhood" we hear of in the FDNY or NYPD. It was obvious when DMORT personnel worked together in the morgue and in the support units. We experienced high esprit de corps demonstrated in our morning briefing meetings.

The technical professionals were supported by emergency management personnel in Command, Planning, Logistics, and Finance/Administration. The management group used skills of coordination, budgeting, accounting, resource tracking, communicating, purchasing, and documentation. The Incident Commander conducted daily debrief meetings requiring organization and communication skills.

Of special note was the universal sense of respect operations and management shared. Whether it was the morning music, the shared meals in the mess tent, the religious services, or the nightly report Cliff Oldfield[3] e-mailed for distribution to our families (see the tribute to Cliff in the box below). We bridged the gap between emergency management and tactical response operations, even if we were only one small piece of the larger puzzle that was and is Katrina.

A Niece's Tribute to Cliff Oldfield

I made an extremely important promise to myself on December 30, 2005. This is the day we buried my uncle, my godfather, John Clifford Oldfield. He was a member of DMORT and his last "project" was in Louisiana, helping out after Hurricane Katrina. Some other disasters he worked on were 9/11 and Flight 800.

My promise: one of my first articles is going to be about the DMORT team and how they, their families, and the victims are all affected by the tragedies. People always remember the victims. They always have the stories about the heroes who rode in on their white horses and became the knights-in-shining-armor to the victims. I want to focus on the personal lives of the heroes—how their work impacts them, their families, and the relationships between the two. If someone can help me get a head start on this project, which means so much to me, I would be forever grateful.

John "Cliff" Oldfield, Commander DMORT 2
(June 12, 1946 - December 24, 2005)

I was a mere newcomer.
Fresh on the team.
Unfamiliar, per se, with the DMORT routine.
Katrina blew in, and everything changed.
We all would be needed. It all seemed so strange.
We were told to "Stand By" so I packed up my gear.
I waited by the phone, the order to hear.
Confusion, frustration: When would they call?
If only someone could answer it all.
Then I found the web page. The page for team 2.
And a comforting man told me just what to do.
Each day he wrote something. Sometimes small, sometimes lots.
But never, not ever…he never forgot.
Each day this fine gentleman, regardless of heat, or workload, exhaustion….
He must have been beat…. But each day he wrote, he kept us all posted.
A labor of love, this journal he hosted.
When the call finally came, I bid family goodbye.

Continued

And as tears welled up in my family's eyes,
I said: "Not to worry, you'll be with me each day, just go to team 2's site,
See what Cliff has to say.
He'll make you feel better, he'll keep you informed.
And he did, and like me, their hearts were so warmed.
I arrived in St. Gabriel, his biggest fan.
The first thing I asked: "Can I meet this great man?"
My memories of that day never will end
For on that day in October, I made a great friend.
I worked for a week under Commander Oldfield
I knew all along, that he was the "Real Deal"
We talked and we joked, I thanked him so much
For thinking of everyone…keeping in touch.
When cliff shipped back home, I wrote him some lines
We said we'd exchange some e mail sometime.
That time never came, but I know as I write
He realized he'd touched so many lives.
Not often in life do we meet a great soul
Who gives of himself, no matter the toll.
Somewhere up above, there's no crisis tonight
Cliff's got it all handled, it'll all be alright.
Next time I deploy, I'll miss seeing this man
But, perhaps, the one thing he's made me understand
Is that this is a team, regardless of rank, regardless of status, or what's in the bank
And if you stand proud, and if you stand tall
In the end, that's what matters.
Farewell Cliff…That's all.

Dedicated to the memory of a friend of all too short a time.
What an impression you made on my entire family.
Troy Bastion, DMORT 7[4]

Discussion Questions

1. Explain the ICS use of the terms "branch" and "camp".

2. What are some of the highly specialized skills used in tactical response operations in DMORT?

3. What emergency management functions were required to support DMORTs primary mission?

4. Were emergency management skills necessary to support operations?

5. Why would DMORT be better aligned with the U.S. Department of Health and Human Services than the FEMA and the Department of Homeland Security?

6. Are there other units that might be inappropriately placed in the DHS organization?

7. Can you describe from this case study some of the signs of cooperation that existed between tactical response operations and emergency management?

References

1. See http://www.dmort.org/DNPages/DMORTDPMU.htm retrieved January 1, 2008, for a description and photos of the DPMU.
2. See Dr. Tom Phelan. (2005, Winter). "Hurricane Katrina: Dignity, Respect, and ICS," PPBI Bulletin, 5:3 at http://www.ppbi.org/PPBI%20Newsletter%20Winter%202005%20Final.pdf retrieved January 1, 2008.
3. Cliff Oldfield led the Trailer Management Unit at St. Gabriel. He was the Region II Commander from New York and sadly passed away the following December, Christmas Eve, 2005.
4. See http://sarahsmusing.blogspot.com/ for more about Cliff on his niece's blog site retrieved January 26, 2008.

Chapter 10

The "Manager" In Emergency Management

Objectives of this chapter:

- Apply the concept of "management by objectives" (MBO) to emergency management.

- Describe the degree to which command and control are used in emergency management; in tactical response operations.

- Explore the roles played by emergency managers in the case studies in Chapters 7–9.

- List the ways in which crisis and emergency management skills can aid general managers.

- Compare and contrast the role of a chief to a manager in emergency services and emergency management.

- Note the role of education in teaching and learning management skills.

☑ Summary

☑ Discussion Questions

☑ References

Introduction

The skills of management are used in many fields. Emergency management is only one type of management. General managers in business, industry, health services, government, and faith-based organizations use many of the same concepts and principles. Emergency managers may benefit greatly from the broader definitions of management found in other fields. One reason college education is recommended for the study of emergency management is the opportunity colleges provide to explore multiple approaches and disciplines to gain an understanding of a subject. Training is often more narrowly focused on the job at hand, whereas many college courses draw from a broad range of authoritative sources. Therefore, the "manager" in emergency management deserves exploration.

In the case studies presented in Chapters 7–9, observations of emergency management illustrated the different skill sets required of emergency managers as opposed to those in tactical response operations. Whether at Ground Zero, in Sri Lanka, or in response to Hurricane Katrina, management principles and practices were employed to accomplish emergency management functions in support of tactical response operations.

For example, the concept of management by objectives (MBO) is central to the Incident Command System (ICS). In this chapter, the use of MBO, command and control, and crisis management for general managers will be explored. We will reflect upon the managers encountered in the previous case studies to explore their application of MBO.

Management by Objectives

As discussed in Chapter 3, The ICS is designed to structure a response to an incident by meeting the needs of those involved in tactical response operations. The ICS 200 course has as one of its required objectives,

> *Delegation of Authority and Management by Objectives*: Describe scope of authority and the process by which authority is delegated. MBO must be described and explained.[1]

One of the core elements of ICS is the Incident Action Plan (IAP). It is important to discuss the IAP at this point because the IAP is the document that lists and addresses the objectives for a single operational period. The IAP identifies the resources needed to achieve those objectives. MBO in ICS includes a series of steps.

Establishing and Implementing Objectives

The steps for establishing and implementing incident objectives include:

- Step 1: Understand agency policy and direction.

- Step 2: Assess incident situation.

- Step 3: Establish incident objectives.

- Step 4: Select appropriate strategy or strategies to achieve objectives.

- Step 5: Perform tactical direction.

- Step 6: Provide necessary follow–up.[2]

The purpose is to determine the objectives for the next operational period (usually 24 hours), and have all units involved in the emergency response direct their efforts toward these common objectives. Although the responsibility for determining the objectives rests with the Incident Commander, the objectives are often the result of the combined input and efforts of all members of the Command and General Staff. The focus of the objectives should be to support the Operations Section in resolving the incident. Subobjectives may address management duties and actions required of other sections involved in supporting the Operations Section. For example, when Operations needs additional personnel, either due to an expansion of the incident or due to the need for current personnel to be relieved, an objective may be written for the Planning Section to source the required personnel. Similarly, if Operations needs expanded medical services for first responders, an objective may be written for the Logistics Section to provide an expanded medical unit.

Once the objectives are determined, they are listed in the IAP, which is then distributed to all units involved in the incident response. The goal is to have all objectives for an operation period clearly communicated to all levels of supervision deployed on the incident. All activities, whether by tactical response operations or support units, should be geared toward achieving the stated objectives. Unit leaders or Section Chiefs who identify other objectives should communicate them to the Planning Section Chief for consideration for the next operational period or for immediate consideration for approval by the Incident Commander. When new objectives are created, they must be approved by the Incident Commander before being included in the next IAP.

The system is designed to create clarity of purpose. It enhances cooperation when multiple units are engaged in a single incident. An IAP is highly supportive of

MBO because it builds upon the objectives by listing all resources (apparatus and personnel) engaged in the response. It enhances accountability, safety, and finance. With MBO as the framework for responding to an incident, there are no surprises. Everyone on the response team knows what the objectives are and the approved resources for achieving them.

MBO can mean different things in different settings. In business, for example, one aspect of MBO has to do with evaluation of personnel performance. It is common in business for objectives to be used to measure the performance of an individual employee or of an entire department. Performance is tracked to determine if objectives are met in a timely fashion. For example, if a manager wants his sales staff to make a required number of sales in a month (operational period), a salesperson might track daily activity to see if the objective will be or is met by the end of the month.

Table 10.1 shows the performance of two salespersons for the first three weeks of the month of March. The objectives for the month are set for each individual (Leslie at 20; Larry at 30). Results are shown for the first three weeks (Leslie has 14; Larry has 28). Leslie is at 70% of quota (objective), and Larry has achieved 93% of quota. With this information, a manager might set new objectives for Week 4. Larry needs only 2 sales to achieve his objective, whereas Leslie needs 6. Since Leslie has been able to achieve 6 sales in only one of three prior weeks, she made need Larry's assistance to meet the objective of a total of 50 sales for the month. The manager may have many options, but one could be to have Larry help Leslie. This is how MBO might be used in a sales environment.

The illustration above suggests that managers might adjust their use of personnel or other resources as a situation progresses (in this case, the sales for the month of March). Emergency management might apply the same principle. An Incident Commander, looking at the degree to which a fire, for example, is being controlled, might choose to redeploy certain resources for the next operational period so the

Table 10.1 Sales Objectives Using MBO

Salesperson	Month	# Sales Required	Week 1	Week 2	Week 3	Week 4	Tally	% to Date	Total to Date
Leslie	March	20	2	4	8		14	70%	14
Larry	March	30	15	5	6		28	93%	28

overall goal or objective can be met on time. The same could be applied to a flood, the identification of victims from an incident, debris removal following a tornado, or any other disaster response.

It is not common in emergency management to use MBO to track the performance of an individual responder, but the principle might be applied to tracking the progress on each section, branch, or division deployed in response to a disaster. The value added is to gather data to assist in making management decisions based on the approved objectives for the operational period, or for the entire operation.

MBO can be applied to emergency management functions other than disaster response. It has value in project management of such projects as developing a mitigation plan, completing a comprehensive emergency management plan for a jurisdiction, monitoring progress in an exercise program, or in tracking the annual budget. These are management functions requiring management concepts that are not typically associated with tactical response operations.

Emergency managers may acquire the knowledge and skills applicable to MBO in a number of ways. One way is to take management courses at a college or university. Emergency Management Degree programs, particularly at the master's degree level, typically include courses from the business management department as a requirement for graduation. At Elmira College, for example, the emergency and disaster preparedness concentration requires core courses as follows:

- Evaluating Research in Management

- Human Resource Management and Development

- Planning and Project Management

- Leadership

- Organizational Economics, Budget and Finance, and

- Application of Technology in a Business Setting.

Emergency management students at Elmira should have ample opportunity to explore the use of MBO in a number of settings. This exposure contributes to a broader understanding that the students may then apply in all aspects of an emergency manager's duties.

Command and Control

A common misconception in emergency management stems from the use of the title, "Incident Commander." My perspective on command and control may differ greatly from the perspectives of others in the field. If I had written the ICS, I might have used the term "Incident Manager" to identify the leader in incident response because a manager and a commander provide very different functions. With the historical roots of ICS in the fire service, I do not believe my perspective would have been helpful. For emergency management, however, it has value. We must first accept that an emergency manager is NOT in command or control of tactical response operations at the scene of an emergency (fire, flood, airline crash, train derailment, terrorist bombing, or other serious incident). Tactical response operations are normally under the command and control of a fire chief, police chief, or other emergency services professional unit leaders. This is often determined by statute wherein the lead agency is a matter of law as in "Home Rule" states.

Background Information: Home Rule

"Home Rule" is widely used as a term to identify the lead agency, especially in the fire service. A simplified meaning is that the fire chief of the department in whose jurisdiction the fire occurred is in charge of the fire scene and the resources deployed to suppress it. The local chief need not transfer command and control to an authority outside the jurisdiction.

It is interesting to note the broader definition from an historical perspective. Home Rule has been in existence for centuries in one context or another.

"Main Entry:
home rule
Function:
noun
Date:
1860
: self-government or limited autonomy in internal affairs by a dependent political unit (as a territory or municipality)"[3]

"It has been a common feature of multinational empires or states—most notably, the ancient Roman Empire and the British Empire—which have afforded measured recognition of local ways and measured grants of self-government..."[4]

For purposes of this discussion, we will use a fire scene and a fire chief, rather than including the other possible emergency services. The fire chief commands those members of the local fire department, and frankly any other fire departments dispatched to the scene. The fire chief, in a larger incident, when ICS is established, is most likely assigned to be the Operations Section Chief. In larger departments, a fire chief might assign a Battalion Chief to be the Operations Section Chief, leaving the fire chief free to become the Incident Commander. Once assigned to the Incident Commander position, however, the fire chief must not continue to serve as the Operations Section Chief, commanding and controlling the firefighters, but, instead, takes on the larger responsibility of managing the entire incident including all of the support functions (Safety, Public Information, Liaison, Planning, Logistics, and Finance/Administration). In order to do this effectively, the fire chief must begin to use management and leadership skills quite different from those used as the fire chief in the Operation Section Chief's position.

There is often confusion if this difference in function and position assignment is misunderstood. It is common in smaller jurisdictions for a fire chief (or a police chief or sheriff) to handle both responsibilities (Operations and Incident Command). With this confusion, at larger incidents, some expect an Incident Commander to direct the activities of first responders. Any conflict between the command and control authority of a chief and the managerial role of an Incident Commander could have serious consequences.

According to my perspective, command and control are NOT the main responsibilities of an Incident Commander, except as they pertain to management issues. When the role of Incident Commander is seen as a management function, command and control are seen more as a matter of management style than of responsibility. Leadership in the form of management knowledge and skill is what is needed from the Incident Commander. It is often said that tactical response operations are most effective when responders operate based on discipline and training, much the same as a military unit. Leaders of such "quasi-military" units are aptly applying the practices of command and control. Not so for the Incident Commander.

Incident Commanders are artfully seeking to achieve cooperation amongst many, diverse groups. They must provide leadership and direction to such varied personnel as safety officers, public information officers, planners, finance and administration personnel, and the agency administrators, often political leaders. They are well-served by applying management skills and various leaderships styles to coordinating of the incident. For example, in DMORT following Katrina, the DMORT Incident Commander provided direction, coordination, and information through daily briefing meetings, keeping all personnel up to date on the contents of the IAP for the next operational period. Though some may use militaristic styles, more commonly associated with command and control, they must focus on objectives as well as the strategies, cooperation, and communication necessary to successfully achieve those objectives.

The Role of "Manager" in the Case Studies

In the three case studies presented in Chapters 7–9, management skills were exhibited and observed at several levels. At Ground Zero, the management of public relations was clearly handled by Mayor Rudy Giuliani. He was not, however, the Incident Commander. That role was left to emergency management professionals while the tactical response operations were the responsibility of the Operations Section Chief and divisions dealing with fire, search and rescue, crime scene investigation, victim identification, and debris removal. In Sri Lanka, Incident Command was a function of the Centre for National Operation (CNO), under the direction of Dr. Tara De Mel, the Secretary of Education, in all respects, a manager. Tactical response operations were the responsibility of the Ministry of Defense, the military. In response to Hurricane Katrina, emergency management was distributed amongst the city, the state, and the Federal Government (FEMA). The absence of the clear establishment of unified or area command as per ICS was problematic. Many units acted autonomously with adequate command and control of tactical response operations. Search and rescue, evacuation, and medical care of victims were conducted on scene as well as any one unit could perform under the circumstances.

Management at Ground Zero

Countless volumes of documentation, analysis, and criticism have been compiled about what happened on September 11, 2001, at the World Trade Center in Manhattan. The analysis has been detailed, based on information gathered from multiple sources, digested and argued by many interested parties. When considering the management roles at Ground Zero, the focus should be on identification of management opportunities and functions, rather than on the immediate response to the attacks. The focus here is to identify the differences between emergency management and tactical response operations, not to evaluate how they were performed. Tactical response operations, as a matter of history, began immediately and proceeded, though not flawlessly, from the first fire alarm to the last bit of debris removal, a period of years.

In order to support the tactical response operations, emergency management had to perform well. With September 11, the work of emergency managers continues to this day. How, you ask? Emergency management extends beyond the scene of an incident, both before and after it. In the larger sense, emergency managers are involved in mitigation, preparedness, recovery, and restoration phases, in addition to the response phase. Plans created by emergency management before September 11 were evident on September 11 even though the incident was unprecedented. For example, at Pier 92, the Emergency Operations Center (EOC), one could observe the structure of the ICS in action. Even though the state-of-the-art EOC in WTC 7 had been destroyed, its framework could be replicated at Pier 92 because of prior planning and training in ICS. The presence of emergency management personnel from other jurisdictions (local and state SEMO personnel), was evidence that ICS training had taken place across the state, well in advance of September 11.

In my unit, DMORT, years of training and professional education were evident in the performance of our duties. We were organized, equipped with a portable morgue (DPMU), and experienced. We knew how to set up, access supplies, and coordinate with NDMS and DMAT personnel.[5]

National Disaster Medical System

The National Disaster Medical System (NDMS) is a federally coordinated system that augments the Nation's medical response capability. The overall purpose of the NDMS is to establish a single integrated National medical

Continued

> response capability for assisting State and local authorities in dealing with the medical impacts of major peacetime disasters and to provide support to the military and the Department of Veterans Affairs medical systems in caring for casualties evacuated back to the United States from overseas armed conventional conflicts.
>
> The National Response Plan utilizes the NDMS, as part of the Department of Health and Human Services, Office of Preparedness and Response, under Emergency Support Function #8 (ESF #8), Health and Medical Care, to support Federal agencies in the management and coordination of the federal medical response to major emergencies and federally declared disasters including: Natural Disasters, Technological Disasters, Major Transportation Accidents, and Acts of Terrorism including Weapons of Mass Destruction Events.[6]

We also knew how to plan, staff, organize, transport, document, and communicate. We had those specialists who performed highly skilled forensic work in the morgues, and a command post where those with managerial skills performed support tasks. In the command post, we documented our objectives, tracked personnel needs, made travel and lodging arrangements, responded to the media, and communicated within our unit and externally to other units and the Emergency Operations Center at Pier 92. We coordinated our efforts with the Medical Examiner's Office, the Mayor's Office, various fire and police leaders, Federal representatives from HHS, the clergy, and the Office of Emergency Management. We arranged for administrative services such as computer equipment, office machines, phone lines, security, and liaison with local churches, the hotel management, and the New York Mets. Clearly, we had emergency management tasks to perform that were quite different from our tactical operations activities in the morgues.

Our leader was DMORT's National Commander, Tom Shepardson. He had four or five direct reports (e.g. Dale Downey, Fred Berry, Christie Whittaker, and Susan Rivera). Most of us were new to ICS, and Tom, at one point, asked me to help create an ICS organization chart for the unit and to organize the command post on the 8th Floor of the La Guardia Marriott according to ICS command and general staff structure. Tom was familiar with my ICS training (ICS 100, 200, 300, and 400 at that time). We did our best to handle the management tasks while the personnel in the morgues attended to tactical response operations.

Based on my perspective with DMORT, the management function at Ground Zero, though not initially, was "by the book." The ICS was evident, especially in the emergency management ranks and particularly at Pier 92. The National Response

Plan was adhered to with Federal support arriving as requested by the Mayor Giuliani and the Governor George Pataki. The large and diverse workforce at Ground Zero included emergency responders, steel workers, truckers, telecommunications workers, heavy equipment operators, the media, clergy, food service personnel, private sector personnel at all levels, humanitarian organizations (Red Cross and Salvation Army), counselors, sanitation workers, Army Corps of Engineers, the National Guard, and many, many more. It was the responsibility of emergency management to manage that workforce, arranging payroll, maintaining safe working conditions, feeding, and following up on all the details. Successfully addressing the immediate tasks of September 11 overlapped with the on-going efforts, even today, of preparing for, training, planning, and mitigating for any future incident.

Management in Sri Lanka following the Indian Ocean Tsunami

The tsunami was different in many ways than the September 11 Attack on the World Trade Center. The disaster was a natural disaster, not a terrorist attack. The death toll was nearly 31,000 at the time I was there, but greater now. The devastation was not confined to a single, 16-acre site; it spanned the entire east coast of the country. The tsunami affected several nations simultaneously, making the need for support and assistance highly complex. Several national governments and international agencies were involved in the response. Victims and their families spoke several languages. Homes and businesses were destroyed, some swept away completely. Many of the survivors were children, orphaned by the storm. Though the tactical response operations involved emergency response units, with similar goals to those on September 11, the duties and skills required of the first responders were again quite different from those of the emergency management team in the capital city, Colombo.

The management of the disaster response was under the supervision of the President, the Prime Minister, and the Ministry of Defense. On most issues they worked together, but it was evident that in many ways they had different agendas. The President appeared to be focused on humanitarian relief issues. She directed the establishment of the Centre for National Operations (CNO) in the same complex with her office. She appointed an Incident Commander who served as a manager of the CNO, Dr. Tara De Mel. Dr. De Mel organized the government response with the assistance of experienced technical advisors from the United Nations. The military had other concerns pertaining to the on-going dispute with the Tamils in the Northern provinces. As the military undertook missions related to disaster response and recovery, they had to be constantly on guard for possible Tamil activities. The Prime Minister had responsibilities to members of Parliament who represented the provincial interests. There was tension, possibly even opposition to the President in Parliament. All three units, CNO, the military, and Parliament had to work toward the response, recovery, and restoration of tsunami devastated citizens.

Nonetheless, the management functions in Colombo, Sri Lanka were the same as at Ground Zero. People in authority, with management skills, needed to organize and lead the response to the disaster. As American consultants from the IBM Crisis Response Team, we were there to provide any assistance we could on behalf of IBM. I was included on the team due to my experience with incident management, particularly ICS. My task was to assist in delivering to the government a means of organizing the response and restoration using time-tested emergency management principles and practices. The CNO in Sri Lanka was new, created in response to the tsunami. There had been no prior structure devoted to emergency management. A management system was needed, especially one for managing disaster response.

Like most large disasters, first responders handled tactical response operations, while emergency management specialists handled management tasks. The tasks involved the same areas as provided for in ICS—command, safety, public information, liaison, operations, planning, logistics, and finance/administration. Some of the areas handled matters quite different from what I had seen elsewhere. For example, logistics needed to deal with Sri Lankan Customs for most of the donated goods and supplies coming into the airport. Liaison needed to coordinate the efforts of NGOs; foreign faith-based organizations; colleges and universities; foreign military support from the United States, Canada, Australia, and others; private sector assistance (some donated, some fee-based); the United Nations and USAID; and victims and their families. Public information officers were needed for internal Sri Lankan communication and a host of international media.

As one can see, the matters of managing such a massive response effort were enormous. Over 100 personnel were present in the CNO daily. The need for management and diplomacy knowledge and skill was tremendous. There were also the cultural issues. Respecting the cultural norms was difficult when dealing with approximately 31,000 fatalities, when burials were rapid and often without notification to families, some Sri Lankan, some foreign, some Buddhist, some Christian, some of other faiths. Camps recorded over 500,000 displaced persons in the days immediately following the tsunami. Railroads, highways, and telecommunications infrastructure along the coast were destroyed. The one extremely positive factor was the limited damage in Colombo, the seat of the national government.

Management of DMORT
in St. Gabriel following Hurricane Katrina

It was similar to Ground Zero for DMORT as far as the forensics were concerned. Forensic personnel perform the professional duties in much the same manner regardless of the nature of the disaster. The setting was quite different, a rural area along the Mississippi River, north of New Orleans, not at all like New York City. Morgue operations proceeded on a larger scale, with many more victims' remains to identify.

There was one major change. Since the September 11 Attacks in 2001, DMORT leadership and many members had undergone ICS training. We had been moved from HHS to the newly formed Department of Homeland Security and assigned to FEMA prior to Hurricane Katrina. This was a totally new management environment and reporting relationship for DMORT. We had received ICS 100 level training as DMORT members, and many of us had received more training as part of our jobs back home. When I arrived at the morgue in St. Gabriel, Louisiana, on October 8, 2005, the ICS was fully functional. The organization was well defined according to ICS, at least at the command and general staff levels. We had daily briefing meetings conducted by the Incident Commander for DMORT. We had an IAP updated daily with clear management and operational objectives stated.

On page one of our daily IAP forms, six objectives were printed:

- Provide for health and safety of all incident personnel.

- Display reverence, dignity, respect regarding the processing, collection, and recovery of H.R. [sic] (Human Remains).

- Provide for the Decon [sic] of H.R.

- Provide for secure processing of human remains for the purpose of identification.

- Provide for appropriate transportation and destination of human remains.

- Provide for the collection of missing person data.[7]

In order to achieve these objectives, the command post was staffed a minimum of 12 hours daily. Management personnel worked to support tactical response operations in the morgue by providing payroll, logistics, staffing, planning, transportation, documentation, telecommunications, supplies, food, shelter, medical support, facilities, and security. The personnel in the morgue would have been taken away from the main objective—to identify the deceased and return their remains to their families—if they had to perform managerial tasks. The skills applied by those in tactical response operations differed greatly from those in emergency management.

How Crisis and Emergency Management Expertise Aid General Managers

ICS training and emergency management education are relevant for many different types of managers, in addition to those in disaster management. In the preface to his book, *The Crisis Manager: Facing Risk and Responsibility*, Otto Lerbinger says of the book, "It is also written for all managers because the lessons learned in crisis management add to their qualifications as policy makers and decision makers."[8] Crises and emergencies requiring management skills are not unusual in business. General managers are required to direct the activities of personnel responding to all sorts of crises, from market value changes, to product tampering, to fires and floods in corporate facilities. Ed Devlin lists dozens of such incidents in his book, *Crisis Management Planning and Execution.*[9] In many private sector organizations, managers are adopting ICS principles and practices for use in corporate emergency operations centers.

In my work with corporations, first in the power utility industry, I found the same need for coordinating incident response. In business, things happen that threaten the company—fires, earthquakes, IT failures, ethical problems, product tampering, strikes, floods—even the unexpected, such as terrorist bombings. In fact, most business executives deal with crises more often than one might think. Most are totally internal, and never make the news. Most corporate responses to incidents occur without warning and with little time to conduct a coordinated response. Nonetheless, incident management or crisis management is necessary to successfully deal with the incident.[10]

Working as the instructional designer for Private & Public Businesses, Inc. (PPBI), I designed a two-day course for business executives and business continuity planners called, "NIMS ICS for Business and Industry." In addition to teaching the course at Disaster Recovery Journal conferences, Deidrich Towne, Jr., John Jackson and I made a DVD for BCP Media of the course. The same concept has been introduced to corporate clients across America—to pharmaceutical companies, colleges, manufacturing firms. Some companies have adapted ICS for their crisis management teams from internal experts in security and fire protection. In other companies, ICS expertise has been imported by hiring veteran emergency managers to serve as crisis management team leaders. In the courses I have taught at colleges, even at the

Associate's Degree level, corporate presidents and other business and education leaders have enrolled to gain emergency management expertise. Whether in two-day training classes or college degree programs, private sector managers are seeking to develop emergency management knowledge and skill.

An example of a public program wherein business executives have expressed satisfaction with the acquisition of emergency management principles and practices is the CERT Program. The Community Emergency Response Team, a Citizens Corps partnership. As stated earlier in Chapter 6,

> Using the training learned in the classroom and during exercises, CERT members can assist others in their neighborhood or work-place following an event when professional responders are not immediately available to help. CERT members also are encouraged to support emergency response agencies by taking a more active role in emergency preparedness projects in their community.[11]

Marianne Guinee, an experienced business continuity professional, wrote of the CERT orientation she attended,

> As business continuity professionals, we know what the "unexpected" can do, and unfortunately some of us have seen it for real. We prepare by building partnerships with recovery vendors, software vendors, and with our own corporate divisions and partners. What about our partnerships with other human beings and for the good of our fellow workers, families, neigh-bors, and communities? There are a limited number of profes-sional emergency services workers and time can be critical. What you do, and do not do, could save someone's life, and maybe even your own. Isn't that worth 20 hours of your time?[12]

Similarly, Peter Laz CBCP, wrote,

> While there are finer details of ICS that may not be needed or appropriate for your given private sector company, the core of the system can be applied to your emergency management environ-ment for the purpose of creating an effective and efficient system to manage incidents.[13]

There is growing interest in the adaptation of most ICS principles to the private sector crisis management team setting, all of which requires a type of education which is distinctly different from first responder training.

Summary

Emergency management requires the effective application of managerial principles and practices. Management is necessary to support tactical response operations. It is the framework of support on scene, during response to an incident, as well as before and after. Effective emergency management involves MBO as noted in the ICS. Emergency managers can learn to manage by objectives in college management courses. Such courses often draw management principles and practices from a variety of fields and management settings, providing a student of emergency management a broader perspective than is normally available in a training program.

Command and control are not essential elements of emergency management, though they may be highly effective and characteristic of leaders of tactical response operations units. Emergency managers are not in command of an incident response as much as they are leading the management functions supporting tactical response operations. They are not first responders in the traditional sense, but are supporting first responders. They are responsible for issues of mitigation, preparedness, response planning, recovery, and restoration. Their management functions extend beyond the on scene response to an incident.

Several business practitioners have recognized the importance of crisis and emergency management expertise for their general managers. Crises occur in business and throughout the private sector often enough to require general managers and corporate executives to apply such expertise. Corporations are adopting ICS and other emergency management practices in increasing instances to ensure effective crisis management team performance.

The "manager" in emergency management is one who has studied, learned and applied management principles and practices. An emergency manager demonstrates the concepts of coordination, budgeting, delegation, cooperation, communication, and supervision in directing the performance of others to achieve the stated objectives in response to a crisis, an emergency or a disaster.

Discussion Questions

1. What is meant by "management by objectives"?
2. Where are written objectives found in response to an incident?
3. Explain the difference between "command and control" and leadership?
4. Who is in command of an incident according to ICS?

5. Why is the Operations Section Chief seen as the commander of the tactical operations units?

6. How were the emergency management duties similar at Ground Zero, in Sir Lanka, and in DMORT Operations at Hurricane Katrina?

7. What might a general manager find as a benefit of learning about emergency management?

8. Explain how the roles of a Planning Section Chief or a Finance/Administration Section Chief are more managerial than tactical.

References

1. "Fact Sheet," *The NIMS Integration Center,* Federal Emergency Management Agency, Department of Homeland Security, December 2005.
2. "Establishing and Implementing Objectives," ICS 200, Unit 3. "Delegation of Authority and Management by Objectives," http://training.fema.gov/EMIWeb/IS/ICS200CR/ICS200Visuals/03ISC200DelegationSept05.pdf retrieved January 1, 2008.
3. Merriam-Webster's Online Dictionary. http://www.m-w.com/dictionary/home+rule retrieved January 6, 2008.
4. "Home Rule." Encyclopedia Britannica Online. http://www.britannica.com/eb/article-9040873/home-rule retrieved January 6, 2008.
5. NDMS and DMAT are acronyms for National Disaster Medical System, and Disaster Medical Assistance Team.
6. http://www.hhs.gov/aspr/opeo/ndms/index.html retrieved January 6, 2008.
7. *Incident Action Plan, Hurricane Katrina DMORT Operations, Saint Gabriel, LA, Saturday October 8, 2005 0700 to October 9, 2005 0700.* ICS 202. p. 1.
8. Lerbinger, Otto. (1997). *The Crisis Manager: Facing Risk and Responsibility.* Mahwah, New Jersey, Lawrence Erlbaum Associates. p. ix.
9. Devlin, Edward S. (2007). *Crisis Management Planning and Execution.* Boca Raton, Florida, Taylor & Francis Group, Auerbach.
10. Phelan, Dr. Tom. (2007, Fall). "The Internal Partnership: Business Continuity Planners and Emergency Managers Working Together." *Disaster Management Canada,* 1:3. p. 21.
11. Community Emergency Response Teams (CERT). https://www.citizencorps.gov/cert/ retrieved January 6, 2008.
12. Guinee, Marianne C. CBCP. (2005, Winter). "CERT: Another Kind of Partnership." *Disaster Recovery Journal,* 18:1. http://www.drj.com/articles/win05/1801-ppbi.html retrieved January 6, 2008.
13. Laz, Peter CBCP. (2006, Summer). "NIMS/ICS in a Private Sector Company," *Disaster Recovery Journal,* 19:3. http://www.drj.com/articles/sum06/1903-ppbi.html retrieved January 6, 2008.

Chapter 11

Resistance

Objectives of this chapter:

- Describe the nature of the resistance to college preparation for emergency managers.
- List the arguments against college-prepared emergency managers.
- List the argument supporting college emergency management programs.
- Identify the recommendations for "bridging the gap" between the two.
- Formulate your own position on college preparation for emergency managers.
- Describe how research has impacted emergency management.
- Compare and contrast the skill sets required for emergency managers to those of personnel in tactical response operations, and the ways to acquire both.

☑ Summary

☑ Discussion Questions

☑ References

Introduction

In the field of emergency management, there is a need for high degrees of cooperation. It does not take a disaster situation or an emergency declaration to require cooperation, coordination, and leadership. Emergency managers do things other than respond to disasters. Their work begins in advance of an emergency and continues long after one has been resolved. There is work to be done in mitigation, preparedness, planning, and restoration that expands the role of an emergency manager far beyond the period of response to a disaster. The management skills used during a disaster response are applied differently in pre- and post-disaster situations. For example, the emergency manager who leads a community meeting to "kick off" a mitigation planning process engages in public relations, diplomacy, communication, organization, encouragement, information dissemination, scheduling, recruiting, and gaining cooperation. Such a meeting is similar to forming a community advocacy organization. It requires knowledge of the Federal program under which a mitigation plan is directed and funded. Preparing such a meeting requires understanding of the mitigation planning process; coordination with local, state and Federal government representatives; working with the media; and presentation skills. Mitigation planning requires the ability to establish rapport with all interested parties (government, emergency response units, public works, environmental groups, historical societies, educational institutions, businesses, nonprofit organizations, humanitarian organizations, and the general public). Mitigation planning is different from emergency planning. It illustrates the expanded role of the emergency manager beyond responding to a disaster.

Sometimes there is a gap between emergency managers educated in college and chiefs of first response units who came up through the ranks of emergency response (fire, police, EMS). It is most notable in disaster or emergency response. The issue centers on the struggle over command and control. Emergency managers provide leadership and managerial skills during response to an incident. Fire and police chiefs provide command and control of those in tactical response operations. Bridging the gap lies in understanding the difference between the two.

The Growing Gap between First Responders and Emergency Managers

The gap between emergency management and tactical response operations indicated very different perspectives on how to respond to a disaster. It is only when confronted by the need for competent emergency response that college educated emergency managers and first responders appear to be working with different rule books and score cards. If the gap between emergency management and first responders is growing, it may be in part a matter of greater urban and social complexity. Or it may be the increasing turnover in emergency managers' positions. Like most other fields, emergency management is engaged in the mass retirement of the "Baby Boomer" generation. With the Baby Boomer retirements, whether in public service or business, there is a growing concern about the loss of practical knowledge, sometime referred to as intellectual capital. With so many retiring, there is a concern that highly developed skill sets will be lost. In the past, such skill sets may have been acquired over years of on-the-job training and experience. When turnover or retirement rates were lower, there was time for younger workers to learn enough to become seasoned veteran employees who could take on the tasks of their predecessors. When so many retire in a short period of time, as we are experiencing with the great number of Baby Boomers, we do not have the time to "season" those who will replace them. There is a concern that irreplaceable knowledge will leave with them as the "Boomers" retire.

Yet, if it were simply a matter of training replacements to do the same jobs as done by those retiring, perhaps the gap might not be so great. The duties, particularly in emergency management, have changed dramatically. What was once characteristic of the job is no longer applicable. The increasing complexity of multi-jurisdictional response is just one aspect. This has made it difficult for new emergency managers to obtain a position by following the same route or career path of those who entered at an earlier time. Since the roles of emergency managers have changed, the degree to which a current emergency manager can prepare a successor is limited. In many cases, there is no provision for that to happen. In smaller communities, for example, the emergency manager works alone. There is not another employee in the department to groom as a replacement. In larger municipalities, the retiring emergency manager may have been trained in emergency response, for example, as a firefighter and possibly a chief. The retiring emergency manager may not have been educated in management. With rapid turnover, there simply is not time to transfer the acquired knowledge and skill one developed in a position to a successor. The successor should be educated elsewhere, before being selected and appointed or hired as an emergency manager.

The question is not how do we prepare the next generation of emergency managers, but, "What do we prepare them to do?" Herein is the origin of the gap. Since today's emergency management positions have a different framework than the skill sets acquired in tactical response operations, the emergency managers who will enter the field need to be educated so as to acquire the appropriate concepts and principles. It is far more likely that a management education will prepare an emergency manager than any number of years in service in tactical response operations. Still, there are many who feel that an experienced first responder makes the best emergency manager. It need not be all one or the other. Those with experience as a first responder, when augmented with a college degree in emergency management, may be the most highly recruited candidates for emergency management positions. The combination of the two may also be the path to bridging the gap.

Overcoming Resistance to College Preparation for Emergency Managers

When attempting to overcome resistance to almost anything, one key is to seek to understand it. As discussed in earlier chapters, the gap in emergency management is similar to gaps between "blue collar" and "white collar" workers in some industries; between enlisted personnel and officers in the military, especially when the officers did not come up through the enlisted ranks. There was a time when the best technical performer on the plant floor was promoted to supervisor or manager. In the 1970s the concept of the "Peter Principle" suggested that such promotions to management positions only served to raise employees to a level of incompetence. They performed well in the technical area, but did not have the skills for management.[1] To avoid this in emergency management, a college certificate or degree program in emergency management may prepare first responders and others to become qualified candidates for emergency management positions.

In order to see the benefits of college preparation, the tasks required of emergency managers need to be compared to the educational goals established by college programs. The management objectives should then be compared to the skills being acquired by first responders in tactical response operations training. If such a comparison were undertaken, one could see that the desired outcomes are quite different (see Chapter 2). To avoid the hiring of emergency managers with inappropriate preparation, a comparison should be made of qualifications listed in management job descriptions to the content of college courses and degree program requirements. College programs are doing a better job of preparing emergency managers than might be provided in the traditional 20 years of experience in tactical response operations.

The successes of those who have come into emergency management from first responder career paths appear to reduce the gap. Many have acquired the necessary management skills through various forms of learning such as the FEMA online and independent study courses. Some have taken management seminars, attended conferences where management training was offered, or acquired skills through participation in community organizations. Many are self-directed, adult learners, who have undertaken adult learning projects outside of structured educational institutions. Several have earned college degrees, some at the graduate level. It is appropriate to say that successful emergency managers have sufficiently learned to handle management duties and responsibilities. Many of them have also reported that administrative duties have overwhelmed them, requiring nearly all of their time. By their very successes, they have indicated that management skills are required, no matter how one learns them.

Adult Learning Projects: Focusing on highly deliberate efforts to learn

According to Professor Allen Tough, a futurist, scientist, and author in adult learning, "Almost everyone undertakes at least one or two major learning efforts a year, and some individuals undertake as many as 15 or 20. The median is eight learning projects a year, involving eight distinct areas of knowledge and skill. A learning project is simply a major, highly deliberate effort to gain certain knowledge and skill (or to change in some other way). Some learning projects are efforts to gain new knowledge, insight, or understanding. Others are attempts to improve one's skill or performance, or to change one's attitudes or emotional reactions. Others involve efforts to change one's overt behavior or to break a habit. Many learning projects are initiated for highly practical reasons: to make a good decision, build something, or carry out some task related to one's job, home, family, sport, or hobby. Adult learning is also motivated by credit toward a degree or certificate."[2]

Regardless of the motivation to learn or the way in which skills are acquired, there is a demonstrated need for emergency managers to have management skills. To overcome the resistance to the use of college courses to acquire the necessary management skills, one need only recognize that learning and skill acquisition can occur as the result of taking college courses. To further the credibility of such courses, one might examine the topics of study presented in them. As stated earlier, an excellent source of this information is the FEMA Higher Education Project website, http://training.fema.gov/EMIWeb/edu/collegelist/. On this site, the College List contains course titles, descriptions, and syllabi for some courses. An example from the FEMA Higher Education Project College List is from Elmira College's Master's Degree with a concentration in Emergency and Disaster Preparedness Management.

Elmira College—Master of Science (M.S.) in Emergency and Disaster Preparedness Management and Advanced Certificate in Emergency and Disaster Preparedness Management

Elmira College offers the Master of Science (M.S.) in Emergency and Disaster Preparedness Management and an Advanced Certificate in Emergency and Disaster Preparedness Management. This master's degree requires satisfactory completion of 12 courses totaling 36 semester credits. The Advanced Certificate in Emergency and Disaster Preparedness Management requires satisfactory completion of 5 courses totaling 15 semester credits.

The degree and certificate are comprised of performance-based learning experiences intended to develop the essential knowledge and skill competencies required for emergency managers. The program is designed for entry and mid-level managers as well as individuals with aspirations for career advancement. For individuals possessing a baccalaureate or advanced degree in another discipline, the advanced certificate may be attractive for career change or advancement.

This program is designed to be integrated with three other graduate level degrees: M.S. Health Services Management, M.S. Information Technology Management, and M.S. General Management. All four programs require the same 21 credits in Core Management Courses. Additionally, the capstone Graduate Seminar will bring together small groups of students from each discipline in an interdisciplinary environment to foster a paradigm of collaborative management.

Core Management Courses (21 credits):

Human Resource Management and Development	3 credits
Planning and Project Management	3 credits
Evaluating Research in Management	3 credits

Continued

Leadership	3 credits
Budget and Finance	3 credits
Application of Technology	3 credits
Graduate Seminar (Multidisciplinary)	3 credits
Subtotal	21 credits

Emergency and Disaster Preparedness Courses (15 credits)

Crisis Management, Disaster Recovery, and Organizational Continuity	3 credits
NIMS Compliance, Planning, and Strategies for Emergency Management	3 credits
Organizational Risk and Crisis Management In both Public and Private Enterprise	3 credits
Health Services and IT Issues in Emergency Management for the Non-Medical Emergency Manager	3 credits
Homeland Security and the Management of Mass Terrorism Preparedness and Response	3 credits
Subtotal	15 credits
Total Required for Graduation	36 credits

Elmira College is accredited by the Middle States Commission on Higher Education.[3]

An example at the undergraduate level is from American Public University's Bachelor of Arts in Emergency and Disaster Management.

American Public University—Bachelor of Arts in Emergency and Disaster Management

The American Public University is offering a Bachelor of Arts in Emergency and Disaster Management. The Bachelor of Arts in Emergency and Disaster management seeks the following specific learning outcomes of its graduates. With reference to each of the respective areas of emergency and disaster management, graduates in this degree program will be able to:

Continued

- Identify and apply the disaster planning and management cycle from mitigation through recovery.

- Assess response strategies for nuclear, biological, chemical, and natural disaster incidents.

- Critically assess the intergovernmental and interagency responsibilities for disaster management support.

- Analyze the psychological and sociological factors and associated coping strategies for natural and manmade disasters.

All courses for the Bachelor of Arts in Emergency and Disaster Management are offered through distance learning only.

Emergency and Disaster Management Curriculum:

RQ295/COL 100 Academic and Career Planning – Required as the first course in all undergraduate programs (3 semester hours)

General Education Requirements (30 semester hours)

English Composition – 6 semester hours

EN101/ENG101 – Proficiency in Writing (3 semester hours)

EN102/ENG102 – Effectiveness in Writing (3 semester hours) or

EN202/ENG200 – English Composition and Literature (3 semester hours)

Social and Behavioral Science – 6 semester hours

Approved course from the Social and Behavioral Science list (6 semester hours)

Science – 3 semester hours

SC112/SCI - 190 Introduction to Environmental Science (3 semester hours)

Mathematics – 3 semester hours

MA110/MAT110 – Introduction to College Algebra and Trigonometry (3 semester hours) or

MA111/MAT111 – College Algebra and Trigonometry (3 semester hours) or

MA125/MAT125 – Math for Liberal Arts Majors (3 semester hours) or

MA 225/MAT225 – Calculus (3 semester hours)

History – 6 semester hours

Approved courses from the History list (6 semester hours)

Humanities – 6 semester hours

Approved courses from the Humanities list (6 semester hours)

Core Courses (30 semester hours)

CJ395/EDM220 – Emergency Planning

EDM498 – Senior Seminar in Emergency and Disaster Management

GM464/EDM320 – Natural Disaster Management

GM465/FCS413 – Special Operations in Emergency Medical Services

MC477/EDM230 – Emergency and Disaster Incident Command

MM325/EDM340 – Consequence Management

Continued

POL 410 - Public Policy
PY 431/PSY431 – Psychology of Disaster
SS489/HLS301 – Homeland Security Organization
RQ300/COL300 – Research, Analysis, and Writing
Major Courses (12 semester credits)
General Program Course List
CJ 188/HLS231 – History of Explosive Ordinance Disposal
CJ214/HLS232 – Electronics, Electricity, and Explosives
CJ215/HLS233 – Explosives: Methods, Practice and Protocols
CJ216/HLS234 – Organization of Explosive Ordnance Disposal
CJ410/HLS311 – Border and Coastal Security
GM160/HLS211 – Emergency Response to Terrorism
GM260/HLS212 – Chemical, Biological, & Radiological Hazards
GM261/HLS213 – Weapons of Mass Destruction Incident Command
GM263/HLS215 – Regulatory Issues in Weapons of Mass Destruction
MC406/TLM381 – Hazardous Materials Management
MC444/EDM420 – Risk Communications
MC445/HLS312 – Port Security
SC223/HLS230 – Chemistry of Explosives
SC403/EDM240 – Chemistry of Hazardous Materials
SS440/HCM -426 – Quarantine
Electives (45 semester hours)
Select any courses that have not been used to fulfill core or major require-ments. Credits applied toward a minor or certificate in an unrelated field may be used to fulfill elective credit for the major.
Total = 120 semester hours
American Public University System is accredited by the Higher Learning Association of the North Central Association of College and Schools and by the Accrediting Commission of the Distance Education and Training Council (DETC). American Public University System is a distance learning institution that includes American Military University (AMU) and American Public University (APU).[4]

First responders and emergency management personnel will feel less resistant to graduates of college programs entering emergency management positions when they understand how comprehensive the degree programs are. It is important to recognize that the requirements for management and tactical response operations are quite different.

What Research and Study Have to Offer Tactical Operations

Today's emergency managers need to know the best practices and principles that directly apply to their profession. Traditional means of sharing valuable lessons learned have served emergency management well in the past. Today, there is more demand for scientific evidence to support planning, response, recovery and restoration. There are new technologies, new hazardous materials, new personal protection devices and equipment, new developments in communication, greater social complexity, and interdependency. What works and what does not are sometime confounding questions. Should our communication systems be more interoperable? How effective is an early warning system? What should a community budget for disaster management? Where is the safest place to locate a data center or a radio tower? Should we use web-based emergency operations centers, or plan on face-to-face centers? Should we invest in satellite phones or Blackberries? What is the best way to notify the public of an evacuation order? How high should homes be elevated to be safe from floods?

There are so many questions to be answered. Who will seek the answers? There are vast research studies funded by and undertaken by government agency researchers. Private enterprise has funded and engaged in research studies. In many instances, college and university students and professors engage in significant research. How does an emergency manager learn about the findings of researchers or the significance of the research?

In other fields where scholarly or scientific research is conducted, it is often reported in scholarly or research journals. Such journals are relatively new to emergency management. There are highly informative magazines, newsletters, and websites, most of which in the past published articles and news stories, not formal research studies. In scholarly publications, papers submitted as potential articles are reviewed by qualified members of an editorial review board. Such journals are referred to as "peer reviewed" journals. Two have emerged in the field of emergency management, and they are relatively recent: *Journal of Emergency Management* (www.emergency managementjournal.com) and *Journal of Homeland Security and Emergency Management* (http://www.bepress.com/jhsem/).

There are many fine informative magazines that include articles on recent developments, but they are not necessarily scholarly research journals. Some are listed below.

- Continuity Central, www.continuitycentral.com
- Disaster Management Canada, http://www.ccep.ca/ccepdmc.html

- Disaster Recovery Journal, www.drj.com

- Disaster Resource Guide, http://www.disaster-resource.com/

- Government Technology's Emergency Management, www.emergencymgmt/com

Many organizations publish newsletters regularly that include articles on emergency management topics and links to research reports. Examples are listed below.

- The Bulletin of the International Association of Emergency Managers (IAEM), www.iaem.com

- The PPBI Newsletter, www.ppbi.org

- University of Minnesota Center for Infectious Disease Research and Policy, CIDRAP, http://www.cidrapsource.com/source/index.html

- Michigan State University, Critical Incident Protocol, http://www.cip.msu.edu/

An example of a university-based disaster research center is the Natural Hazards Center at the University of Colorado.

The mission of the Natural Hazards Center at the University of Colorado at Boulder is to advance and communicate knowledge on hazards mitigation and disaster preparedness, response, and recovery. Using an all-hazards and interdisciplinary framework, the Center fosters information sharing and integration of activities among researchers, practitioners, and policy makers from around the world; supports and conducts research; and provides educational opportunities for the next generation of hazards scholars and professionals.[5]

Another example is the Disaster Research Center at the University of Delaware.

The Disaster Research Center (DRC), the first social science research center in the world devoted to the study of disasters, was established at Ohio State University in 1963 and moved to the University of Delaware in 1985. The Center conducts field and survey research on group, organizational and community preparation for, response to, and recovery from natural and technological disasters and other community-wide crises. DRC researchers have carried out systematic studies on a broad range of disaster types, including hurricanes, floods, earthquakes, tornadoes, hazardous chemical incidents, and plane crashes. DRC has also done research on civil disturbances and riots, including the 1992 Los Angeles unrest.

Staffs have conducted nearly 600 field studies since the Center's inception, traveling to communities throughout the United States and to a number of foreign countries, including Mexico, Canada, Japan, Italy, and Turkey.[6]

The contributions of research institutions is complemented by hundreds of government and private sector research reports and published findings following major disasters. In emergency management, research must inform practice. Often, it does not, because it is not read or applied by practitioners in emergency management or by first responders. An excellent way to bridge the gap between emergency management and tactical response operations would be to find a way to report research findings to a wide audience in both groups.

Understanding the Different Requirements of Emergency Management and Tactical Response Operations

Much of this book has been devoted to identifying and describing the different requirements for success in emergency management and in tactical response operations. Clearly, first responders do different work than emergency managers. In general, first responders acquire skills through training and practice. Emergency managers may acquire knowledge through training, education or on-the-job. Where it might be dangerous to have a first responder learning on the job, it is not as threatening to have someone new to emergency management learning on the job. Since emergency management involves many duties before and after an incident, there are opportunities to apply key concepts in less threatening environments.

For example, at a recent mitigation planning orientation meeting, attended by 70+ community members, there were three emergency management personnel in attendance from the state emergency management office. One was a Regional Director, one a fairly new regional assistant, and one a 20-year veteran mitigation planner. The planner provided technical expertise and experience; the regional assistant provided logistical and administrative support, and the Regional Director provided direction, support to the municipal emergency managers, and increased credibility for the project. The mitigation orientation meeting was filled with representatives of local government, private enterprise, fire, law enforcement, environmental, transportation, education, Red Cross, social services, and public works units. They were presented with an overview of the benefits of mitigation planning, the mitigation planning process, the law requiring it, the funding mechanisms, and the roles they could play in developing a plan. This type of activity provides a great opportunity for students of emergency management to participate and learn about the process without risk to public safety. Though none of this was tactical response operations, all of it could support operations in future disasters. The skills involved in conducting such a meeting and the planning following it are clearly managerial by definition.

As discussed earlier (see Chapter 3), knowledge of management is also required during response to a disaster or emergency. In short, one need only observe an Emergency Operations Center in action during a major incident. There is much work to be done in planning, communicating, liaison with agency representatives, procurement, documentation (particularly of labor hours and log sheets), and coordination. Yet, in an emergency operations center there is no one engaged in tactical response operations, only in supporting operations.

A few of my graduate students have expressed the belief that the best preparation for emergency management should include some experience in tactical response operations. They feel that a manager who has not been in the trenches cannot possibly understand what tactical operations are about. They are not confident that such an emergency manager would make proper policy and management decisions. For certain, some experience on scene, whether in fire, law enforcement, HazMat, or EMS can provide a valuable perspective. With the differences amongst the first responder's disciplines, which one would provide the best experience for management? Would experience on scene as a firefighter have applicability to management that would differ from on-scene experience as a law enforcement officer? Does experience in the trenches create a bias toward one emergency service or resistance from the groups in which one did not serve? Will firefighters have any greater respect for an emergency manager who came from law enforcement than they would for one who came from a Master's Degree program in emergency management? These are important questions. To respond to my students, I recommend that a tactical operations responder who chooses to enter emergency management, enroll in an emergency management degree program. Many of my students at the undergraduate and graduate levels are practitioners in tactical response operations studying part-time in traditional classroom, instructor-led courses, and in online degree programs. They are applying their on-scene experience to management situations using the principles, practices, and research they are studying in the emergency management or homeland security degree program. This is an excellent approach to emergency management career positions.

Summary

Overcoming resistance in any field is a challenge. In emergency management, like in business or the military, those engaged in tactical response operations want the support of a management team that is responsive to their needs. A familiar, classic gap scenario is the auto mechanic who feels the engineer who designed the car never had to change the oil. It can be frustrating if the gap makes it more difficult for one to get the job done. Emergency management is about support of tactical response operations, not about micromanaging so as to make the job harder. When one understands the roles played by both, and the tasks required of both, the job gets easier.

College degree programs in emergency management are designed and developed to promote the learning of crucial management concepts and principles to equip a graduate to successfully apply them in practice. In many colleges, the professors in such programs have experience on scene in either operations or management. Many of the students are in emergency response, the military, or in business where they have gained valuable experience.

Research is increasing in disaster response, geological hazards, sociological impacts, prevention, technology, communication, and psychological aspects of emergency response and management. There are many questions being asked and answered. Scholarly research and scholarly writing to report it should be part of every emergency manager's preparation and in-service education. We need to find better ways to distribute research findings to the emergency response and management practitioners.

As we better understand the roles and responsibilities of emergency managers, we will more clearly see the need to educate them in management principles and best practices. Such education can be provided by college degree programs. There is, in additional, added value when college students of emergency management have on-scene experience in tactical response operations.

Is there a way for the colleges and those in tactical response operations to work together? We will discuss this in Chapter 12.

Discussion Questions

1. What are the factors associated with resistance to management educated in classrooms rather than coming up through the ranks?

2. How might the Peter Principle apply to emergency management?

3. Can you list examples of Adult's Learning Projects undertaken by first responders? By you?

4. Read and summarize a research study in emergency management.

5. What value did you find in the research study you selected?

6. What research questions might you recommend for researchers to study?

7. What recommendations do you have for the best way to distribute research findings to practitioners in tactical response operations? In emergency management?

8. What system might be useful to keep emergency managers up to date on current research findings?

9. How would you go about creating a better understanding of the differences and similarities in the roles of those in tactical response operations and those in emergency management?

10. How significant is the surge in retirements of Baby Boomers currently in emergency management positions?

References

1. Peter, Laurence J. (1969). *The Peter Principle*. William Morrow and Company. "The theory that employees within an organization will advance to their highest level of competence and then be promoted to and remain at a level at which they are incompetent." Printed in *The American Heritage® Dictionary of the English Language: Fourth Edition*. 2000. http://www.bartleby.com/61/4/P0220400.html retrieved January 13, 2008.

2. Tough, Allen. (1979). *The Adult's Learning Projects* (2nd Edition). Austin, Texas: Learning Concepts. P 1. http://ieti.org/tough/books/alp/chapt01.pdf retrieved January 13, 2008.

3. Elmira College, printed in http://training.fema.gov/EMIWeb/edu/collegelist/EMMasterLevel/ retrieved January 13, 2008.

4. American Public University printed in http://training.fema.gov/EMIWeb/edu/collegelist/embadegree/ retrieved January 13, 2008.

5. http://www.colorado.edu/hazards/ retrieved January 13, 2008.

6. http://www.udel.edu/DRC/index.html retrieved January 13, 2008.

Chapter 12

Working Together

Objectives of this chapter:

- Identify the events that have encouraged colleges and Community Emergency Managers to work together.

- List the ways in which colleges have supported both tactical response operations and emergency management.

- Explore cases where management has undertaken administrative responsibilities to support first responders.

- Examine the role of emergency management personnel on scene during a disaster or emergency.

- Summarize the ways in which working together is in the best interest of all citizens and for the safety of our nation.

☑ Summary

☑ Discussion Questions

☑ References

Introduction

When it comes to safety, homeland security, and emergency management, no one should be alone. Partnerships, arranged in advance, help to provide resources, information, and support before, during, and following a disaster. There are numerous, highly valuable opportunities for partnerships to add value, to mitigate loss, to better prepare, to enhance response capabilities, to foster mutual aid, to provide relief personnel, and to offer follow-up assistance to victims, families and responders. Partnerships exist on all levels – local, state, regional, national, and international. They can be amongst public sector entities, private sector, or public/private partnerships. Whatever the structure, they can benefit all parties. In my experience, it has been best to develop partnerships in peacetime (before the next disaster strikes), rather than in the throes of a disaster. On the other hand, disasters have spawned partnerships on the spot, spontaneously created to meet a need. Partnerships may be formal, with written agreements, or informal as in neighbor helping neighbor.

In this chapter, we will explore partnerships that have proven to be beneficial to several aspects of emergency management. Some are well-established, and some are just coming together. Many have brought tactical operations responders together with emergency managers and college emergency management programs. Most recently, colleges are beginning to join in emergency management and response planning, especially since the unfortunate incident at Virginia Tech on April 16, 2007. That incident seems to have convinced college and emergency management leaders that they must work together.

Working together will address questions that may help bridge the gap between those in tactical response operations and emergency management. What are the best practices? Where are the successful models? What might happen if we were to focus our attention on cooperation and partnering?

Partnering between College Programs and Community First Response Organizations

Businesses have business continuity plans. Computer data centers have disaster recovery plans. Agencies have continuity of operations plans. Communities have comprehensive emergency management plans. They all focus on preparedness, response, and recovery. Some extend to mitigation and restoration. Some organizations, corporations, or communities have no plans at all. Many times, plans are found to be outdated or too narrow in scope to deal with major disasters. Some disasters can overwhelm a community or private sector organization, making their planning appear inadequate. Some organizations plan for internal response and recovery without recognizing their dependencies on outside agencies. They have not considered the potential need for external assistance, and therefore have not considered forming a partnership or working together with a neighbor, a business partner, or a supplier.

In some cases, vulnerability assessment has been inadequate. Risks have not been properly identified, making the perceived need for assistance underestimated. It sometimes appears that our resources may be overwhelmed, as the universe of new threats increases. Who predicted the 9/11 attackers would use commercial airliners? Who predicted that so many residents of New Orleans would remain in the city following the hurricane conditions leading to the flooding when the levees broke? Who could have imagined the death toll of the Indian Ocean Tsunami? Who sent their young sons and daughters to high school or college knowing of the tragedies of Columbine and Virginia Tech? If the harm of these incidents were known in advance, maybe they would have been prevented or appropriate partnerships might have been created to help us cope with them. In some cases, there were excellent plans and partnerships. We learn from such experiences.

The Local Level: The Public Safety Training Center Model

In Onondaga County, where Syracuse, New York is located, the Public Safety Training Center has brought private and public organizations together for years offering training programs such as the Public Safety Critical Incident Management course (PSCIM). For a time, the course enrolled equal groups from fire, law enforcement, EMS, government, education, and private sector business and industry. Rich Flanagan, the program's director, saw the benefit of having first responders, emergency management, and private sector participants in the same course, working together to apply ICS methodology to disaster and emergency response. The program trained hundreds of participants, introducing all parties to ICS and to common concerns and issues. The program grew to include courses in emergency response to terrorism, weapons of mass destruction, and ICS levels 100—400. School districts, colleges, businesses, humanitarian organizations, utilities, hospitals, and pharmaceutical companies joined in the training with local fire departments, police departments, EMS services, and New York State Emergency Management Office (NYSEMO) officials. Local government officials and representatives from the county emergency management office also participated. After a number of years of providing these courses, the Center at Onondaga Community College developed an Associate Degree program in emergency management. This program expanded the existing police and fire academies already in existence. At this one center, tactical response operations personnel have worked together with emergency management personnel from both pubic and private sectors.

The State Level: NY-ALERT

Colleges in New York State raised their levels of concern following the Virginia Tech incident in 2007. Many formed crisis management committees to explore methods of mitigating or preventing similar incidents from occurring on their campuses. The Chancellor of the State University of New York convened a Task Force to conduct a review of campus preparedness, and the Task Force issued a report containing several recommendations. Among them was a recommendation to implement an emergency alert system to send emergency warnings and instructions to all members of the campus community. Some campuses purchased notification systems for delivering emergency alerts via telephone, cell phone, e-mail, fax, and instant text messaging. Some campuses installed sirens to alert the community. Colleges and school districts are using NY-ALERT, a free, rapid notification system to which individuals can either subscribe or "opt out" when the institution provides contact information.

NY-ALERT

The New York State Emergency Management Office (SEMO) provides the NY-ALERT Web site for informational purposes only and makes every effort to post accurate and reliable information. Other state and local agencies are authorized to post information to the NY-ALERT Web site and utilize communication gateways within the Web site to disseminate information. SEMO makes neither warranties, guarantees nor representations of any type as to the content, accuracy or completeness of the information contained in its Web site, disseminated through the Web site, or any related links. SEMO assumes

Continued

no responsibility for any error, omissions or other discrepancies between the electronic and printed versions of documents.

The User understands when subscribing to the service that SEMO cannot guarantee 100 percent delivery of the message in a timely manner. SEMO utilizes third parties' infrastructure to deliver messages such as faxing, Short Message Service (SMS), and voice calls that may be unavailable due those third parties' infrastructure issues. These may be due to weather, power, acts or war, etc. SEMO will make every effort to ensure this delivery but due to above unforeseen circumstances, cannot guarantee 100 percent delivery in a timely manner.

The NY-ALERT Web site links to Web sites maintained by other entities. Reasonable precautions are taken to link only to Web sites that are appropriate, accurate and maintained by reputable organizations. However, those Web pages are not under the control of the New York State Emergency Management Offices and the New York State Emergency Management Office is not responsible for the information or opinions expressed in these linked sites.

SEMO does not endorse services and products; no such endorsement should be implied by the presence of advertising that may appear on links from its Web site.

Upon clicking the link below you are acknowledging you understand the above statements and are agreeing to register for the NY-Alert Civilian Portal. You may also copy and paste it into your Web browser to complete the registration process.[1]

Following the receipt of the above message, an individual user can subscribe to the service, listing all forms of contact desired—phone, cell phone, fax, e-mail, or instant text message. The secure site allows for users to enter personal contact information, select a password, and choose security questions and answers. The system is being used by colleges and public school districts. It is an excellent example of how emergency management supports safety, mitigation, preparedness and response in the college community and the community at large.

The National Level: The Academic Continuity Model

Since Hurricane Katrina impacted college campuses at Tulane University, Xavier University, LSU's Health Science Center, the University of New Orleans and others, college leaders have become aware of the potential for having to close campuses for extended periods due to damage from natural hazards. In the past, closing for a few days might have been an inconvenience, but closing for weeks or months presented major problems for the entire campus community. Students had their programs of study interrupted; professors were out of work; researchers lost valuable equipment, evidence, and data; and financial administrators had to find ways to recover both physical plant and financial losses. For the first time, colleges became aware of the impact of losing the academic program for an extended period of time.

A working group held a meeting at the University of Maryland on June 27, 2007, to discuss the concept of academic continuity. Funded by a grant from the Alfred P. Sloan Foundation, it may have been the first group convened on this topic in the nation.

Participants attending the workshop included representatives from a variety of sectors and constituencies, including the U.S. Department of Education, the U.S. Department of Homeland Security, National Association of Counties, International Association of Emergency Managers, EDUCAUSE, Southern Regional Education Board, emergency management professionals at the national, regional and state levels, academic institutions from across the country, national education organizations, and nongovernmental organizations. Several stakeholders made formal presentations about their organization/constituency and its responsibilities—the Department of Homeland Security, Maryland Emergency Management Association (MEMA), National Association of Counties, and higher education—to assure everyone had a basic knowledge of the varied roles and challenges each faced in disaster situations.[2]

The working group defined several issues regarding cooperation between emergency management and colleges. Among the recommendations were those pertaining to ways colleges can prepare and those pertaining to strengthening relationships between colleges and emergency management.

The workshop laid the groundwork for developing long-term, sustainable approaches dealing with the issue of academic continuity and emergency management. A priority was identified: the development of a national center for academic continuity that would build upon the experiences of Sloan Semester and other academic programs, serve as an information clearinghouse, and engage in other relevant activities. The workshop also identified a core group of organizations and individuals who could be called upon to develop other approaches and raise awareness of the need to plug the gap between the two communities.

Recommendations:

1. Develop a national center for academic continuity to make information and resources available to higher education institutions, emergency managers, and professional associations. The national center would also serve as a catalyst for institutions addressing academic continuity in the context of broader campus emergency preparedness planning, and as a mechanism to support academic continuity needs at colleges, universities and other institutions affected by disasters.

2. Encourage institutions of higher education to proactively pursue academic continuity planning, including preparedness planning; to work collaboratively with local and state emergency managers to ensure that the needs and capabilities of educational institutions (including available resources) are shared with their local emergency management agencies and incorporated into community emergency plans. Groups such as the National Association of Counties or state emergency management offices have specialists who can provide advice, and identify local experienced contacts.

3. Engage regional accrediting agencies to include continuity of operations planning as part of the accreditation process. For example, a one-day informational session on academic continuity should be convened to consider emergency management issues and the varied applications via the accreditation process.

4. Support the development of updated emergency preparedness standards, including academic continuity guidelines, via an expert panel of representatives from higher education, relevant government bodies, emergency management community, and telecommunications specialists. These standards should allow colleges, universities, and other higher education institutions to maintain teaching and learning in an emergency, to improve resilience and recovery capacities.

5. Pursue strategies to secure funding for higher education preparedness planning, and particularly for academic continuity planning, such as amending existing Department of Homeland Security grant language to enable educational institutions to apply and make use of such funds.

6. Encourage educational institutions and associations to work with the Department of Education and the Department of Homeland Security to elevate the priority of education (from its current status) to ensure that its needs and concerns are addressed in federal planning. Appoint a federal lead for higher education preparedness issues.

7. Engage leadership in higher education and state and local emergency management entities to meet and develop protocols for joint action.

8. Identify and expand the number of national educational organizations that are engaged in campus preparedness and higher education resilience, including academic continuity planning. This would include organizations such as regional accrediting agencies, non-governmental organizations.

9. Higher education institutions should move quickly to develop relationships (operational, contractual, information sharing, etc.) with state and local authorities and public and private sector institutions that can offer emergency support and "back-up" capacities and operations, such as those that provide effective communications support.[3]

As one can see, colleges are reaching out to emergency management sources for information, advice, and partnerships to prepare for unforeseen incidents. The meeting at the University of Maryland is an excellent example of a budding partnership—colleges and emergency management working together.

The Administrative Chief Model

An example of how emergency management concepts might be brought to a tactical response operations unit exists in the model of the "administrative chief" in volunteer fire departments. Volunteers have traditionally elected their fire chiefs from amongst their own ranks. A relatively new concept is to hire an administrative chief to oversee the management issues in the volunteer department. The administrative chief is to a volunteer fire department as an emergency manager might be to first responder units at a large incident. They both provide support before, during and following the emergency. Volunteer fire departments are well-established institutions in America. They have provided fire protection and emergency medical response since the nation was founded. George Washington is said to have been a member of the Alexandria, Virginia Volunteer Fire Department:

> The volunteer fire service holds a special place in the history of Alexandria. Founded in 1774, Alexandria's first volunteer fire company [sic] counts President George Washington among its earliest members.[4]

The work of volunteer firefighter extends far beyond responding to a fire. The work includes training, equipment maintenance, fund raising, community relations, recruitment, and department social activities. In recent years, support for the volunteer departments has included grant writing, liaison with local governments, tax issues, procurement, human resources, credential documentation, and, in some cases, contracting for career firefighter and EMS services. Volunteer chiefs have been overwhelmed, if for no other reason than they are often fully employed outside the fire district. To meet the administrative responsibilities, volunteer departments hire an administrative chiefs—a paid employee to administratively supervise a volunteer department. The model is common in humanitarian organizations and foundations, but not as common in the fire service outside of larger municipalities. It is an excellent example of management objectives supporting first responder goals. In the cases I have observed, the administrative chiefs are experienced, veteran firefighters. Some were educated in college-based fire academies. Some have college degrees. Their role illustrates one way those with emergency management skills and/or degrees can work together with personnel in tactical response operations.

The Role of Emergency Management on Scene

On scene, emergency management duties and responsibilities are conducted in the background, while first responders attend to their duties at the forefront of the disaster response. Nonetheless, the roles played by emergency management personnel are vital to the incident response and the recovery and restoration that will follow. What do emergency managers do at the scene of a disaster? What is their role, and what are the expectations of those in tactical response operations? What does the public perceive the role to be? Emergency management personnel have a responsibility to activate and operate an Emergency Operations Center when required on or near the scene of an emergency. Forward Command Posts are often established early in a response. They are usually functions of single departments or possibly others in a mutual aid response. When the incident begins to grow, ICS is established at an EOC, with tactical response operations continuing to function under the first responders' chief, while the support of an ICS management unit is being shifted to the EOC. The support functions are critical to the success of the incident response. They are often accomplished using emergency plans created by emergency management personnel far in advance of an incident, and applicable to several types of incidents.

Management functions extend beyond the incident both before and after. Sometimes emergency management personnel are staged so as to be in position should a disaster occur. In such cases, emergency management roles and responsibilities are being met, using management skills, but the incident has not yet happened. This was the case in the contingency planning that took place for the NCAA Men's Basketball Tournament (Round of 16) at Syracuse University's famed Carrier Dome.

Special Events Planning: Syracuse University & the NCAA Basketball Tournament

After September 11, the NCAA engaged in enhanced preparedness planning when the number of nationally televised venues was reduced to four. At Syracuse University, an emergency planning Task Force was formed to review and enhance the Carrier Dome Emergency Plan. The threat of a possible terrorist attack required prudent contingency planning. Working together, representatives from the University's Security Department, the Carrier Dome management, City Fire, law enforcement, utilities, the FBI, the Secret Service, the Onondaga County Emergency Management Department, the New York State Health Department, Rural Metro (private EMS provider), and the neighboring College of Environmental Science and Forestry (ESF). Though the tournament progressed without interruption, emergency management stood by in an Emergency Operations Center set up on campus a safe distance from the Dome. The tournament was monitored the entire weekend, though an emergency did not occur. This is typical for emergency managers when special events draw large crowds and media attention. The risks warrant professional emergency planning.

Examples of two of the specific items required to be addressed by the Task Force follow:

- "Establish a security command post in or near the competition venue. All agencies should be represented in the command post. Create a direct communications link between the facility management and the command post."[5]

- "Working with local authorities, establish evacuation routes for pedestrians and vehicles."[6]

Similar planning occurs in large cities for such events as the Republican and Democratic National Conventions, the Super Bowl, the Olympics, and the New Year's Eve celebration in several cities. Emergency management is on scene with a host of first responders as preparedness for any possible emergency. Emergency management personnel carry out carefully developed plans by supporting tactical response operations from the EOC during the event. In my experience, emergency management personnel have supported tactical response operations in events ranging from a large, local fishing derby to Hurricane Katrina. Management skills have played a part in the Emergency Operations Centers supporting each.

EOC Operation and Emergency Management On-Scene Support

During the response to a large emergency or disaster, the Emergency Operations Center is a busy place. Whether during an ice storm, a devastating wind storm, September 11 at Ground Zero, the Indian Ocean Tsunami at the capitol in Colombo, Sri Lanka, or at the DMORT facility following Katrina, emergency management personnel were kept busy around the clock supporting tactical response operations on scene. The roles and responsibilities as listed in the Incident Command System literature are clear for command and general staff. They are management roles.

Command Staff is responsible for overall management of the incident. *Command*, although the chosen term of the ICS system, is perhaps misleading. It is important to remember that incidents are managed; personnel are commanded. Incident Command (IC), whether conducted by an individual or through **Unified Command (UC)**, is a management and leadership position. IC is responsible for setting strategic objectives and maintaining a comprehensive understanding of the impact of an incident as well as identifying the strategies required to manage it effectively.[7]

Regardless of the incident, if the job requires the response and recovery services of multiple agencies from multiple jurisdictions, an EOC is established in accordance with ICS and the Incident Commander assumes the management functions required to manage the incident. There may also be a joint information center (JIC), a family reception or assistance center, and sometimes a separate facility for agency representatives. All are part of the management function supporting on scene operations.

Forward command posts are often established early in a response to a disaster. They are usually set up by fire or police departments. They continue until the incident is determined to be in need of greater response efforts than can be handled by a single department. Often, the early, on-scene command posts are converted to Operations Section command posts when the incident command is transferred to an Emergency Operations Center (EOC). Once the EOC is activated, the Incident Commander is in charge of managing the incident.

In power utility companies, the EOC is often at a regional control center or at corporate headquarters, far from the affected area. At Ground Zero on 9/11, the EOC was destroyed due to its location in World Trade Center 7. It was relocated twice to temporary sites. When established at Pier 92, it served as the EOC for the duration of the incident. It has since been moved twice again, first to Water Street in Brooklyn and then to its new permanent location in Cadman Plaza.

In Sri Lanka, a temporary EOC was established in the President's office facilities in Colombo, called the Centre for National Operations (CNO). Though much of the response was conducted by the military and provincial government officials, the management of the response was conducted at the CNO.

Following Katrina, there were separate command posts for the State of Louisiana and for FEMA in Baton Rouge. There were management activities at both sites. While FEMA adjusted its leadership, the State hired the services of former FEMA Director James Lee Witt as a private contractor to manage the state's EOC. There was a pressing need for these governments to partner for better coordination.

The Best of Both Worlds for the Safety of the Nation

There is a pressing need for a better understanding of emergency management by all parties. If there were one thing I could change, it would be the use of the term "incident commander" in the Incident Command System. The term has contributed to a significant confusion concerning the role of emergency managers when used to name the position. The "command" term applies in the fire service where ICS was created. When first responders require the support of an EOC or of emergency management personnel, the term commander would still be appropriate for operations. As discussed in Chapter 10, the emergency management function might be better served if the leader were called the "incident manager." Since ICS does not use the term "incident manager," we must all try to understand the role and responsibility of the incident commander. The incident commander's position is one of leadership and management, not command and control. It is a position of coordinating multiple entities through section chiefs, all of whom direct their resources toward resolving the emergency, disaster, or crisis. With the exception of the Operations Section, everyone involved in the Incident Command System is there to support Operations. Bridging the gap between emergency management and tactical response operations might be best accomplished by understanding that both play critical roles in emergency and disaster response. The emergency management roles extend beyond response to mitigation, preparedness, recovery and restoration. Tactical response operations are largely focused on incident response, though the response requires training, maintenance, and exercising that are continuous and ongoing. Just as expertise is required in the fire service and law enforcement, special expertise is also required in emergency management. The best of both worlds must work together for the safety of the nation.

Lessons Learned

What have I learned from writing this book? What are the recommendations for emergency management going forward? My first lesson learned is a confirmation that in emergency management, like in other fields, it is best to be a lifelong learner. If we think we know all we need to know, we run a serious risk. There are new developments in legislation, technology, communication, and research findings every day. Emergency managers need to be informed of such developments and the opportunities they present for effective emergency and disaster management. Professional development should be part of every emergency manager's budget and job description. Whether that development is through conference attendance, reading journals, completing training, or continuing one's education in a college degree program, emergency managers can enhance their capabilities, improve their support of first responders and victims, and further emergency management as a profession by continuing to acquire knowledge, skills, and abilities through lifelong learning.

The issue is not how many emergency managers have college degrees, but how we will educate the next generation of emergency managers. Prior to writing this book, as a consequence of some articles and presentations on the subject of educating emergency managers, I received valuable feedback from practitioners, colleagues and educators. One such message was a reminder from a prominent emergency management professional that many emergency managers have advanced degrees. Specifically, I was contacted through the editor of Disaster Recovery Journal by a reader with a Master's Degree, years of service in emergency management, and a record of leadership in the professional organizations such as the National Emergency

Managers' Association (NEMA) and the International Association of Emergency Management (IAEM). He was more than justified in his comment on my oversight. There is no survey that I know of that reports the number of emergency managers who have college degrees. I have written this book to advocate for educating future emergency managers in college management-centered degree programs. Why? First, I am concerned about the number of emergency managers who may retire in the next few years. Second, I have a firm belief that the future will be more demanding of management concepts and principles than skills acquired from years of service in tactical response operations. From my research, I have learned that there is an increasing requirement for candidates to have college degrees, particularly in management, governmental administration, finance, and emergency management.

I have learned that job descriptions for positions in emergency management, whether local, state, or Federal, list required competencies that closely align with lists of management skills taught in college courses. The lists of requirements do not match skills and abilities required of tactical response operations positions. The exception, I learned, is in the job descriptions for fire and police chiefs. In those fields, leadership positions are also characterized by management duties. It was surprising to learn that undergraduate degrees were listed on fire and police chief job postings, whereas graduate degrees were required for leadership in emergency management.

In response to large disasters, or catastrophes to use Quarantelli's definition, it is amazing to see the number of emergency management responders who are engaged in management functions, supporting first responders. In the case studies presented in Chapters 7–9, large contingencies of emergency management personnel were assembled in Emergency Operations Centers and various command posts to perform administrative, planning, logistics, communications, liaison, safety and coordination functions. Hundreds of personnel were involved at Pier 92 in New York City following September 11; in the CNO in Colombo, Sri Lanka following the tsunami; and in Baton Rouge in response to Hurricanes Katrina and Rita. For certain, the same would have been true for responses to incidents such as the 2007 California Wildfires, the bridge collapse in Minneapolis, and earthquake in Pakistan. In each instance, tactical operations responders required the support of management personnel.

In conversations with emergency response personnel, the view has been expressed that an emergency manager would benefit from some experience in tactical response operations. "They need to know what it's like to be on the ground," one student commented. I agree that some experience in first response would be valuable for an emergency manager. The concern is that experience in one discipline, such as law enforcement or fire, does not necessarily provide an understanding of what other disciplines may require. A law enforcement background is not the same as fire, hazmat, search and rescue, EMS, or the military. In some cases, identification with a specific discipline may create resistance from those serving in a different discipline. In certain instances, leadership by those with military, legal, and political backgrounds proved to be effective. In the case studies, the leadership of Rudolph Giuliani at Ground Zero, a long-term Federal prosecutor and the Mayor proved effective, though he was not directly responsible for emergency management. In the tsunami, the leader of the CNO in Sri Lanka was the Minister of Education. Following Katrina, Admiral Thad Allen, from the Coast Guard, provided exemplary leadership to FEMA. In each case, the leaders brought experience largely from management roles rather than from first responder roles.

I have learned that there are many professionals, particularly professors in college emergency management programs, who have a passion for developing future emergency managers. They have designed and taught courses to provide an excellent knowledge base to their students. They have appreciated, in particular, those students currently employed in emergency service who are continuing their education to earn degrees that prepare them to handle the management responsibilities in emergency management careers. They also have graduate students with undergraduate degrees in communication, meteorology, geology, public administration, and a host of other disciplines who are bringing specialized knowledge to the field of emergency management. The professors are encouraging and participating with their students in research studies. Research will inform practice to improve disaster response.

Recommendations

To bridge the gap between emergency management and tactical response operations, there are some steps that should be taken.

1. Recognize that there are emergency managers with considerable knowledge of managerial principles and practices. Some have college degrees that have prepared them for their positions. Many have experience as first responders.

2. Recognize that the duties of emergency managers are largely managerial in nature, not synonymous with tactical response operations.

3. Whereas tactical response operations skills and abilities might best be acquired in training programs, emergency management knowledge can be

acquired in educational programs such as those provided in college degree programs.

4. Recognize that first responder experience may be valuable for an emergency manager to have, but it will not provide the required management training.

5. Recognize that first responders in disasters need the support of an Emergency Operations Center or a similar structure for providing the management support they require.

6. Find a way to convey the findings of researchers in emergency management to the field of practitioners both in emergency management and in tactical response operations. The significance of research must be enhanced by broader dissemination of research findings.

7. Encourage first responders with management capabilities to enroll in college degree programs in emergency management as a career development measure.

8. Support the development of emergency management as a profession by requiring candidates and incumbent emergency managers to achieve certification from recognized sources, as in the case of the Certified Emergency Manager (CEM) credential available from the International Association of Emergency Managers. Note that this credential will soon require a college degree.

9. Wherever possible, encourage first responders and emergency management personnel to train and exercise together so as to better understand each others roles.

10. Recognize that there will be an increased need for emergency management personnel in the future and that preparing them through college degree programs with a focus on management and a concentration on emergency management may be the best way to meet that need.

Summary

There never used to be a gap. Complexities in government, proximity, and technology have contributed to a clear difference between emergency management and tactical response operations. In disasters, when response efforts demand the cooperation of multiple agencies and jurisdictions, there is a need for coordination and management to support the work of first responders and their chiefs. There is a need to understand the political and social contexts of disaster response. To best utilize the resources available, emergency managers need to know the laws and regulations that apply. Managing a multi-jurisdictional disaster response is not the same as performing tactical response operations. The management knowledge and skill pertinent to disaster and emergency management are different from those applied to tactical response operations. They are best acquired in a management educational program such as those offered at more the 140 colleges and universities across the United States and in other countries. First responders with management career aspirations should consider enrolling in a college program in emergency management. Their experience as first responders will be valuable as they acquire the emergency management perspective.

As individuals prepare for emergency management careers, research should continue and expand to discover new findings and recommendations in order to strengthen disaster mitigation, preparedness, response, recovery and restoration efforts. Additional means of building personal responsibility orientation in all citizens should be the focus of such research. Greater emphasis on mitigation should be at the forefront, to reduce the impact and the cost of disasters.

Emergency responders and emergency managers must learn to work together, to understand and appreciate each others contributions. The forces of nature that continue to cause disasters will not pause to wait for us to work together. We must realize our collective responsibility and know that it will take our combined efforts to effectively reduce the impact of future disasters.

Daniel Hoffman wrote of Stephen Crane's description of the challenge before us and our insignificance as we combat the forces of nature. "Nature's malignity and omnipotence are accentuated in Crane's work by the gnatlike stature of man. The world has no need for man, and can readily dispense of his strivings:

A man said to the universe:

"Sir, I exist!"

"However," replied the universe,

"The fact has not created in me

A sense of obligation."[8]

The gap between emergency management and tactical response operations seems so small when viewed in the greater context of the task confronting us: to save lives and protect communities. Together we stand, dedicated to that mission.

Discussion Questions

1. List three disastrous incidents that have encouraged Colleges and Community Emergency Managers to work together.

2. List the types of programs in which colleges have supported both tactical response operations and emergency management.

3. Describe the role of emergency management personnel on scene during a disaster or emergency.

4. Summarize the ways in which working together is in the best interest of all citizens and for the safety of our nation.

References

1. http://www.nyalert.gov/SiteText/SiteTextDisplay.aspx?text=AboutSite retrieved January 20, 2008.
2. Academic Continuity and Emergency Management: *Improving Higher Education's Ability to continue teaching and learning When confronted by Disasters*, Report of Working Group (June 2007), p. 1.
3. Academic Continuity and Emergency Management: *Improving Higher Education's Ability to continue teaching and learning When confronted by Disasters*, Report of Working Group (June 2007), p. 4.
4. http://departments.firehouse.com/dept/AlexandriaVA retrieved January 15, 2008.
5. *Syracuse University Carrier Dome 2002 NCAA Division I Men's Basketball-East Regional Security Plan.* (March 20, 2002). p. 3.
6. *Syracuse University Carrier Dome 2002 NCAA Division I Men's Basketball-East Regional Security Plan.* (March 20, 2002). p. 2.
7. Donald W. Walsh, et al. (2005). *National Incident Management System: Principles and Practice.* Boston: Jones and Bartlett. p.24.
8. Stephen Crane printed in Daniel Hoffman. (1957). *The Poetry of Stephen Crane.* New York: Columbia University Press. p. 93. ISBN 0231086628.

National Incident Management System (NIMS):

Five-Year NIMS Training Plan

National Integration Center (NIC), Incident Management Systems
Integration (IMSI) Division

Preface

On 1 March 2004, the Department of Homeland Security published the *National Incident Management System* (NIMS). The NIMS provides a consistent nationwide template to enable Federal, State, tribal, and local governments, the private sector, and nongovernmental organizations to work together to prepare for, prevent, respond to, recover from, and mitigate the effects of incidents, regardless of cause, size, location, or complexity, in order to reduce the loss of life, property, and harm to the environment. This consistency provides the foundation for utilization of NIMS for all incidents, ranging from daily occurrences to incidents requiring coordinated Federal response. The NIMS was updated in 2007 based on input from stakeholders at every level within the nation's response community and lessons learned during recent incidents.

A critical tool in promoting the nationwide implementation of NIMS is a well-developed training program that facilitates NIMS training throughout the nation. Closely related to the training, core competencies will form the basis of the training courses' learning objectives and personnel qualifications that validate proficiency.

The National Integration Center (NIC) Incident Management Systems Integration (formerly known as the NIMS Integration Center) is charged with the development of NIMS core competencies, training courses, and personnel qualifications. This document describes the operational foundations of these efforts; defines NIMS core competencies, training courses, and personnel qualifications as part of the National Training Program for NIMS; assembles and updates the training guidance for available NIMS courses (organized as a core curriculum); and lays out a plan for the next five years to continue development of the National Training Program.

Introduction

The National Incident Management System (NIMS) represents a core set of doctrine, concepts, principles, terminology, and organizational processes that enables effective, efficient, and collaborative incident management across all emergency management and incident response organizations and disciplines.[1] The President of the United States of America has directed Federal agencies to adopt NIMS and encouraged adoption of NIMS by all stakeholders[2]—Federal, State, territorial, tribal, sub-state regional, and local governments, private sector organizations, critical infrastructure owners and operators, and nongovernmental organizations involved in emergency management and/or incident response. As initially laid out in Homeland Security Presidential Directive (HSPD)–5, *Management of Domestic Incidents*, which established NIMS, adoption and implementation of the NIMS by State, tribal, and local organizations is one of the conditions for receiving Federal preparedness assistance (through grants, contracts, and other activities).[3]

Adequately trained and qualified emergency management/response personnel are critical to the national implementation of NIMS.[4] In particular, the *NIMS* document describes the National Integration Center's (NIC) responsibility to develop "a national program for NIMS education and awareness," and to facilitate common national standards for personnel qualification.[5] The Five-Year NIMS Training Plan will guide the NIC's activities to support NIMS training and education. The Plan is comprehensive, covering NIC responsibilities and actions as well as those of all stakeholders.

A critical piece of the Five-Year NIMS Training Plan is the description of a National Training Program for NIMS. This document introduces a National Training Program for NIMS, which compiles the NIC's existing and on-going development of NIMS training and guidance for personnel qualification.[6] Previous guidance on NIMS training[7] has been updated and is issued as Appendices of this document. The National Training Program for NIMS will develop and maintain a common national foundation for training and qualifying emergency management/response personnel. To achieve a national goal of well

---

[1] *National Incident Management System.* Washington, DC: Department of Homeland Security, March 2004 (hereafter cited as *NIMS*); and *National Incident Management System,* revision. Washington, DC: Department of Homeland Security, FEMA 501, Draft August 2007, *http://www.fema.gov/pdf/emergency/nrf/nrf-nims.pdf* (hereafter cited as *NIMS*, revised), p. 3 & 6.

[2] Throughout this document, following *NIMS*, revised, the term "stakeholders" refers to all organizations involved in emergency management and incident response. Stakeholders are Federal, State, territorial, tribal, substate regional, and local governments, private sector organizations, critical infrastructure owners and operators, and nongovernmental organizations.

[3] *Homeland Security Presidential Directive (HSPD)-5: Management of Domestic Incidents.* Washington, DC: White House, February 2003; and *NIMS,* revised, p. 3.

[4] "NIMS implementation" means that NIMS is institutionalized in a sustainable manner within every organization, agency, and jurisdiction in order to be effectively and efficiently used for emergency management and incident response activities.

[5] *NIMS*, revised, p. 76

[6] The National Training Program for NIMS is described more fully in a later section.

[7] Federal Emergency Management Agency, *National Incident Management System (NIMS)—National Standard Curriculum Training Development Guidance—FY07,* Washington, DC: Department of Homeland Security, March 2007.

trained and qualified emergency management/response personnel, able to work together effectively and efficiently during any incident, the National Training Program for NIMS has three broad objectives.

These objectives are:

1. Support NIMS education and training for all stakeholder emergency management/response personnel;

2. Adapt the functional capabilities defined by the NIMS into guidelines and courses that help stakeholders develop personnel training and credentialing plans that yield the desired capabilities; and

3. Define the minimum personnel qualifications required for service on complex multi-jurisdictional incidents nationwide, a term used in this document to denote incidents that require responders to hold credentials under the National Emergency Responder Credentialing System, in development by FEMA.[8]

To meet the broad objectives for the National Training Program for NIMS, this Plan describes a sequence of goals, objectives, and action items that translates the functional capabilities defined in the NIMS into positions, core competencies, training, and personnel qualifications. The NIMS defines functional capabilities necessary for emergency management and incident response; it is organized into components and subcomponents: Preparedness; Communications and Information Management; Resource Management; and Command and Management, including Incident Command System (ICS), Multiagency Coordination Systems, and Public Information. For each NIMS component and subcomponent, the National Training Program will define typical position titles for personnel fulfilling each functional capability, and specify the core competencies for these personnel. Based on these core competencies, the Program will define standard training courses and minimum personnel qualifications for each position. Personnel qualifications specify the combination of training, experience, and evaluation that a candidate must complete to become qualified to fill a position on a complex multi-jurisdictional incident, and are recommended to fill the position in other types of incidents.

The Program relies on a process to develop training and personnel qualifications, based on functional needs specified in the NIMS. Personnel need adequate training to gain the knowledge, skills, and abilities to fulfill NIMS functions, and the experience to demonstrate proficiency and become qualified to serve in a position that fulfills NIMS functions. **Figure 1** represents the relationship between functional capabilities, positions, core competencies, training curriculum, and personnel qualifications. Positions and core competencies will be derived from functional capabilities. Starting from core competencies for positions, the Program will specify appropriate training courses and guidelines for personnel qualification for each position. The training and personnel qualification guidelines should be developed in tandem, since each affects the other and personnel qualification typically includes specific training requirements.

Once appropriate training courses have been defined within the National Training Program, the NIC will support development of these courses. In addition to developing the courses, the NIC will issue training guidance for them. This will allow stakeholders to develop equivalent training, if they wish to

---

[8] Some information about the forthcoming National Emergency Responder Credentialing System is available at: *http://www.oes.ca.gov/Operational/OESHome.nsf/PDF/NIMS%20Credentialing/$file/credentialingFAQ.pdf*. It is also recommended that stakeholders adopt the same qualification and credentialing for service on smaller, day-to-day incidents.

develop training that encompasses specific stakeholder needs in addition to the general NIMS training requirements. In general, this plan assumes that states will be the only stakeholders interested in developing equivalent courses. Stakeholders that develop equivalent training are responsible for ensuring course equivalence. A course will be considered equivalent if it meets the training guidance specified in the appropriate Course Summary (cf., Appendix C). Training guidance describes the course objectives, topics covered, and minimum requirements of instructional time and instructor qualifications for instructor-led courses to shape development of equivalent courses.[9]

Personnel-qualification guidelines will provide a national standard model for credentialing organizations and will eventually be the foundation for a national credentialing system.[10] While the NIC is in the process of developing this national credentialing system, stakeholders hold the responsibility and authority for issuing credentials. However, once NIMS implementation is mature (including a mature state for the National Training Program for NIMS), participation in national incidents will require credentials based on personnel qualifications that meet or exceed the NIC guidelines for personnel qualification.

Figure 1 schematically shows the link between elements in the National Training Program for NIMS. This figure emphasizes the operational basis (Needed Functional Capabilities) as the foundation for the development of training and definition of personnel qualifications.

---

[9] For computer-based training, the course needs to meet all equivalence standards defined in the training guidance, except for instructor guidelines, because there is no instructor.

[10] The NIC is developing a national credentialing system that will help verify, quickly and accurately, the identity and qualifications of emergency personnel responding to an incident. The National Emergency Responder Credentialing System will document minimum professional qualifications, certifications, and training and education requirements that define the standards required for specific emergency response functional positions. *http://www.fema.gov/emergency/nims/rm/credentialing.shtm.*

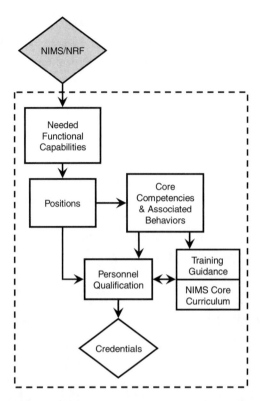

Figure 1: Operational Foundation for NIMS Training and Personnel Qualification Guidelines

The heart of the Five-Year NIMS Training Plan is to develop the complete foundation of the National Training Program for NIMS, which consists of:

- Core competencies for typical positions;

- A national core curriculum for NIMS;

- Training guidance for specific courses within the core curriculum; and

- Personnel qualification guidelines.

Definition of the National Training Program begins with collection of the elements that already exist or are currently in development. Core competencies for ICS positions were published on September 11, 2007. Initial definition of the national core curriculum includes awareness-level courses spanning all NIMS components and subcomponents; advanced courses in ICS; and position-specific courses for ICS (in pilot testing). Training guidance for all existing courses exists (cf., Appendix C). Personnel qualifications guidelines are not yet published.

The National Training Program for NIMS—and this Plan which guides the development, maintenance, and sustainment of the Program—recognizes the shared responsibilities between the NIC and all stakeholders. Though the Five-Year NIMS Training Plan guides specific NIC actions to develop, maintain, and sustain the National Training Program for NIMS, it also provides critical guidance to all stakeholders so that they are able to develop plans, budgets, and schedules for their own training programs. Stakeholder training plans can include directing personnel to online or in-person NIMS courses and/or completing stakeholder-developed NIMS-equivalent courses consistent with national training guidance. Stakeholder emergency management and incident response credentials for service in incidents with national implications will be based on NIC guidelines for personnel qualifications.

A critical driver for stakeholder training plans should be NIMS compliance requirements for training. NIMS compliance requirements are specific activities designed to measure an organization or jurisdiction's degree of implementation of NIMS.[11] Training is one such compliance activity. These training requirements fall into two categories: awareness-level training required of many stakeholder personnel; and training related specifically to personnel qualification. In the first case, compliance requirements encompass a broad requirement for awareness-level training for many emergency management/response personnel. In the second case, training will only be required of those personnel seeking credentials issued under the guidance of the National Emergency Responder Credentialing System. As the National Training Program for NIMS matures, more awareness-level training courses will be required. In addition to such jurisdiction-wide or organization-wide requirements, NIMS will require that stakeholder emergency management and incident response credentials be based on NIC guidelines for personnel qualification for service in complex multi-jurisdictional incidents nationwide, a term used in this document to denote incidents that require responders to hold credentials under the National Emergency Responder Credentialing System, in development by FEMA.

The National Training Program for NIMS is in its initial development phase, but the Five-Year NIMS Training Plan should guide a transition from the Program's initial phase into a more mature state. Currently, NIMS training primarily provides awareness-level training; no national all-hazards personnel-qualification guidance exists. Ultimately, the fully formed Program will contain a comprehensive core curriculum for NIMS training spanning all the components and subcomponents, along with national guidance for personnel qualification in all-hazards emergency management and incident response, both based on defined core competencies. In this more mature state, the ongoing support of the Program will be maintenance and sustainment of its elements, plus an additional element of assessing the effectiveness of courses, the core curriculum, and the National Training Program for NIMS.

In the mature state, qualification guidelines in the National Training Program will be based on a stair-step approach, as shown in **Figure 2**. Personnel entering jobs in emergency management and incident response will gain initial NIMS training as part of their intake or introductory training. As a person gains experience and takes identified training, that person's qualifications to serve during incidents should similarly progress.

[11] The NIMS document specifies that NIC/IMSI (formerly known as the NIMS Integration Center) is responsible for "developing . . . compliance requirements and compliance timelines for Federal, State, local and tribal entities regarding NIMS standards and guidelines." *NIMS*, p. 64.

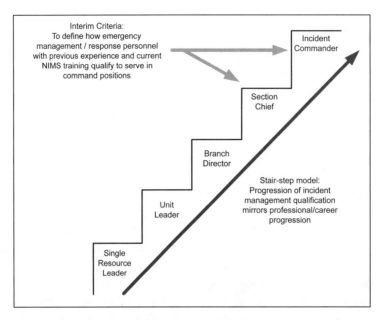

Figure 2: Personnel qualification steps

Position qualifications need to be developed that both define a mature state for the Training Program, when personnel may follow the stair-step model shown in Figure 2; and recognize interim criteria that will be suitable to fill senior positions based on training and experience predating establishment of position-qualification guidelines within the National Training Program for NIMS.

In general, then, the Plan expands on the training that is available and lays down the operational foundation for more advanced personnel training and qualification. Out-year compliance requirements will allow sufficient time for course development, instructor training, and course distribution to stakeholders.

The Plan was developed in conjunction with a working group of representative stakeholders[12] and was made available for national review and public comment. The Plan is based on an analysis of the current state of NIMS-related training, compared to a specification of a desired state of the National Training Program for NIMS. This document describes both the desired state and current state of NIMS training, and then identifies the goals, objectives, and action items that constitute the active portion of the Five-Year NIMS Training Plan.

INTENDED AUDIENCE

The primary audience for the Five-Year NIMS Training Plan is the NIC and stakeholder personnel directly involved in the planning, budgeting, and execution of NIMS training at all levels (Federal, State,

---

[12] The Working Group of representative stakeholders met on May 1-2, 2007, in Arlington, Virginia, to discuss issues relevant to this initial Five-Year NIMS Training Plan.

tribal, local, private sector, and NGOs). The secondary audience includes all stakeholder personnel who require NIMS training. Both groups are encouraged to use this Five-Year NIMS Training Plan to anticipate, plan, and prepare for the NIC's implementation of the National Training Program for NIMS.

AUTHORITIES AND BACKGROUND

On 28 February 2003, Homeland Security Presidential Directive (HSPD)–5, *Management of Domestic Incidents*, was issued, directing the Secretary of Homeland Security to establish a National Incident Management System. Initially published in March 2004, the NIMS provides a consistent national approach for Federal, State, tribal, and local governments; the private sector; and NGOs to work together to prepare for, prevent, respond to, recover from, and mitigate the effects of incidents, regardless of cause, size, location, or complexity, in order to reduce the loss of life, property, and harm to the environment..[13] Based upon emergency management and incident response practices, the NIMS represents a core set of doctrine, concepts, principles, terminology, and organizational processes that enables effective, efficient, and collaborative incident management.[14]

Initially, the Department of Homeland Security established the NIMS Integration Center to coordinate training and support NIMS implementation. Subsequently, this office was renamed the Incident Management Systems Integration (IMSI) and placed within the NIC of the Federal Emergency Management Agency (FEMA).

Incidents' lessons learned and the *NIMS* document recognize that successful implementation relies upon development and maintenance of NIMS training nationally.[15] Furthermore, NIMS implementation relies upon comprehensive NIMS training and standardized personnel qualification. In 2007, the NIC supervised and coordinated an update to the NIMS document to better meet the needs of all stakeholders.

SCOPE OF FIVE-YEAR NIMS TRAINING PLAN

The Five-Year NIMS Training Plan defines the National Training Program for NIMS. It specifies NIC and stakeholder responsibilities and activities for developing, maintaining, and sustaining the National Training Program for NIMS. Besides spanning NIC and stakeholder responsibilities and actions, the Plan defines the process for developing both training and personnel qualification requirements for emergency management/response personnel.

The NIC's responsibilities within the National Training Program for NIMS include defining a core curriculum, descriptions of the curriculum's courses, and training guidance in the form of Course Summaries suitable to guide development of equivalent courses. The NIC also has responsibility to

---

[13] *NIMS*, revised version, p. 3.

[14] Ibid.

[15] "DHS should institute a formal training program on the NIMS and NRP for all department and agency personnel with incident management responsibilities" (Recommendation 2 of *The Federal Response to Hurricane Katrina: Lessons Learned,* Washington, DC: The White House, February 2006); "The NIC is responsible for ... developing a national program for NIMS education and awareness, including specific instruction on ... NIMS in general" (*NIMS*, revised version, p. 76).

develop personnel qualification guidelines for stakeholder-issued incident management credentials. [16]

While the Plan defines stakeholder responsibilities, the details of stakeholder plans and activities are not specified. However, it does provide out-year training-related NIMS compliance requirements as targets for stakeholders to attain. Existing and future documents and guidance are, and will be, designed to assist stakeholder development of jurisdictional, agency, and/or organizational training plans for NIMS.

The Five-Year NIMS Training Plan has the following strategic objectives:

1. Establish specific goals, objectives, and action items to guide the NIC as it develops and implements the National Training Program, thus providing national leadership.

2. Provide sufficient planning and documentation to guide stakeholders' long-term training plans, budgets, and schedules.

3. Define a national core curriculum for NIMS and provide explicit guidelines for NIMS courses in the core curriculum, applicable to all levels of government, the private sector, and NGOs.

4. Provide national guidelines for emergency management/response personnel qualifications, based on development of core competencies for NIMS-defined incident-management positions. Personnel qualifications following these guidelines will be required for service on complex multi-jurisdictional incidents nationwide (incidents that require responders to hold credentials under the National Emergency Responder Credentialing System) and are recommended for service on all incidents.

5. Serve as a single-source, regularly updated compilation of training within the national core curriculum for NIMS and personnel-qualification guidance.

ORGANIZATION OF FIVE-YEAR NIMS TRAINING PLAN DOCUMENT

Preceding the description of the goals, objectives, and action items that constitute its substance, the Five-Year NIMS Training Plan has the following descriptive sections.

- *Desired State of National Training Program for NIMS.* This introduces the overall idealized picture of NIMS training nationally; the NIC and stakeholder responsibilities and interactions are highlighted. Following the initial picture, the steps encompassing the development of a National Training Program for NIMS are described. These aspects of the program include the basis for core competencies and the training courses and objectives to meet the competencies. It concludes with a discussion of personnel qualifications.

- *Current State of NIMS Training.* This describes existing training efforts, following essentially the same structure as the *Desired State of National Training Program for NIMS* section.

- *NIMS Compliance Objectives for Training.* This section describes the evolution of NIMS compliance objectives (requirements) for training, culminating in a table of out-year compliance objectives for training. By verifying stakeholder engagement with the National Training Program for NIMS, these compliance objectives drive stakeholder activities. As the National Training Program matures, the compliance objectives will shift accordingly.

Following these descriptive sections are the tables of goals, objectives, and action items directed at closing that gaps between the current state of NIMS training and the desired state of training and personnel qualification.

Desired State of National Training Program for NIMS

National coordination among the stakeholders and the NIC must occur to reach a state of consistent and systematic implementation of NIMS training and personnel qualification. Ultimately, operational needs require qualified personnel to serve in emergency management and incident response roles. While training is necessary to produce qualified personnel, this Plan recognizes that qualified personnel are more than simply the sum of their training. Training is necessary to develop qualified personnel, but qualification also requires experience through exercises or time in the field and development of discipline-specific skills in emergency management and incident response.

Figure 3 is a visual depiction of the national coordination process for NIMS training and personnel qualification. The NIC provides national leadership and resources, particularly training and qualification guidance. Stakeholders plan, implement training programs, and train, qualify, and credential personnel.

Figure 3 highlights the following key elements of the process:

- Foundational national documents—e.g., the NIMS and the National Response Framework (NRF)—are maintained and distributed by the NIC and provide national doctrine and strategy. These documents, in conjunction with stakeholder assessments of specific hazards, risks, and vulnerabilities, guide stakeholder plans.

- Based on NIMS, the NIC specifies core competencies and their associated behaviors to provide a foundation for both personnel qualification and a national core curriculum for NIMS training.[17] Personnel qualification guidance, in the form of position task books, defines tasks that measurably demonstrate a candidate's proficiency.

- Stakeholder plans and foundational national documents dictate functional capabilities for emergency management and incident response that stakeholders should develop and maintain.

- Personnel qualification guidance specifies means for demonstrating minimum capabilities for stakeholder personnel assigned to NIMS positions. Personnel credentialed to serve on complex multi-jurisdictional incidents nationwide (incidents that require responders to hold credentials under the National Emergency Responder Credentialing System) must be qualified within a system that meets or exceeds the national qualification guidance. It is recommended that national qualification guidance also be used for incidents of other sizes.

- Stakeholders, based on guidance provided by the NIC, determine who should be trained and seek qualification for emergency management and incident response positions, based on their own plans, qualification, and credentialing policy. With consideration of the national training guidance published by the NIC, stakeholders develop a training plan for their personnel. These plans often have significant programmatic, schedule, and budget implications for the stakeholder.

---

[17] The national core curriculum will be defined more completely below, but it currently constitutes the following courses: IS-700, IS-800, ICS-100, ICS-200, ICS-300, ICS-400, IS-701 through IS-707, and position-specific courses currently in pilot testing or under development.

For example, States may decide to develop their own training courses to suit their specific needs while still meeting the national training guidance.[18]

- Stakeholders execute the training plans, resulting in trained, qualified, and credentialed personnel.

- Training and experience for personnel qualification are acquired through course-based knowledge development; risk-free practical application, such as tabletop exercises and planned exercises; and on the job training, such as job shadowing, planned events, and IC experience during small incidents.

- Once trained, personnel will test and practice their skills during specific exercises and demonstrate their skills by effective management of and response to actual incidents.

- Exercise and mission/incident after-action reports should include an evaluation of the effectiveness and performance of incident-management personnel. Recommendations for improvements should be incorporated throughout the national coordination process for NIMS training to tailor stakeholder training plans as well as training and qualification of specific personnel, provide feedback to the national curriculum for NIMS and training courses, and perhaps suggest modifications of the NIMS, National Response Framework, and stakeholder plans.

---

[18] This Plan supersedes the previous guidance: Federal Emergency Management Agency, *National Incident Management System (NIMS)—National Standard Curriculum Training Development Guidance—FY07*, Washington, DC: Department of Homeland Security, March 2007.

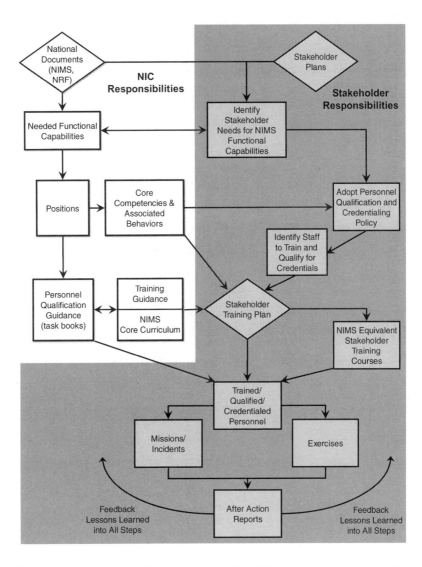

Figure 3: Coordinated responsibilities to support NIMS training and personnel qualification

NATIONAL TRAINING PROGRAM FOR NIMS

The NIMS Five-Year Training Plan defines the process for developing the National Training Program for NIMS. The Program, in turn, is guided by three broad objectives: to support NIMS education and training; to develop NIMS curriculum and training guidance; and to define personnel qualifications.

To meet these broad objectives, this Training Program will develop and maintain the national core curriculum for the NIMS and personnel-qualification guidelines. Both the curriculum and guidelines are based on core competencies and associated behaviors. Taken together, core curriculum and qualification guidelines specify "who" needs NIMS training and "what" the courses, training objectives, and minimum instructional standards are for NIMS training.

The desired state of the National Training Program for NIMS is to create a sustained program of training and personnel qualification that is well coordinated, continually maintained, and meets the operational needs of the emergency management and incident response community under the NIMS. It is envisioned that at the end of Fiscal Year 2012 (FY12), the Training Program will be fully developed and NIMS training will be consistently delivered throughout the community of emergency management/response personnel at the levels identified by the core competencies—at which point, the National Training Program for NIMS will include:

- Core competencies and associated behaviors to describe capabilities required of emergency management/response personnel within the NIMS;
- A national core curriculum for the NIMS, with each course having course objectives that meet training needs set by the core competencies;
- Complete training guidance for all courses in the core curriculum for the NIMS; and
- Qualifications guidelines for individual emergency management/response positions or functions within the NIMS.

The Program also requires additional elements to measure stakeholder participation and evaluate progress of the Program and Plan.

- NIMS compliance requirements for training to assure maintenance and sustainment of stakeholder training programs, including ongoing qualification of emergency management/response personnel. [19]
- Program assessment and evaluation systems for gauging the effectiveness of the National Training Program for NIMS.
- Periodic evaluations and updates to maintain the effectiveness of the Five-Year NIMS Training Plan.

OPERATIONAL NEEDS DEFINE CORE COMPETENCIES AND ASSOCIATED BEHAVIORS

The NIMS document specifies an emergency management and incident response framework and specific functions to be conducted within this framework. In most general terms, NIMS functions align with major components and subcomponents of NIMS: Preparedness; Communications and Information Management; Resource Management; and Command and Management, including Incident Command System, Multiagency Coordination Systems, and Public Information. Within each major component and subcomponent, emergency management/response personnel responsibilities and activities are further delineated.

This set of functions, responsibilities, and activities, in conjunction with an incident's size and/or complexity, identifies operational or mission needs. Based on these operational/mission needs, NIMS

---

[19] Stakeholders will define the emergency management/response personnel within their jurisdiction, agency, or organization who require ongoing training.

personnel capabilities—skills and knowledge necessary to fulfill these needs—can be defined for typical positions within the NIMS structure.

For the purposes of developing training guidelines, operational needs and NIMS position capabilities are expressed in the form of core competencies for the position, along with behaviors associated with these competencies. The core competencies are quite general, usually encompassing broad leadership and/or management skills. The associated behaviors provide more specific descriptions of how a competency is expressed.[20] However, overall performance is measured by "tasks," which are evaluated activities that demonstrate proficiency. The specificity of tasks makes it difficult to develop them for all hazards. Typically, tasks will be incident-specific, often even discipline-specific, especially for operational and some planning tasks. The NIC will develop personnel qualifications, likely based on tasks, which take into account this distinction of discipline specificity.

CORE CURRICULUM FOR NIMS

The core curriculum for the NIMS represents those courses critical to train personnel capable of implementing emergency management and incident response within the NIMS. The current curriculum's courses are shown in **Table 1**, and Course Summaries are listed in **Appendix C**.

---

[20] Appendix B lists core competencies and their associated behaviors for sample positions: the eight ICS Command and General Staff positions, for type I & II incidents.

Table 1: Core Curriculum for the NIMS

Course Grouping	Course ID	Course Title
Overview	IS-700	National Incident Management System (NIMS) an Introduction
	IS-800	National Response Framework (NRF), an Introduction
ICS Courses	ICS-100	Introduction to the Incident Command System
	ICS-200	ICS for Single Resources and Initial Action Incidents
	ICS-300	Intermediate ICS
	ICS-400	Advanced ICS
NIMS Components and Subcomponents	IS-701	NIMS Multiagency Coordination System
	IS-702	NIMS Public Information Systems
	IS-703	NIMS Resource Management
	IS-704	NIMS Communication and Information Management
	IS-705	NIMS Preparedness
	IS-706	NIMS Intrastate Mutual Aid, An Introduction
	IS-707	NIMS Resource Typing
ICS Position-Specific Courses	P-400	All-Hazards Incident Commander
	P-430	All-Hazards Operations Section Chief
	P-440	All-Hazards Planning Section Chief
	P-450	All-Hazards Logistics Section Chief
	P-460	All-Hazards Finance Section Chief
	P-480	All-Hazards Intelligence/Investigations Function
	P-402	All-Hazards Liaison Officer
	P-403	All-Hazards Public Information Officer
	P-404	All-Hazards Safety Officer

The core curriculum courses cover all the components and major subcomponents of NIMS and are further classified into levels of training. Each level of training is based upon the expected level of learning the students will achieve:[21]

- "Awareness" training presents NIMS topics and concepts at an introductory level, with evaluations typically provided via written or computer-based examinations (e.g., multiple-choice, true-false, or fill-in-the-blank tests[22]) to determine student comprehension.

---

[21] "Levels of training" organization is drawn from analysis of course objectives, activities (e.g. practical exercises), depth of material, and evaluations criteria.

- "Advanced" training is oriented to skills development and includes practical exercises to test application level of NIMS subject matter. For the most part, courses provided at this level are geared towards fulfilling NIMS credentialing tracks.
- "Practicum" training emphasizes exercises that practice the skills learned in the other levels of training. In general, this training will be in the form of exercises directed at certifying or qualifying personnel and will include discipline-specific courses.

Table 2: Core Curriculum Aligned with NIMS Components and by Level of Training

				Levels of Training		
				Awareness	Advanced	Practicum
Components of NIMS	Preparedness		IS-700	IS 800 IS 705		
	Communications & Info Management			IS 704		
	Resource Management			IS 703 IS 706 IS 707		
	Command & Management	ICS		ICS 100 ICS 200	ICS 300 ICS 400	Position-specific courses
		MACS		ICS 701		
		Public Info		ICS 702		
	Ongoing Management & Maintenance					

COURSE DEVELOPMENT AND TRAINING GUIDANCE

The Emergency Management Institute (EMI), the United States Fire Administration (USFA), the National Wildfire Coordination Group (NWCG), and Federal agencies in coordination with the NIC have developed, and are continuing to develop, NIMS-related training courses. In conjunction with courses developed by these agencies and departments, the IMSI issues training guidance in the form of Course Summaries (cf., Appendix C), which include descriptions and guidelines for specific courses.

---

[22] Examinations for equivalent courses must be based on the course learning objectives and covering the same material as examinations for NIC-developed core curriculum courses. Passing grade for examinations is 75%.

Each course-developing agency works with the IMSI to assure that the courses meet appropriate instructional standards. Course Summaries describe the courses developed with IMSI support in sufficient detail to guide development of equivalent courses by other stakeholders. The Course Summaries include:

- Intended student audience for the course;
- Course objectives supported by the topical content descriptions and intended learner outcomes;
- Cross-reference to NIMS topics. [23]

Course Summaries also determine the means to deliver course material, including consideration of:

- Minimum contact hours; and
- Instructor qualifications (for instructor led courses).

NIMS training development guidance states that training may be offered through government agencies and/or private training vendors. It is not necessary to meet training requirements by attending a Federal course; however, courses must meet course objectives, activities (e.g. practical exercises), and depth of material described within this Plan. This Plan supersedes the previously published *National Standards Curriculum Training Development Guidance*. [24]

PERSONNEL QUALIFICATION

Personnel qualification relies on a combination of training, operational experience (during exercises or incidents), job shadowing, and administrative requirements (such as agency association and criminal background checks). The Plan considers qualified personnel to be more than simply the sum of their training, and developing minimum expectations for functional qualification of personnel is an important part of the National Training Program for NIMS. Incident experience must supplement training for a candidate to meet minimum expectations to qualify for service in an all-hazards NIMS position during a complex multi-jurisdictional incident nationwide (incidents that require responders to hold credentials under the National Emergency Responder Credentialing System).

Personnel qualification is closely related to credentialing, which is inherently a stakeholder responsibility. For personnel to be credentialed so they can serve in NIMS-defined positions on a complex multi-jurisdictional incident (incidents that require responders to hold credentials under the National Emergency Responder Credentialing System), a stakeholder's credentialing system must meet the minimum personnel-qualification guidelines specified by the NIC.

Personnel qualification guidance will list the performance requirements, through position task books or tasks, for specific positions in a format that allows a trainee to be evaluated against written guidelines. These tasks, based on core competencies and associated behaviors, are the measurable activities that demonstrate proficiency associated with the competencies and behaviors. Successful performance of all tasks during exercises, job shadowing, and/or operations for a relevant position, as observed and

---

[23] Appendix A is an annotated outline of the revised NIMS document, to be used for the cross-references found in the Course Summaries contained in Appendix C.

[24] Federal Emergency Management Agency, *National Incident Management System (NIMS)—National Standard Curriculum Training Development Guidance—FY07,* Washington, DC: Department of Homeland Security, March 2007, p. 5.

recorded by an evaluator, results in a recommendation to the certifying agency that the trainee be qualified in that position.

Current State of NIMS Training

A great deal of NIMS training exists, especially at the awareness level, and stakeholders are training personnel in the NIMS to varying degrees.

CORE COMPETENCIES AND ASSOCIATED BEHAVIORS

The IMSI has drafted core competencies for ICS positions (for examples, cf., Appendix B). These are the only NIMS positions to have their core competencies and behaviors fully defined. A change management board has been chartered by the IMSI to provide ongoing maintenance of the ICS core competencies.[25] The board is responsible for determining appropriate minimum competencies and behaviors required to enable interoperability between emergency management and incident response functions. Core competencies will be republished by the board every three years, or as needed.

CORE CURRICULUM FOR NIMS

Many courses in the core curriculum are available. **Table 3** lists the status of each course. A number of the courses are still being developed, but some are closer to completion than others. The courses that are in the latter stages of development are shown within the table to be in "pilot testing." All other courses that have not reached this stage are shown to be "in development."

Several of the courses have versions tailored to align with disciplines. The course material remains consistent, but the examples and representative scenarios are drawn from a specific discipline, to increase familiarity to the students.[26] Stakeholders that develop equivalent training are responsible for ensuring course equivalence. A course will be considered equivalent if it meets the training guidance specified in the appropriate Course Summary (cf., Appendix C).

REFRESHER TRAINING

Refresher training is recommended on a regular basis to ensure that knowledge and skills are maintained, especially for personnel who are not regularly involved in complex multi-jurisdictional incidents nationwide (incidents that require responders to hold credentials under the National Emergency Responder Credentialing System). Refresher training may be considered for inclusion as a requirement beginning in FY09. This is a point for analysis and development in the future.

---

[25] Information on the group, including how membership is determined and how to petition for membership is available at *http://www.fema.gov/emergency/nims/ics_competencies.shtm*.

[26] In general, these courses have the same course number, with a disciplinary suffix added. Some older courses that have been determined to be equivalent have numbering outside the core curriculum numbering scheme. These will be renumbered or be given an auxiliary number to align with the core curriculum for the NIMS.

Table 3: Status of Core Curriculum for NIMS

Course Grouping	Course ID	Course Title	Course Status
Overview	IS-700	National Incident Management System (NIMS) an Introduction	CBT, C
	IS-800	National Response Framework (NRF), an Introduction	CBT, C
ICS Courses	ICS-100	Introduction to the Incident Command System	CBT, C
	ICS-200*	ICS for Single Resources and Initial Action Incidents	CBT, C
	ICS-300	Intermediate ICS	C
	ICS-400	Advanced ICS	C
NIMS Components and Subcomponents	IS-701	NIMS Multiagency Coordination System	CBT, C
	IS-702	NIMS Public Information Systems	CBT, C
	IS-703	NIMS Resource Management	CBT, C
	IS-704	NIMS Communication and Information Management	D
	IS-705	NIMS Preparedness	D
	IS-706	NIMS Intrastate Mutual Aid, An Introduction	CBT, C
	IS-707	NIMS Resource Typing	D
ICS Position-Specific Courses	P-400	All-Hazards Incident Commander	P
	P-430	All-Hazards Operations Section Chief	P
	P-440	All-Hazards Planning Section Chief	P
	P-450	All-Hazards Logistics Section Chief	P
	P-460	All-Hazards Finance Section Chief	P
	P-480	All-Hazards Information and Intelligence Function	P
	P-402	All-Hazards Liaison Officer	P
	P-403	All-Hazards Public Information Officer	P
	P-404	All-Hazards Safety Officer	P

* It is recommended that IS-200 be taken in a classroom

Key: CBT = computer-based training;[27] C = classroom; D = initial development period; P = pilot testing period

COURSE DEVELOPMENT AND TRAINING GUIDANCE

Although it is recommended that stakeholders use EMI, USFA, CDP, and other federal sources for courses in the NIMS core curriculum, equivalent courses may be provided by stakeholders and private vendors. These courses are expected to cover the topics and meet the course objectives as listed in the Course Summaries (cf., **Appendix C**). Because of the wide array of potential providers, the issue of standards for course equivalencies is often raised. Courses provided through vendors outside of pre-recognized equivalent courses must meet the standard course minimums described in the Course Summaries. Stakeholders are responsible for validating that vendor courses meet the proscribed course minimums.

---

[27] Computer-based training includes interactive web-based courses.

Guidelines have been developed to ensure that NIMS training courses, provided outside of NIC venues, meet the appropriate "as taught by the NIC" standard. These guidelines are developed and issued by the NIC, through the IMSI. The consequences for failing to meet this standard could result in participants having to retake these courses from another compliant source.

PERSONNEL QUALIFICATION

The NIC has not yet developed an all-hazards qualification guide that shows the specific progression and provisions of the all-hazard stair-step training program envisioned. The NWCG's *Wildland Fire Qualification System Guide*, utilized by the wildland fire discipline, is a good example of what is likely to be adopted by the NIC.[28]

A key requirement of a performance-based training program is a tool to document successful completion of performance requirements for any given position. This education and evaluation tool leads to qualification and certification upon successful completion of all required tasks and training for the position. Position task books are used for this documentation, as they identify the requirements for positions based on competencies and behaviors. The NIC has developed model all-hazard position task books for Command and General Staff positions (in draft as of this document's publication), and is in the process of developing model task books for the other ICS positions identified in the NIMS ICS competencies.[29]

---

[28] National Wildfire Coordination Group, *Wildland Fire Qualifications System Guide*, PMS 310-1 (April 2006). Available for download at *http://www.nwcg.gov* (click on "Publications" then "Qualifications").

[29] All-Hazard Position Task Books are available for download at *http://www.usfa.dhs.gov/fireservice/subjects/incident/imt/imt-training.shtm*.

NIMS Compliance Objectives

To ensure that stakeholders implement NIMS, the NIC evaluates implementation using NIMS Compliance Objectives (requirements). These compliance objectives are regulated at the organizational or jurisdictional level, and Federal policy requires jurisdictions and organizations to meet NIMS compliance requirements as a condition for receiving Federal preparedness assistance (through grants, contracts, and other activities). The NIMS compliance objectives for training typically require that stakeholders are providing their personnel with appropriate NIMS training.

Initially, compliance objectives for training have been focused on the broad awareness-level courses in the NIMS core curriculum. These initial objectives sought to provide awareness of NIMS to the entire emergency management/response community. In FY07, the compliance objectives began a shift toward emphasizing compliance through advanced ICS training of personnel deemed likely to fill certain ICS roles. This represents the beginning of a trend toward emphasis on compliance objectives that emphasize developing qualified personnel.

As the National Training Program for NIMS progresses, stakeholders will be able to train more personnel to greater depth. Compliance objectives will then need to shift accordingly. Compliance objectives will increasingly ensure that stakeholder personnel are meeting published qualifications and then, in turn, receiving credentials. This shift in the compliance objectives for NIMS training must be linked to the National Training Program's maturity to ensure, for example, that there are sufficient numbers of NIMS-related courses and qualified instructors to satisfy the training needs of emergency management/response personnel nationwide.[30]

Coordinating this shift in compliance and the maturity of the National Training Program for NIMS, the Five-Year NIMS Training Plan describes a complementary evolution of compliance requirements as the Program evolves. As the National Training Program for NIMS reaches its desired state—a sustained, consistent, well-coordinated training program that meets operational needs—compliance requirements will also evolve. Early NIMS compliance objectives required all or most emergency management/response personnel to take IS-700 and IS-800. Once the desired state is reached, NIMS compliance objectives for training will focus on orderly qualification and credentialing of personnel and maintenance and sustainment of stakeholders' training plans for NIMS. **Table 4** shows the NIMS Compliance Objectives for training, as currently envisioned.

---

[30] IMSI recognizes that some stakeholders may have difficulty maintaining a pool of qualified instructors to conduct all courses. If so, gaining necessary training via NIC-delivered courses may be the best course of action.

Table 4: Out-Year NIMS Compliance Objectives for Training

Fiscal Year	Compliance Requirement
FY08	Complete IS-700; IS-800; Complete ICS-100; ICS-200 – Awareness Training Complete ICS-300 – Advanced Training Complete ICS Position-Specific Training – Practicum[†]
FY09	Complete IS-700; IS-800; ICS-100; ICS-200 – Awareness Training Complete ICS-300; ICS-400 – Advanced Training Complete Emergency Management Framework Course – Awareness Training Complete ICS Position-Specific Training – Practicum[†]
FY10	Complete IS-700; IS-800; ICS-100; ICS-200 – Awareness Training Complete IS 701; IS-702; IS-703; IS-704 – Awareness Training Complete ICS-300; ICS-400 – Advanced Training Complete Emergency Management Framework Course – Awareness Training Complete ICS Position-Specific Training – Practicum[†]
FY11	Complete IS-700; IS-701; IS-702; IS-703; IS-704; IS-705; IS-706; IS-707; IS-800; ICS-100; ICS-200 – Awareness Training Complete Emergency Management Framework Course – Awareness Training Complete ICS-300; ICS-400 – Advanced Training Complete ICS Position-Specific Training – Practicum[†] Complete EOC Position-Specific Training – Practicum[†]
FY12	Complete IS-700; IS-701; IS-702; IS-703; IS-704; IS-705; IS-706; IS-707; IS-800; ICS-100; ICS-200; Emergency Management Framework Course – Awareness Training Complete ICS-300; ICS-400; ICS/EOC Course – Advanced Training Complete ICS Position-Specific Training – Practicum[†] Complete EOC Position-Specific Training – Practicum[†]

[†] Stakeholders are not required to complete ICS Position-Specific Training (or EOC Position-Specific Training in future years) for NIMS compliance. However, the completion of ICS Position-Specific Training is required for those stakeholders who desire to be credentialed as part of the national credentialing system.

Five-Year Training Plan: Goals, Objectives, Action Items

A comparison of the current state to the desired state of the National Training Program for NIMS suggests a set of goals, objectives, and action items are necessary to achieve the desired state.

A great deal of NIMS training exists, especially at an awareness/introductory level, and some stakeholders have taken the initiative to train their personnel beyond the scope of the current compliance requirements, while others are still striving to meet training requirements. As a result, personnel are trained in NIMS to varying degrees. In general terms, some objectives and action items for FY08 and FY09 are aimed at fostering continued development of these awareness-level training efforts. Additional objectives and action items for FY08 and FY09 lay a foundation for supporting qualification of emergency management/response personnel by ensuring that qualification guidelines and sufficient instructors and course offerings are available to train these personnel. Objectives and action items for FY10-FY12 focus on reaching a mature implementation of the National Training Program for NIMS, including the sustained and enhanced NIMS proficiency of the stakeholder community. FY10-FY12 will emphasize ongoing development of a national cadre of emergency management/response personnel holding stakeholder-issued NIMS credentials.

One major goal guides NIC development of courses and training guidance to support stakeholder training nationally and development of personnel qualification guidance for credentials under the National Emergency Responder Credentialing System. **Table 5** specifies objectives and action items to meet this goal, for each NIMS component or subcomponent. Note that the degree of maturity for each of the components and subcomponents varies. As an example, the Incident Command System subcomponent is further along in development than this generic version of **Table 5** represents.

The other major goal addresses aspects of the National Training Program for NIMS outside curriculum development and personnel qualifications, such as updates and maintenance of the plan itself, including specification of the evolution of compliance requirements. The corresponding objectives and action items are shown in **Table 6**.

The objectives under each goal serve as building blocks directed toward developing, maintaining, and sustaining the National Training Program for NIMS. Each goal's objectives follow a logical sequence of development.

Action items are specific tasks that help meet the objectives. These are assigned a specific target year for work, noted by an "X" in the Action Item table for a particular objective as shown in **Tables 5 and 6** below. In some cases, action items may be identified for work over multiple years. This indicates that there is an expectation that the task will take in excess of one year to complete or that the task is required for ongoing maintenance of the training program.

MAJOR GOALS GUIDING NIMS TRAINING PLAN (TABULAR FORM)

The NIC will:

1. Provide guidance and support so that stakeholder personnel can be appropriately trained in all NIMS components and subcomponents; and

2. Maintain and update the Plan annually.

Table 5: Training Goal, To Be Met for Each NIMS Component and Subcomponent

Goal 1:	The NIC will provide guidance and support so that stakeholder personnel can be appropriately trained in all NIMS components and subcomponents.							

Objective 1 — Define Core Competencies

	Action Items	Done	FY08	FY09	FY10	FY11	FY12	FY12+
N,S	Identify mission space	X						
N,S	Determine functional domains within Component		X					
N,S	Identify individual responsibilities/skills needed to work within functional domains		X					

Objective 2 — Define and Publish Position Qualifications

	Action Items	Done	FY08	FY09	FY10	FY11	FY12	FY12+
N	Link functional roles to typical position titles		X					
N	Publish guidance linking functional roles tied to position titles		X					
N	Determine skills and knowledge needed for each position			X				
N	Identify levels of training and experience each position will require, including refresher training			X				
N	Publish Position Task Book					X		

Objective 3 — Develop guidelines to assist Stakeholders to define the training each personnel level requires

	Action Items	Done	FY08	FY09	FY10	FY11	FY12	FY12+
N	Identify positions requiring awareness training		X					
N	Identify positions requiring basic knowledge training		X					
N	Identify positions requiring advanced training		X					
N	Publish guidance associating typical positions and recommended levels of training			X				

Objective 4 — Analyze existing courses

	Action Items	Done	FY08	FY09	FY10	FY11	FY12	FY12+
N	Identify gaps where competencies are not covered by existing courses		X	X	X	X	X	X
N	Determine Instructor qualifications		X	X				
N	Specify course minimum standards		X	X				
N	(Re)Publish existing course guidelines		X	X	X	X	X	X
N	Report recommendations for course development/improvement		X	X	X	X	X	X

Objective 5 — Develop courses

	Action Items	Done	FY08	FY09	FY10	FY11	FY12	FY12+
N	Develop individual courses		X	X	X	X	X	X
S	If stakeholder adapts courses, assess courses compared to objectives and standards provided by the NIC		X	X	X	X	X	X

Objective 6 — Expedite course availability

	Action Items	Done	FY08	FY09	FY10	FY11	FY12	FY12+
S	Identify qualified instructors			X	X			
S	Identify actual course offerings			X	X			
S	Determine availability of course alternatives			X	X			
N	Provide resources to train instructors and offer courses							

Objective 7 — Train Personnel to appropriately identified level

	Action Items	Done	FY08	FY09	FY10	FY11	FY12	FY12+
S	Identify positions needed to fulfill functional roles			X	X			
S	Determine number of course offerings needed			X	X			
S	Set plans to provide identified levels of training to personnel			X	X			
S	Train Personnel					X		

N = NIC responsibility

S = Stakeholder responsibility

N,S = Shared responsibility of the NIC and stakeholders

B = Baseline metric collected through compliance metrics

R = Required training in NIMS Compliance Requirements

Table 6: Plan Maintenance Goal

Goal 2: The NIC will maintain and update the Plan annually.									
Objective 1	**Ensure mechanisms are developed to assess or measure training implementation**								
		Action Items	Done	FY08	FY09	FY10	FY11	FY12	FY12+
	WG	Assess current year (CY) compliance requirements (CR) for proper support of CY plan expectations		X	X	X	X	X	X
	WG	Measure CY CR for baseline data collection, providing updates to the scope of the plan		X	X	X	X	X	X
	WG	Provide adjustments/recommendations for future CR		X	X	X	X	X	X
Objective 2	**Assess progress made toward goals of Five-Year NIMS Training Plan**								
		Action Items	Done	FY08	FY09	FY10	FY11	FY12	FY12+
	WG	Review current & previous Five-Year NIMS Training Plan action items assigned to the NIC	X	X	X	X	X	X	X
	WG	Review stakeholder training progress via compliance data	X	X	X	X	X	X	X
	WG	Identify any problems/delays reaching goals or objectives	X	X	X	X	X	X	X
	WG	Analyze the identified problems/delays for trends or patterns	X	X	X	X	X	X	X
	WG	Recommend updates to the overall plan	X	X	X	X	X	X	X
Objective 3	**Update Five-Year NIMS Training Planí s goals and objectives as needed**								
		Action Items	Done	FY08	FY09	FY10	FY11	FY12	FY12+
	WG	Review plan objectives		X	X	X	X	X	X
	N	Review and integrate new and updated NIMS related material	X	X	X	X	X	X	X
	WG	Update plan with incorporation of stakeholder input	X	X	X	X	X	X	X
	N	Publish updated plan	X	X	X	X	X	X	X
Objective 4	**Revise and update Training Guidance (i.e., Five-Year NIMS Training Plan Appendices)**								
		Action Items	Done	FY08	FY09	FY10	FY11	FY12	FY12+
	N	Review and integrate new and updated NIMS related material	X	X	X	X	X	X	X
	N	Review and update training guidance for existing courses	X	X	X	X	X	X	X
	N	Update material on courses in development	X	X	X	X	X	X	X
	N	Publish updated guidance	X	X	X	X	X	X	X
Objective 5	**Integrate Five-Year NIMS Training Plan with other NIMS implementation planning activities**								
		Action Items	Done	FY08	FY09	FY10	FY11	FY12	FY12+
		TBD							

N = NIC responsibility

WG = NIC-convened Working Group

Appendix A: NIMS Components

I. COMPONENT I OVERVIEW: PREPAREDNESS

The following concepts and principles of the NIMS relating to the Preparedness component need to be addressed in NIMS training offered by other Federal agencies; State, tribal, and local agencies; and private vendors. If these concepts and principles are addressed in non-DHS training, the training will meet the standards established by the NIC. An overview and means to evaluate NIMS training content relevant to Preparedness follow.

I.A.   Preparedness focuses on the following elements: planning, procedures and protocols, training and exercises, personnel qualifications and certification, and equipment certification. The core concepts and principles of preparedness as taught by DHS (and as defined in the NIMS document) incorporate the following components:

I.A.1.   *Unified approach*: Preparedness requires a unified approach to emergency management and incident response activities. The unified approach concept is at the core of the command and management system, as it is based on chain of command, unity of command, unity of effort, and, when implemented, unified command.

I.A.2.   *Levels of capability*: Preparedness involves actions to establish and sustain necessary capabilities to execute a full range of emergency management and incident response activities.

I.B.   Achieving preparedness: Individual jurisdictions are responsible for preparing in advance of an incident, in coordination with and support from the private sector and nongovernmental organizations (NGOs), as appropriate.

I.B.1.   To achieve national preparedness and coordinated response, emergency management and incident response activities must be coordinated at all levels of government and should include the private sector and NGOs, where appropriate. HSPD-5, *Management of Domestic Incidents*; HSPD-7, *Critical Infrastructure Identification, Prioritization, and Protection*; and HSPD-8, *National Preparedness*; all direct DHS to establish a comprehensive approach to incident management.

I.B.2.   NIMS provides the template for the management of incidents, regardless of cause, size, location, or complexity. The National Response Framework is an all-hazards plan built upon the NIMS framework. Both documents are designed to improve the Nation's incident management capabilities and overall efficiency.

I.B.3.   Preparedness activities should be coordinated among all appropriate agencies and organizations within the jurisdiction, as well as across jurisdictions. The NIMS provides the tools to ensure and enhance preparedness through the following roles:

I.B.3.a.   Preparedness Organizations
I.B.3.b.   Elected and Appointed Officials
I.B.3.c.   Nongovernmental Organizations
I.B.3.d.   Private Sector

I.B.4.   There are five preparedness elements that build the foundation necessary for efficient and effective response and recovery: Preparedness Planning, Procedures and Protocols, Training and Exercises, Personnel Qualifications and Certification, and Equipment Certification.

I.B.5.   Mitigation is an important element of emergency management and incident response and provides a critical foundation in the effort to reduce the loss of life and property from natural and/or manmade disasters by avoiding or lessening the impact of a disaster and providing value to the public by creating safer communities.

II. Component II Overview: Communications and Information Management

The following concepts and principles of the NIMS relating to the Communication and Information Management component need to be addressed in NIMS training offered by other Federal agencies; State, tribal, and local agencies; and private vendors. If these concepts and principles are addressed in non-DHS training, the training will meet the standards established by the NIC. An overview and means to evaluate NIMS training content relevant to Communication and Information Management follow.

II.A.   The underlying concepts and principles of communications and information management reinforce the use of a flexible communications and information system in which emergency management/response personnel can maintain a constant flow of information throughout an incident. The core concepts and principles of communication and information management as taught by DHS (and as defined in the NIMS document) incorporate the following components:

II.A.1.   A *common operating picture* is established and maintained by gathering, collating, synthesizing, and disseminating incident information to all appropriate parties involved. Having a common operating picture during an incident helps to ensure consistency for all emergency response providers engaged in an incident.

II.A.2.   *Interoperability* allows emergency management/response personnel and their affiliated organizations to communicate within and across agencies and jurisdictions via various communications systems.

II.A.3.   *Reliability, scalability, and portability*: Communication and information systems should be designed to be flexible, reliable, and scalable in order to function in any type of incident, regardless of cause, size, location, or complexity. They should be suitable for operations within a single jurisdiction or agency, a single jurisdiction with multiagency involvement, or multiple jurisdictions with multiagency involvement.

II.A.4.   *Resiliency and redundancy* are critical to ensuring communications flow during an incident.

II.B.   Emergency management/response personnel must be able to manage incident communications and information effectively using the following:

II.B.1.   Standardized Communication Types
II.B.2.   Policy and Planning
II.B.3.   Agreements
II.B.4.   Equipment Standards and Training

II.C.   Organization and Operations

II.C.1.   *Incident information*: During an incident, information is vital to assist the IC, UC, and/or supporting agencies and organizations with decision making. Examples include incident notification, situation and status reports, analytical data, and geospatial data.

II.C.2. *Communications standards and formats*: Common terminology, standards, and procedures should be established and detailed in plans and/or agreements that enable diverse organizations to work together effectively.

III. COMPONENT III OVERVIEW: RESOURCE MANAGEMENT

The following concepts and principles of the NIMS relating to the Resource Management component need to be addressed in NIMS training offered by other Federal agencies; State, tribal, and local agencies; and private vendors. If these concepts and principles are addressed in non-DHS training, the training will meet the standards established by the NIC. An overview and means to evaluate NIMS training content relevant to Resource Management follow.

III.A. Emergency management and incident response activities require carefully managed resources (personnel, teams, facilities, equipment, and/or supplies) to meet incident needs.

III.A.1. The underlying concepts of resource management as taught by DHS (and as defined in the NIMS document) are

- Consistency
- Standardization
- Coordination
- Inclusion
- Information management
- Credentialing

III.A.2. The foundations of resource management are based on the following five principles: planning, use of agreements, categorizing resources, resource identification and ordering, and effective management of resources.

III.B. The Resource Management process can be separated into two parts: (1) resource management activities as an element of preparedness and (2) managing resources during an incident. Resource management during an incident is a finite process, with a distinct beginning and ending specific to the needs of the particular incident, and includes the following seven steps:

III.B.1. *Identify requirements*: Involves accurately identifying what and how much is needed, where and when it is needed, and who will be receiving or using it.

III.B.2. *Order and acquire*: Requests for resources that cannot be obtained locally are submitted using standardized resource-ordering procedures.

III.B.3. *Mobilize*: This process may include planning for deployment, equipping, training, designating assembly points, and obtaining transportation.

III.B.4. *Track and report:* Resource tracking provides a clear picture of where resources are located; helps staff prepare to receive resources; protects the safety and security of equipment, supplies, and personnel; and enables their coordination and movement.

III.B.5. *Recover and demobilize*: Recovery involves the final disposition of resources, including rehabilitation, replenishment, and disposal and/or retrograding and pertains to both expendable and nonexpendable resources.

III.B.6.   *Reimburse*: When applicable, reimbursement provides a mechanism to recoup funds expended for incident-specific activities.

III.B.7.   *Inventory*: Resource management uses various resource inventory systems to assess the availability of assets provided by jurisdictions. The inventory process includes credentialing and identifying and typing resources.

IV. COMPONENT IV OVERVIEW: COMMAND AND MANAGEMENT

The following concepts and principles of the NIMS relating to the Command and Management component need to be addressed in NIMS training offered by other Federal agencies; State, tribal, and local agencies; and private vendors. If these concepts and principles are addressed in non-DHS training, the training will meet the standards established by the NIC. An overview and means to evaluate NIMS training content relevant to Command and Management follow.

The Incident Command System (ICS), Multiagency Coordination Systems (MACS), and Public Information are the fundamental elements of incident management. These elements provide standardization through consistent terminology and established organizational structures and are the most visible aspects of incident management. The Command and Management component describes the systems used to facilitate Command and Management operations.

The NIMS relies on the relationships among the three elements. These relationships must be clearly defined and documented as each element evolves during an incident.

The following provides an overview of each element as taught by DHS (and as defined in the NIMS document).

IV.A.   The ICS is a widely applicable management system designed to enable effective and efficient incident management by integrating a combination of facilities, equipment, personnel, procedures, and communications operating within a common organizational structure.

IV.A.1.   *Management characteristics*: ICS is based on 14 management characteristics:

IV.A.1.a.   Common terminology: The ICS establishes common terminology that allows diverse incident management and support organizations to work together across a wide variety of incident management functions and hazard scenarios. ICS common terminology covers the organizational functions, resources descriptions, and incident facilities.

IV.A.1.b.   Modular organization: The ICS organizational structure develops in a modular fashion that is based on the size and complexity of the incident, as well as the specifics of the hazard environment created by the incident.

IV.A.1.c.   Management by objectives: The establishment of specific, measurable objectives for various incident management functional activities and directing efforts to attain them is essential to a successful operation.

IV.A.1.d.   Incident action planning: Incident Action Plans (IAPs) guide all response activities and provide a concise and coherent means of capturing and communicating the overall incident priorities, objectives, strategies, and tactics in the contexts of both operational and support activities. Every incident must have an action plan.

IV.A.1.e.   Manageable span of control: The span of control of any individual should range from three to seven subordinates, with the optimum being five.

IV.A.1.f.   Incident facilities & locations: Various types of operational support facilities are established in the vicinity of an incident, depending on its size and complexity, to accomplish a variety of purposes.

IV.A.1.g.   Comprehensive resource management: Maintaining an accurate and up-to-date picture of resource utilization is a critical component of incident management.

IV.A.1.h.   Integrated communications: Incident communications are facilitated through the development and use of a common communications plan and interoperable communications processes and architectures.

IV.A.1.i.   Establishment and transfer of command: The command function must be clearly established from the beginning of incident operations.

IV.A.1.j.   Chain of command and unity of command: These principles clarify reporting relationships and eliminate the confusion caused by multiple, conflicting directives.

IV.A.1.k.   Unified command: Unified command allows agencies with different legal, geographic, and functional authorities to work together effectively without affecting individual agency authority, responsibility, or accountability.

IV.A.1.l.   Accountability: The ICS accountability principles include check-in/check-out, IAP, unity of command, personal responsibility, span of control, and resource tracking.

IV.A.1.m. Dispatch/deployment: Resources should respond only when requested or when dispatched by an appropriate authority through established resource management systems.

IV.A.1.n.   Information and intelligence management: The incident management organization must establish a process for gathering, analyzing, assessing, sharing, and managing incident-related information and intelligence.

IV.A.2. *Incident command (IC) and command staff*: Incident command is responsible for overall management of the incident. Overall management includes command staff assignments required to support the command function.

IV.A.2.a.   Incident command: The command function may be conducted in one of two general ways: single incident commander and unified command.

IV.A.2.a.1.   *Single incident commander:* When an incident occurs within a single jurisdiction and there is no jurisdictional or functional agency overlap, a single IC should be designated with overall incident management responsibility by the appropriate jurisdictional authority.

IV.A.2.a.2.   *Unified command (UC):* UC is an important element in multi-jurisdictional or multiagency incident management and allows all agencies with jurisdictional authority or functional responsibility for the incident to jointly provide management direction to an incident through a common set of incident objectives and strategies and a single IAP.

IV.A.2.b. Command Staff: The Command Staff typically includes a public information officer, a safety officer, and a liaison officer, who report directly to the IC/UC and may have assistants as necessary. Additional positions may be required, depending on the nature, scope, complexity, and location(s) of the incident(s), or according to specific requirements established by the IC.

IV.A.2.c. Incident command organization: The incident command and management organization is located at the Incident Command Post (ICP). One ICP is established for each incident, where the incident command directs operations.

IV.A.3. *General Staff*: The General Staff is responsible for the functional aspects of the incident command structure and typically consists of Operations, Planning, Logistics, and Finance/Administration Section Chiefs. The Command Staff and General Staff must continually interact and share vital information and estimates of the current and future situation and develop recommended courses of action for consideration by the IC.

IV.A.3.a. Operations Section: The Operations Section is responsible for all activities focused on reducing the immediate hazard, saving lives and property, establishing situational control, and restoring normal operations. The NIMS document provides an organizational template for an Operations Section, which includes the following elements: a section chief, branches, divisions/groups, and resources.

IV.A.3.b. Planning Section: The Planning Section collects, evaluates, and disseminates incident situation information and intelligence to the IC/UC and incident management personnel. It prepares status reports, displays situation information, maintains the status of resources assigned to the incident, and prepares and documents the IAP. The section has four primary units (resource, situation, demobilization, documentation), as well as technical specialists to assist in evaluating the situation.

IV.A.3.c. Logistics Section: This section is responsible for all service support requirements needed to facilitate effective and efficient incident management. The Logistics Section provides facilities, security (of the incident command facilities and personnel), transportation, supplies, equipment maintenance and fuel, food services, communications and information technology support, and emergency responder medical services, including inoculations, as required. It has six primary units that fulfill the functional requirements: Supply, Facilities, Ground Support, Communications, Food, and Medical.

IV.A.3.d. Finance/Administration Section: The Finance/Administration Section is established when the incident management activities require on-scene or incident-specific finance and other administrative support services. When established, this section has four primary units that fulfill functional requirements: Compensation/Claims, Cost, Procurement, and Time.

IV.A.3.e. Intelligence/Investigations Function: This function ensures that all investigative and intelligence operations, functions, and activities within the incident response are properly managed, coordinated, and directed. It can be embedded in several places within the organizational structure: within the Planning Section; as a separate General Staff section; within the Operations Section; or within the Command Staff. The Intelligence/Investigations Function can be organized in a variety of ways. The following groups can be activated, if needed: Investigative Operations; Intelligence; Forensic; Electronic Communications, Surveillance, and Evidence; Missing/Unidentified Persons and Human Remains; and Investigative Support.

IV.A.4. *Incident Management Teams (IMTs)*: An IMT is an incident command organization made up of the Command and General Staff members and other appropriate personnel in an ICS organization and can be deployed or activated, as needed.

IV.A.5. *Incident Complex—Multiple Incident Management with a Single ICS Organization*: Two or more individual incidents located in the same general area and assigned to a single IC or UC.

IV.A.6. *Area Command*: An organization to oversee the management of multiple incidents that are each being handled by a separate ICS organization or to oversee the management of a very large or evolving incident that has multiple incident management teams engaged.

IV.A.6.a. An area command is activated only if necessary, depending on the complexity of the incident and incident management span-of-control considerations.

IV.A.6.b. Area command has the following responsibilities:
- Develops broad objectives for the impacted area(s)
- Coordinates the development of individual incident objectives and strategies
- Allocates/reallocates resources as the established priorities change
- Ensures that incidents are properly managed
- Ensures effective communications
- Ensures that incident management objectives are met and do not conflict with each other or with agency policies
- Identifies critical resource needs and reports them to the established emergency operations center (EOC)/MAC groups
- Ensures that short-term "emergency" recovery is coordinated

IV.B. Multiagency coordination systems: Multiagency coordination is a *process* that allows all levels of government and all disciplines to work together more efficiently and effectively. Multiagency coordination occurs across the different disciplines involved in incident management, across jurisdictional lines, or across levels of government. The core concepts and principles of the Multiagency Coordination System (MACS) as taught by DHS (and as defined in the NIMS document) incorporate the following components:

IV.B.1. *Description*: The primary function of multiagency coordination systems is to coordinate activities above the field level and to prioritize the incident demands for critical or competing resources, thereby assisting the coordination of the operations in the field. MACS consist of a combination of elements: personnel, procedures, protocols, business practices, and communications integrated into a common system.

IV.B.2. *System elements*: MACS include a combination of facilities, equipment, personnel, and procedures integrated into a common system with responsibility for coordination of resources and support to emergency operations.

IV.B.3. *Examples of system elements*: The most commonly used elements of MACS are EOCs and MAC Groups. An EOC is activated to support the on-scene response during an escalating incident by relieving the burden of external coordination and securing additional resources. Typically, administrators/executives, or their appointed representatives, are brought together and form MAC Groups. MAC Groups may also be known as multiagency committees, emergency management committees, or as otherwise defined.

IV.B.4. *Primary functions of multiagency coordination systems*: There are seven common functions that MACS will generally perform during an incident: situation assessment, incident priority determination, critical resource acquisition and allocation, supporting relevant incident management policies and interagency activities, coordination with other MACS, coordination with elected and appointed officials, and coordination of summary information.

IV.C. Public Information

IV.C.1. Public information consists of the processes, procedures, and systems to communicate timely, accurate, and accessible information on the incident's cause, size, and situation to the public, responders, and additional stakeholders (both directly and indirectly affected). Public information includes processes, procedures, and organizational structures required to gather, verify, coordinate, and disseminate information.

IV.C.2. *System description and components*: Public information consists of five components:

IV.C.2.a. The Public Information Officer (PIO) supports the incident command structure as a member of the Command Staff. The PIO advises the incident command on all public information matters relating to management of the incident. The PIO handles inquiries from the media, the public, and elected officials; emergency public information and warnings; rumor monitoring and response; media monitoring; and other functions required to gather, verify, coordinate, and disseminate accurate, accessible, and timely information related to the incident. The PIO serves as a link to the Joint Information System (JIS).

IV.C.2.b. The JIS provides the mechanism to organize, integrate, and coordinate information to ensure timely, accurate, accessible, and consistent messaging activities across multiple jurisdictions and/or disciplines with the private sector and NGOs.

IV.C.2.c. The Joint Information Center (JIC) is a central location that facilitates operation of the JIS.

IV.C.2.d. Organizational independence: Organizations participating in incident management retain their independence.

IV.C.2.e. Getting information to the public and additional stakeholders: This is an ongoing cycle that involves four steps: (1) gathering information, (2) verifying information, (3) coordinating information, and (4) disseminating information.

IV.C.3. *Public information communications planning*: Plans should include processes, protocols, and procedures that require the development of news releases, media lists, contact information for elected officials, community leaders, private-sector organizations, and leads for public-service organizations to facilitate the dissemination of accurate, consistent, accessible, and timely public information to numerous audiences.

V. Component V Overview: Ongoing Management and Maintenance

The following concepts and principles of the NIMS relating to the Ongoing Management and Maintenance component need to be addressed in NIMS training offered by other Federal agencies; State, tribal, and local agencies; and private vendors. If these concepts and principles are addressed in non-DHS training, the training will meet the standards established by the NIC. An overview and means to evaluate NIMS training content relevant to Ongoing Management and Maintenance follow.

Ongoing Management and Maintenance of the NIMS contains two subsections: National Integration Center (NIC) and Supporting Technologies. The core concepts and principles of ongoing management and maintenance as taught by DHS (and as defined in the NIMS document) incorporate the following components:

V.A.   National Integration Center

   V.A.1.   *Concepts and principles*: The NIC serves as a mechanism for ensuring the ongoing management and maintenance of the NIMS and provides strategic direction for and oversight of the NIMS, supporting both routine maintenance and continuous refinement of the system and its components over the long term.

   V.A.2.   *NIMS revision process*: Proposed changes to the NIMS will be submitted to the NIC for consideration, approval, and publication.

   V.A.3.   *NIC responsibilities* include the ongoing administration and implementation of the NIMS; ensuring the adoption of common national standards and credentialing systems compatible with the NIMS; leading the development of training and exercises that further the knowledge, adoption, and implementation of the NIMS; and NIMS publication management.

V.B.   Supporting Technologies

   V.B.1.   *Concepts and principles*: The NIMS leverages science and technology to improve capabilities and lower costs. It observes the following five key principles: interoperability and compatibility, technology support, technology standards, broad-based requirements, and strategic planning for research and development.

   Supporting incident management with science and technology: Supporting technologies enhance incident management capabilities or lower costs through three principal activities: operational scientific support, technology standards support, and research and development support.

Appendix B: Position Competencies and Behaviors

This section includes all-hazards competencies and behaviors for the eight Command and General Staff positions for a Type 1 or Type 2 incident as defined by IMSI. These positions competencies and behaviors correlate with the position-specific courses currently available or in development. Competencies and behaviors for all ICS positions are available from IMSI and can be found at *http://www.fema.gov/emergency/nims/ics_competencies.shtm.*

Table B-1: Incident Commander

Position	Competencies	Behaviors
I n c i d e n t C o m m a n d e r T y p e 1 & 2	**Assume position responsibilities**	Ensure readiness for assignment.
		Ensure availability, qualifications, and capabilities of resources to complete assignment.
		Gather, update, and apply situational information relevant to the assignment.
		Establish effective relationships with relevant personnel.
		Establish organization structure, reporting procedures, and chain of command of assigned resources.
		Understand and comply with ICS concepts and principles.
	Lead assigned personnel	Model leadership principles of Duty, Respect and Integrity.
		Ensure the safety, welfare, and accountability of assigned personnel.
		Establish work assignments and performance expectations, monitor performance, and provide feedback.
		Emphasize teamwork.
		Coordinate interdependent activities.
	Communicate effectively	Ensure all relevant information is exchanged during check-in, briefings and debriefings.
		Ensure documentation is complete and disposition is appropriate.
		Gather, produce and distribute information as required by established guidelines and ensure understanding by recipient.
		Communicate and assure understanding of work expectations within the chain of command and across functional areas.
		Develop and implement plans and gain concurrence of affected agencies and the public.
	Ensure completion of assigned actions to meet identified objectives	Administer and/or apply agency policy, contracts and agreements.
		Gather, analyze, and validate information pertinent to the incident or event and make recommendations for setting priorities.
		Prepare clear and concise assessments regarding hazards, fire behavior, weather, and other relevant events.
		Make appropriate decisions based on analysis of gathered information.
		Take appropriate action based on assessed risks.
		Modify approach based on evaluation of incident situation.
		Anticipate, recognize and mitigate unsafe situations.
		Develop appropriate information releases and conduct media interviews according to established protocol.
		Transfer position duties while ensuring continuity of authority and knowledge and taking into account the increasing or decreasing incident complexity.
		Plan for demobilization and ensure demobilization procedures are followed.

Table B-2: Operations Section Chief

Position	Competencies	Behaviors
O p e r a t i o n s S e c t i o n C h i e f T y p e 1 & 2	**Assume position responsibilities**	Ensure readiness for assignment.
		Ensure availability, qualifications, and capabilities of resources to complete assignment.
		Gather, update, and apply situational information relevant to the assignment.
		Establish effective relationships with relevant personnel.
		Establish organization structure, reporting procedures, and chain of command of assigned resources.
		Understand and comply with ICS concepts and principles.
	Lead assigned personnel	Model leadership principles of Duty, Respect and Integrity.
		Ensure the safety, welfare, and accountability of assigned personnel.
		Establish work assignments and performance expectations, monitor performance, and provide feedback.
		Emphasize teamwork.
		Coordinate interdependent activities.
	Communicate effectively	Ensure all relevant information is exchanged during check-in, briefings and debriefings.
		Ensure documentation is complete and disposition is appropriate.
		Gather, produce and distribute information as required by established guidelines and ensure understanding by recipient.
		Communicate and assure understanding of work expectations within the chain of command and across functional areas.
		Develop and implement plans and gain concurrence of affected agencies and the public.
	Ensure completion of assigned actions to meet identified objectives	Administer and/or apply agency policy, contracts and agreements.
		Gather, analyze, and validate information pertinent to the incident or event and make recommendations for setting priorities.
		Prepare clear and concise assessments regarding hazards, fire behavior, weather, and other relevant events.
		Make appropriate decisions based on analysis of gathered information.
		Utilize information to produce outputs.
		Take appropriate action based on assessed risks.
		Modify approach based on evaluation of incident situation.
		Plan for demobilization and ensure demobilization procedures are followed.
		Transfer position duties while ensuring continuity of authority and knowledge and taking into account the increasing or decreasing incident complexity.

Table B-3: Planning Section Chief

Position	Competencies	Behaviors
Planning Section Chief Type 1 & 2	**Assume position responsibilities**	Ensure readiness for assignment.
		Ensure availability, qualifications, and capabilities of resources to complete assignment.
		Gather, update, and apply situational information relevant to the assignment.
		Establish effective relationships with relevant personnel.
		Understand and comply with ICS concepts and principles.
	Lead assigned personnel	Model leadership principles of Duty, Respect and Integrity.
		Ensure the safety, welfare, and accountability of assigned personnel.
		Establish work assignments and performance expectations, monitor performance, and provide feedback.
		Emphasize teamwork.
		Coordinate interdependent activities.
	Communicate effectively	Ensure all relevant information is exchanged during check-in, briefings and debriefings.
		Ensure documentation is complete and disposition is appropriate.
		Gather, produce and distribute information as required by established guidelines and ensure understanding by recipient.
		Communicate and assure understanding of work expectations within the chain of command and across functional areas.
		Develop and implement plans and gain concurrence of affected agencies and the public.
	Ensure completion of assigned actions to meet identified objectives	Administer and/or apply agency policy, contracts and agreements.
		Gather, analyze, and validate information pertinent to the incident or event and make recommendations for setting priorities.
		Take appropriate action based on assessed risks.
		Modify approach based on evaluation of incident situation.
		Plan for demobilization and ensure demobilization procedures are followed.
		Transfer position duties while ensuring continuity of authority and knowledge and taking into account the increasing or decreasing incident complexity.

Table B-4: Logistic Section Chief

Position	Competencies	Behaviors
Logistic Section Chief Type 1 & 2	Assume position responsibilities	Ensure readiness for assignment.
		Ensure readiness of self and subordinates [crew] for assignment.
		Ensure availability, qualifications, and capabilities of resources to complete assignment.
		Gather, update, and apply situational information relevant to the assignment.
		Establish effective relationships with relevant personnel.
		Establish organization structure, reporting procedures, and chain of command of assigned resources.
		Understand and comply with ICS concepts and principles.
	Lead assigned personnel	Model leadership principles of Duty, Respect and Integrity.
		Ensure the safety, welfare, and accountability of assigned personnel.
		Establish work assignments and performance expectations, monitor performance, and provide feedback.
		Emphasize teamwork.
		Coordinate interdependent activities.
	Communicate effectively	Ensure all relevant information is exchanged during check-in, briefings and debriefings.
		Ensure documentation is complete and disposition is appropriate.
		Gather, produce and distribute information as required by established guidelines and ensure understanding by recipient.
		Communicate and assure understanding of work expectations within the chain of command and across functional areas.
		Develop and implement plans and gain concurrence of affected agencies and the public.
	Ensure completion of assigned actions to meet identified objectives	Administer and/or apply agency policy, contracts and agreements.
		Gather, analyze, and validate information pertinent to the incident or event and make recommendations for setting priorities.
		Make appropriate decisions based on analysis of gathered information.
		Modify approach based on evaluation of incident situation.
		Plan for demobilization and ensure demobilization procedures are followed.
		Transfer position duties while ensuring continuity of authority and knowledge and taking into account the increasing or decreasing incident complexity.

Table B-5: Finance/Administration Section Chief

Position	Competencies	Behaviors
Finance-Admin Section Chief Type 1 & 2	**Assume position responsibilities**	Ensure readiness for assignment.
		Ensure availability, qualifications, and capabilities of resources to complete assignment.
		Gather, update, and apply situational information relevant to the assignment.
		Establish effective relationships with relevant personnel.
		Establish organization structure, reporting procedures, and chain of command of assigned resources.
		Understand and comply with ICS concepts and principles.
	Lead assigned personnel	Model leadership principles of Duty, Respect and Integrity.
		Ensure the safety, welfare, and accountability of assigned personnel.
		Establish work assignments and performance expectations, monitor performance, and provide feedback.
		Emphasize teamwork.
		Coordinate interdependent activities.
	Communicate effectively	Ensure all relevant information is exchanged during check-in, briefings and debriefings.
		Ensure documentation is complete and disposition is appropriate.
		Gather, produce and distribute information as required by established guidelines and ensure understanding by recipient.
		Communicate and assure understanding of work expectations within the chain of command and across functional areas.
		Develop and implement plans and gain concurrence of affected agencies and the public.
	Ensure completion of assigned actions to meet identified objectives	Administer and/or apply agency policy, contracts and agreements.
		Gather, analyze, and validate information pertinent to the incident or event and make recommendations for setting priorities.
		Make appropriate decisions based on analysis of gathered information.
		Utilize information to produce outputs
		Take appropriate action based on assessed risks.
		Modify approach based on evaluation of incident situation.
		Plan for demobilization and ensure demobilization procedures are followed.
		Transfer position duties while ensuring continuity of authority and knowledge and taking into account the increasing or decreasing incident complexity.

Table B-6: Liaison Officer

Position	Competencies	Behaviors
Liaison Officer	Assume position responsibilities	Ensure readiness for assignment.
		Ensure readiness of self and subordinates [crew] for assignment.
		Ensure availability, qualifications, and capabilities of resources to complete assignment.
		Gather, update, and apply situational information relevant to the assignment.
		Establish effective relationships with relevant personnel.
		Establish organization structure, reporting procedures, and chain of command of assigned resources.
		Understand and comply with ICS concepts and principles.
	Lead assigned personnel	Model leadership principles of Duty, Respect and Integrity.
		Ensure the safety, welfare, and accountability of assigned personnel.
		Establish work assignments and performance expectations, monitor performance, and provide feedback.
		Emphasize teamwork.
		Coordinate interdependent activities.
	Communicate effectively	Ensure all relevant information is exchanged during check-in, briefings and debriefings.
		Ensure documentation is complete and disposition is appropriate.
		Gather, produce and distribute information as required by established guidelines and ensure understanding by recipient.
		Communicate and assure understanding of work expectations within the chain of command and across functional areas.
	Ensure completion of assigned actions to meet identified objectives	Gather, analyze, and validate information pertinent to the incident or event and make recommendations for setting priorities.
		Modify approach based on evaluation of incident situation.
		Plan for demobilization and ensure demobilization procedures are followed.
		Transfer position duties while ensuring continuity of authority and knowledge and taking into account the increasing or decreasing incident complexity.

256

Table B-7: Public Information Officer

Position	Competencies	Behaviors
Public Information Officer Type 1 & 2	**Assume position responsibilities**	Ensure readiness for assignment.
		Ensure availability, qualifications, and capabilities of resources to complete assignment.
		Gather, update, and apply situational information relevant to the assignment.
		Establish effective relationships with relevant personnel.
		Establish organization structure, reporting procedures, and chain of command of assigned resources.
		Understand and comply with ICS concepts and principles.
	Lead assigned personnel	Model leadership principles of Duty, Respect and Integrity.
		Ensure the safety, welfare, and accountability of assigned personnel.
		Establish work assignments and performance expectations, monitor performance, and provide feedback.
		Emphasize teamwork.
		Coordinate interdependent activities.
	Communicate effectively	Ensure all relevant information is exchanged during check-in, briefings and debriefings.
		Ensure documentation is complete and disposition is appropriate.
		Gather, produce and distribute information as required by established guidelines and ensure understanding by recipient.
		Develop and implement plans and gain concurrence of affected agencies and the public.
	Ensure completion of assigned actions to meet identified objectives	Administer and/or apply agency policy, contracts and agreements.
		Gather, analyze, and validate information pertinent to the incident or event and make recommendations for setting priorities.
		Prepare clear and concise assessments regarding hazards, fire behavior, weather, and other relevant events.
		Take appropriate action based on assessed risks.
		Anticipate, recognize and mitigate unsafe situations.
		Follow established and safety procedures revelant to given assignment
		Provide logistical support as necessary
		Develop appropriate information releases and conduct media interviews according to established protocol.
		Transfer position duties while ensuring continuity of authority and knowledge and taking into account the increasing or decreasing incident complexity.
		Plan for demobilization and ensure demobilization procedures are followed.

Table B-8: Safety Officer

Position	Competencies	Behaviors
Safety Officer Type 1 & 2	Assume position responsibilities	Ensure readiness for assignment.
		Ensure availability, qualifications, and capabilities of resources to complete assignment.
		Gather, update, and apply situational information relevant to the assignment.
		Establish effective relationships with relevant personnel.
		Understand and comply with ICS concepts and principles.
	Lead assigned personnel	Model leadership principles of Duty, Respect and Integrity.
		Ensure the safety, welfare, and accountability of assigned personnel.
		Establish work assignments and performance expectations, monitor performance, and provide feedback.
		Coordinate interdependent activities.
	Communicate effectively	Ensure all relevant information is exchanged during check-in, briefings and debriefings.
		Ensure documentation is complete and disposition is appropriate.
		Gather, produce and distribute information as required by established guidelines and ensure understanding by recipient.
		Develop and implement plans and gain concurrence of affected agencies and the public.
	Ensure completion of assigned actions to meet identified objectives	Gather, analyze, and validate information pertinent to the incident or event and make recommendations for setting priorities.
		Prepare clear and concise assessments regarding hazards, fire behavior, weather, and other relevant events.
		Utilize information to produce outputs.
		Take appropriate action based on assessed risks.
		Anticipate, recognize and mitigate unsafe situations.
		Follow established and safety procedures revelant to given assignment
		Ensure compliance with all legal and safety requirement revelavant to air operations
		Ensure functionality of equipment
		Transfer position duties while ensuring continuity of authority and knowledge and taking into account the increasing or decreasing incident complexity.
		Plan for demobilization and ensure demobilization procedures are followed.

Appendix C: Course Summaries

This section provides one-page summaries of the NIMS core curriculum courses, as developed by the NIC. In general, this plan assumes that states will be the only stakeholders interested in developing equivalent courses. Stakeholders that develop equivalent training are responsible for ensuring course equivalence. Each course summary defines the minimum requirements for that course and does not necessarily reflect the entire course. Courses will be deemed equivalent if they meet the minimum requirements outlined in these course summaries. Stakeholders that develop equivalent training are responsible for ensuring course equivalence.

The NIMS core curriculum is expected to grow as more courses are added. This course guidance supersedes the *National Standard Curriculum Training Development Guidance – FY07* (March 2007).

IS-700: National Incident Management System (NIMS), An Introduction

Audience

All personnel with a direct role in emergency management/response must complete NIMS IS-700, including:

- *Executive level*—political and government leaders; agency and organization administrators and department heads; personnel that fill ICS roles as unified commanders, incident commanders, Command Staff, or General Staff in either area command or single incidents; senior MACS personnel; senior emergency managers; and emergency operations center Command or General Staff.

- *Managerial level*—agency and organization management between the executive level and first-level supervision; personnel who fill ICS roles as Branch Directors, Division/Group Supervisors, Unit Leaders, technical specialists, strike team and task force leaders, single resource leaders, and field supervisors; midlevel MACS personnel; EOC Section Chiefs, Branch Directors, Unit Leaders, and other emergency management/response personnel who require a higher level of ICS/NIMS training.

- *Responder level*—emergency response providers and disaster workers, entry level to managerial level, including emergency medical service personnel; firefighters; medical personnel; police officers; public health personnel; public work/utility personnel; and other emergency management response personnel.

Course Objectives	Relation to NIMS Document	
• **Concepts:** Describe the key concepts and principles underlying the NIMS.	I	Preparedness
	I.A	Preparedness Concepts and Principles
• **ICS:** Identify the benefits of using ICS as the national incident management model.	I.B	Achieving Preparedness
	II	Communications and Information Management
• **Area Command**: Describe when it is appropriate to institute an area command.	II.A	Underlying Concepts of Communications and Information Management
	III	Resource Management
• **MACS:** Describe when it is appropriate to institute a Multiagency Coordination System.	III.A.1	Underlying Concepts of Resource Management
	III.A.2	Five Basic Principles of Resource Management
• **JIS:** Describe the benefits of using a JIS for public information.	III.B	Resource Management Process
	IV	Command and Management
• **Preparedness:** Identify the ways in which the NIMS affects preparedness.	IV.A	Incident Management
	IV.A.1	Management Characteristics
	IV.A.2	Incident Command (IC) and Command Staff
• **Resource Management**: Describe how the NIMS affects how resources are managed.	IV A.2.a	Incident Command
	IV A.2.b	Command Staff
• **Communications:** Describe the advantages of common communication and information management systems.	IV.A.2.c	Incident Command Organization
	IV.A.3	General Staff
	IV.C	Public Information
	IV.C.2.b	Joint Information System (JIS)
• **Technology:** Explain how the NIMS influences technology and technology systems.	V	Ongoing Management and Maintenance
	V.A	National Integration Center (NIC)
• **NIC:** Describe the purpose of the NIMS Integration Center.	V.B	Supporting Technologies

Instruction Standards

Minimum course contact hours: 3 classroom hours minimum, or interactive, web-based course

Instructor Qualifications:

1. Successful completion of accredited ICS -100, ICS-200, IS-700.

2. Service in a mid-level emergency management and incident response position within five years in real-world incidents, planned events, or accredited exercises.

3. Recognized qualifications in techniques of instruction and adult education methodologies.

IS-800: National Response Framework (NRF), An Introduction

Audience

All Federal, State, tribal, and local emergency management/response personnel whose primary responsibility is emergency management must complete this training. Specifically, officials who must take the course include:

- Personnel in Federal departments and agencies with emergency management and incident response responsibilities under the NRF.

- Officials in State and Territorial governments with emergency management and incident response responsibilities, personnel from emergency management agencies, and personnel from agencies who support and interact with the NRF's 15 Emergency Support Functions and Support Annexes.

- Officials in tribal entities and local jurisdictions with overall emergency management responsibilities as dictated by law or ordinance, officials with overall emergency management responsibilities through delegation, and officials primarily involved in emergency planning.

Course Objectives	Relation to NIMS Document	
Purpose: The course introduces participants to the concepts and principles of the NRF and the response doctrine.	I	Preparedness
	I.A	Preparedness Concepts and Principles
	I.A.2	Relationship of NIMS to the National Response Plan (NRF)
Roles and Responsibilities: Describe the roles and responsibilities of entities as specified in the NRF and actions that support national response.	I.B	Achieving Preparedness
	IV	Command and Management
Organization: Identify the organizational structure used for NRF coordination. Describe the field-level organizations and teams activated under the NRF.	IV.A	Incident Management
	IV.A.1	Management Characteristics
	IV.A.2	Incident Command (IC) and Command Staff
Incident Management: Identify the incident management activities addressed by the NRF to include multiagency coordination.	IV.A.3	General Staff
	IV.A.3.a	Operations Section
	IV.A.3.b	Planning Section
Planning: Describes how planning relates to national preparedness.	IV.A.3.c	Logistics Section
	IV.A.3.d	Finance/Administration Section
	IV.A.3.e	Intelligence/Investigations Function
	IV.A.5	Incident Complex—Multiple Incident Management with a Single ICS Organization
	IV.A.6	Area Command
	IV.A.6.b	Area Command Responsibilities
	IV.B	Multiagency Coordination Systems

Instruction Standards

Minimum course contact hours: 3 classroom hours, or interactive, web-based course

Instructor Qualifications:

1. Successful completion of accredited ICS -100, ICS-200, IS-700, IS-800.

2. Service in a mid-level emergency management and incident response position within five years in real-world incidents, planned events, or accredited exercises.

3. Recognized qualifications in techniques of instruction and adult education methodologies.

ICS-100: Introduction to the Incident Command System

Audience

- It is incumbent upon Federal, State, tribal, and local emergency management/response personnel to determine who within their organizations requires ICS-100 training, based on local incident management organizational planning.
- *Responder level*—emergency response providers and disaster workers, entry level to managerial level, including emergency medical service personnel; firefighters; medical personnel; police officers; public health personnel; public work/utility personnel; and other emergency management response personnel
- Typically, all Federal, State, tribal, local, private-sector, and nongovernmental personnel at the following levels of responsibility in emergency management and incident response operations: first-line supervisor, mid-level management and command and general staff.

Course Objectives

- **Purpose of ICS:** Identify requirements to use ICS, three purposes of ICS, and common incident tasks.

- **Basic Features of ICS:** Describe the basic features of ICS.

- **Incident Commander and Command Staff Functions:** Describe the role and function of the incident commander and Command Staff.

- **General Staff Functions:** Describe the role and function of the Operations, Planning, Logistics and Finance/Administration sections.

- **Facilities:** Describe the six basic ICS facilities, identify facilities that may be located together, and identify facility map symbols.

- **Common Responsibilities:** Describe common mobilization responsibilities and common responsibilities at an incident, list individual accountability and responsibilities, and describe common demobilization responsibilities.

Relation to NIMS Document

IV	Command and Management
IV.A	Incident Command System
IV.A.1	Management Characteristics
IV.A.1.f	Incident Facilities & Locations
IV.A.2	Incident Command (IC) and Command Staff
IV.A.2.a	Incident Command
IV.A.2.b	Command Staff
IV.A.2.c	Incident Command Organization
IV.A.3	General Staff
IV.A.3.a	Operations Section
IV.A.3.b	Planning Section
IV.A.3.c	Logistics Section
IV.A.3.d	Finance/Administration Section
IV.A.3.e	Intelligence/Investigations Function

Instruction Standards

Minimum course contact hours: 6 classroom hours, or interactive, web-based course

Instructor Qualifications:

1. Successful completion of accredited ICS-100, ICS-200, IS-700.

2. Service in a mid-level emergency management and incident response position within five years in real-world incidents, planned events, or accredited exercises.

3. Recognized qualifications in techniques of instruction and adult education methodologies.

ICS-200: ICS for Single Resources and Initial Action Incidents

Audience

- It is incumbent upon Federal, State, tribal, and local emergency management/response personnel to determine who within their organizations requires ICS-200 training, based on local incident management organizational planning.

- Typically, all Federal, State, tribal, local, private-sector, and nongovernmental personnel at the following levels of responsibility in emergency management and incident response operations: first-line supervisor, mid-level management and command and general staff.

Course Objectives	Relation to NIMS Document	
• **Leadership and Management:** Describe the chain of command and formal communication relationships, identify common leadership responsibilities, describe span of control and modular development, and describe the use of position titles.	IV.A.1	Management Characteristics
	IV.A.1.c	Management by Objectives
	IV.A.1.b	Modular Organization
	IV.A.1.e	Manageable Span of Control
	IV.A.1.i	Establishment and Transfer of Command
• **Delegation of Authority and Management by Objectives:** Describe scope of authority and the process by which authority is delegated. Management by objectives must be described and explained.	IV.A.1.j	Chain of Command and Unity of Command:
	IV.A.1.n	Information and Intelligence Management
	IV.A.3	General Staff
	IV.A.3.a	Operations Section
• **Functional Areas and Positions:** Identify the ICS tools to manage an incident, demonstrate the function of organizational positions within ICS, and demonstrate the use of an ICS 201 form.	IV.A.3.b	Planning Section
	IV.A.3.c	Logistics Section
	IV.A.3.d	Finance/Administration Section
	IV.A.3.e	Intelligence/Investigations Function
• **Briefings:** Give an operational briefing and describe components of field, staff and section briefings/meetings.		
• **Organizational Flexibility:** Explain how the modular organization expands and contracts, complete a complexity analysis given a specific scenario, define the five types of incidents, and describe the importance of preparedness plans and agreements.		
• **Transfer of Command:** List the essential elements of information involved in transfer of command and describe a transfer-of-command process.		

Instruction Standards

Minimum course contact hours: 6 classroom hours, or interactive, web-based course

Instructor Qualifications:

1. Successful completion of accredited ICS-100, ICS-200, IS-700, and IS-800.

2. Service in a mid-level emergency management and incident response position within five years in real-world incidents, planned events, or accredited exercises.

3. Recognized qualifications in techniques of instruction and adult education methodologies.

ICS-300: Intermediate ICS

Audience

Federal, State, tribal, and local emergency management/response personnel determine who within their organizations requires ICS-300 training, based on local incident management organizational planning.

Typically, required personnel include all mid-level management, Federal, State, tribal, local, private-sector, and nongovernmental personnel, including persons serving as command staff, section chiefs, strike team leaders, task force leaders, unit leaders, division/group supervisors, branch directors, and multiagency coordination system/emergency operations center staff.

It is recommended that ICS-300 participants utilize their skills in an operational environment before taking ICS-400. This will provide necessary context and understanding of the skills they will develop when they take ICS-400.

Course Objectives	*Relation to NIMS Document*	
	III	Resource Management
• **ICS Fundamentals Review:** Explain ICS staffing fundamentals and organization, including reporting and working relationships, information flow, and transfer of command. Match responsibility statements to each ICS organizational element.	III.A.1	Underlying concepts of Resource Management
	III.A.2	Five Basic Principles of Resource Management
	III.B	Resource Management Process
	IV	Command and Management
	IV.A	Incident Management
	IV.A.1	Management Characteristics
	IV A.1.a	Common Terminology
• **Unified Command:** Define and identify the primary features of unified command. Describe the unified command organization and functions in a multi-jurisdictional or multiagency incident. Demonstrate roles and reporting relationships under a unified command in single and multi-jurisdictional incidents.	IV A.1.b	Modular Organization
	IV.A.1.c	Management by Objectives
	IV.A.1.d	Incident Action Planning
	IV.A.1.e	Manageable Span of Control
	IV.A.1.f	Incident Facilities & Locations
	IV.A.1.g	Comprehensive Resource Management
	IV.A.1.h	Integrated Communications
• **Incident Management Operations:** Describe methods and tools used to assess incident/event complexity. Describe the five steps in transferring and assuming incident command. Identify the key principles of incident management operations. Describe the process for developing incident objectives, strategies, and tactics.	IV A.1.i	Establishment and Transfer of Command
	IV.A.1.j	Chain of Command and Unity of Command
	IV.A.1.k	Unified Command
	IV.A.1.l	Accountability
	IV.A.1.m	Dispatch/Deployment
	IV.A.1.n	Information and Intelligence Management
	IV.A.2	Incident Command (IC) and Command Staff
• **Resource Management:** Identify and describe four basic principles of resource management. Identify the basic steps involved in managing incident resources. Demonstrate proper use of ICS forms.	IV A.2.a	Incident Command
	IV.A.2.b	Command Staff
	IV.A.2.c	Incident Command Organization
	IV.A.3	General Staff
	IV.A.3.a	Operations Section
• **Planning Process:** Identify the importance of and explain the differences between planning for incidents or events. Discuss major planning steps, including logistical concerns, cost-benefit analysis, situational understanding, plan development, implementation, and evaluation.	IV.A.3.b	Planning Section
	IV.A.3.c	Logistics Section
	IV.A.3.d	Finance/Administration Section
	IV.A.3.e	Intelligence/Investigations Function
• **Demobilization, Transfer of Command, Closeout**		

Instruction Standards

Minimum course contact hours: 18 total hours

Instructor Qualifications:

1. Successful completion of accredited ICS-100, ICS-200, ICS-300, ICS-400, IS-700, and IS-800.

2. Service in a mid-level incident management position within five years in real-world incidents, planned events, or accredited exercises.

3. Recognized qualifications in techniques of instruction and adult education methodologies.

ICS-400: Advanced ICS

Audience

Federal, State, tribal, and local emergency management/response personnel determine who within their organizations requires ICS-400 training, based on local incident management organizational planning.

Typically, required personnel include all Federal, State, tribal, local, private-sector, and nongovernmental personnel, including persons serving as Command and General Staff in an ICS organization, select department heads with multiagency coordination system responsibilities, area managers, emergency managers, and multiagency coordination system/emergency operations center managers.

It is recommended that ICS-300 participants utilize their skills in an operational environment before taking ICS-400. This will provide necessary context and understanding of the skills they will develop when they take ICS-400.

Course Objectives	*Relation to NIMS Document*	
• **Command and General Staff:** Describe how unified command functions in a multi-jurisdictional or multiagency incident. List the major steps involved in the planning process. Describe issues that influence incident complexity and available analysis tools. Describe the primary guidelines and responsibilities of the Command and General Staff positions.	IV.A.2	Incident Command (IC) and Command Staff
	IV.A.2.a	Incident Command
	IV.A.2.b	Command Staff
	IV.A.2.c	Incident Command Organization
	IV.A.3	General Staff
	IV.A.3.a	Operations Section
• **Major and/or Complex Incident/Event Management: Deputies and Assistants:** List the primary factors affecting major and/or complex incidents and events. List the four expansion options for incident/event organization and describe their application.	IV.A.3.b	Planning Section
	IV.A.3.c	Logistics Section
	IV.A.3.d	Finance/Administration Section
	IV.A.3.e	Intelligence/Investigations Function
• **Area Command:** Define and list the principal advantages of area command, and describe how, where, and when area command would be established. Describe area command organization and identify six primary functions of area command.	IV.A.5	Incident Complex—Multiple Incident Management with a Single ICS Organization
	IV.A.6	Area Command
	IV.A.6.b	Area Command Responsibilities
• **Unified Command:** Demonstrate a knowledge of unified command structure and operations.	IV.B	Multiagency Coordination Systems
	IV.B.1	MACS Description
• **Multiagency Coordination:** Describe the kinds of incident/event management problems that can occur due to a lack of multiagency coordination. Identify the major guidelines for establishing and using MAC groups and systems and their primary components. List the responsibilities of key elements with MACS.	IV.B.2	System Elements
	IV.B.3	Examples of System Elements
	IV.B.4	Primary Functions of Multiagency Coordination Systems
• **Organizational Relationships:** Describe the organizational relationships among area command, unified command, multi-entity coordination systems, and emergency operation centers.		

Instruction Standards

Minimum course contact hours: 14 total hours

Instructor Qualifications:

1. Successful completion of accredited ICS-100, ICS-200, ICS-300, ICS-400, IS-700, and IS-800.

2. Service in a mid-level emergency management and incident response position within five years in real-world incidents, planned events, or accredited exercises.

3. Recognized qualifications in techniques of instruction and adult education methodologies.

IS-701: NIMS Multiagency Coordination Systems (MACS)

Audience

All personnel with a direct role in MACS and complex incident management or response must complete NIMS IS-701, including Federal, state, tribal, and local emergency management/response personnel—among them, incident commanders from all emergency management disciplines, private industry personnel responsible for coordination activities during a disaster, and Voluntary Organizations Active in Disaster personnel.

Course Objectives	*Relation to NIMS Document*	
• **Concepts:** Describe the key concepts and principles underlying NIMS.	II	Communications and Information Management
	II.A	Underlying Concepts of Communications and Information Management
• **ICS:** Identify the benefits of using ICS as the national incident management model.	III	Resource Management
	III.A.1	Underlying Concepts of Resource Management
• **Area Command**: Describe when it is appropriate to institute an area command.	III.A.2	Five Basic Principles of Resource Management
	III.B	Resource Management Process
• **MACS:** Describe when it is appropriate to institute a Multiagency Coordination System.	IV	Command and Management
	IV.A	Incident Management
• **JIS:** Describe the benefits of using a JIS for public information.	IV.A.1	Management Characteristics
	IV.A.2	Incident Command (IC) and Command Staff
• **Preparedness:** Identify the ways in which the NIMS affects preparedness.	IV.A.2.a	Incident Command
	IV.A.2.b	Command Staff
• **Resource Management**: Describe how the NIMS affects how resources are managed.	IV.A.2.c	Incident Command Organization
	IV.A.3	General Staff
• **Communications:** Describe the advantages of common communication and information management systems.	IV.B	Multiagency Coordination System (MACS)
	IV.B.1	Description
• **Technology:** Explain how the NIMS influences technology and technology systems.	IV.B.2	System Elements
	IV.B.3	Examples of System Elements
• **NIC:** Describe the purpose of the NIMS Integration Center.	IV.B.4	Primary Function of MACS
	IV.C	Public Information

Instruction Standards

IS-701: Multiagency Coordination Systems (MACS) provides an understanding of MACS components, concepts, and principles, and it outlines the relationships among all elements of the system. IS-701 is composed of six components that require approximately 20 to 40 minutes each, as well as a post-test. Although IS-701 is available as a web-based independent study course, materials may be downloaded and used in a classroom setting. The following instruction standards apply to the classroom setting.

Contact Hours: 16 total hours

Instructor Qualifications:

1. One instructor required, two is recommended.

2. Successful completion of accredited ICS-100, ICS-200, ICS-300, ICS-400, IS-700, and IS-800.

3. Lead and unit instructors performed as EOC staff in at least two level II or higher EOC activations.

IS-702: NIMS Public Information

This course is designed for experienced PIOs. It will touch on the fundamentals of effective public information programs, but only to illustrate or provide examples for the details of NIMS Public Information.

The public information systems described in NIMS are designed to effectively manage public information at an incident, regardless of the size and complexity of the situation or the number of entities involved in the response. The goal of this course is to facilitate NIMS compliance by providing the basic information and tools needed to apply the NIMS public information systems and protocols during incident management.

This course is designed for local and State PIO.

Course Objectives	*Relation to NIMS Document*	
• **Joint Information System & Joint Information Center:** Define NIMS public information systems, including onsite operations, the JIS and the JIC, and how they relate to each other.	II	Communications and Information Management
	II.A	Underlying Concepts of Communications and Information Management
	IV.C	Public Information
	IV.C.1	Public Information Overview
• **JIS/JIC Process:** Describe the JIS/JIC process of gathering, verifying, coordinating, and disseminating information by public information and incident management personnel.	IV.C.2	System Description and Components
	IV.C.2.a	Public Information Officer (PIO)
	IV.C.2.b	Joint Information System (JIS)
• **Agency Participation:** Identify each agency involved in given emergency situations and the role of each in the JIS to ensure that appropriate situational awareness information is communicated to the public.	IV.C.2.c	Joint Information Center (JIC)
	IC.C.2.d	Organizational Independence
	IV.C.2.e	Information Flow to Stakeholders and the Public
	IV.C.3	Public Information Communications Planning
• **Relationship to MACS:** Define key terms related to public information systems, including the relationship with multiagency coordination systems and the field.		
• **Resource Requirements**: Identify typical resource requirements for public information systems.		

Instruction Standards

IS-702: NIMS Public Information is a web-based independent study module course that explains NIMS public information systems components, concepts, and principles. IS-702 takes approximately three hours to complete.

IS-703: NIMS Resource Management

Audience

All personnel with a significant resource management role in emergency management and incident response must complete NIMS IS-703.

Course Objectives	Relation to NIMS Document	
• **Concepts and Principles:** Establishing systems for describing, inventorying, requesting, and tracking resources.	I	Preparedness
	I.A	Preparedness Concepts and Principles
	I.B	Achieving Preparedness
• **Activation:** Activating these systems prior to and during an incident.	III	Resource Management
	III.A.1	Underlying Concepts of Resource Management
• **Dispatch:** Dispatching resources prior to and during an incident.	III.A.2	Five Basic Principles of Resource Management
	III.B	Resource Management Process
• **Deactivation:** Deactivating or recalling resources during or after incidents.	IV	Command and Management
	IV.A	Incident Management
	IV.A.1	Management Characteristics
	IV.A.2	Incident Command (IC) and Command Staff
	IV.A.2.a	Incident Command

Instruction Standards

IS-703: NIMS Resource Management is a web-based independent study module course that explains resource management components, concepts, and principles. The course is divided into six lessons, which each take 10 to 60 minutes to complete. A passing grade on the post-test at the completion of Lesson 6 is required for course credit. Although IS-703 is designed to be taken online interactively, course materials may be downloaded and used in a classroom setting. The following instruction standards apply to the classroom setting:

Contact Hours: 16 total hours

Instructor qualifications:

1. A minimum of two instructors is recommended.

2. Instructors should have experience managing resources at a complex incident.

3. Instructors should have successfully completed ICS-100, ICS-200, IS-700, and IS-800.

4. Instructor should have experience as an instructor teaching adults.

Equivalencies: IS-703 supersedes G-276, Resource Management. For purposes of the Advanced Professional Series, those who have completed G-276 may still claim credit for it as an elective, or IS-703 will count toward that elective.

IS-704: NIMS Communication and Information Management

Audience

IS-704 is designed for: members of the general public; emergency management/response personnel; elected officials of State, tribal, and local governments; appointed officials of State, tribal, and local governments; employees of the Department of Homeland Security; and employees of other Federal agencies.

Course Objectives	Relation to NIMS Document	
At the conclusion of this course, participants should be able to:	I	Preparedness
	I.A	Preparedness Concepts and Principles
• Define communications and information management at the local, tribal, State, and Federal levels of government to include the common operating picture and common communications and data standards.	I.A.1	Unified Approach
	I.B	Achieving Preparedness
	I.B.3	Preparedness Roles
• Identify each agency involved in communications and information management activities before, during, and after a domestic incident.	I.B.4	Preparedness Elements
	II	Communications and Information Management
• Identify typical interoperability standards established by the NIMS Integration Center relative to communications and information management, including incident notification and situation reports, status reports, analytical data, geospatial information, wireless communications, and identification and authentication issues.	II.A	Underlying Concepts of Communications and Information Management
	II.A.1	Common Operating Picture
	II.A.2	Interoperability
	II.A.3	Reliability, Scalability, and Portability
	II.A.4	Resiliency and Redundancy
• Define key terms related to communications and information management, including the relationship with multiagency coordination systems, public information, and the field.	II.B	Effective management of Incident Communications and Information
	II.B.1	Standardized Communication Types
	II.B.2	Policy and Planning
• Identify incident management communications issues relative to the incident command system for individual jurisdictions and for multiple jurisdictions.	II.B.3	Agreements
	II.B.4	Equipment Standards and Training
	II.C	Organization and Operations
• Identify potential coordination and policy issues arising from an incident relative to communications and information	II.C.1	Incident Information
	II.C.2	Communications Standards and Formats
	IV	Command and Management
	IV.A	Incident Command System
	IV.B	Multiagency Coordination System
	IV.C	Public Information

Instruction Standards

Course Hours: 6 classroom hours minimum, or interactive, web-based course

Instructor Qualifications:

1. A minimum of two instructors is recommended, with one instructor having a Law Enforcement background.
2. Instructors should have successfully completed ICS-100, IS-700, and IS-800.
3. Instructors should have served in a mid-level emergency management and incident response position within five years in real-world incidents, planned events, or accredited exercises and performed in the Logistics and/or Planning functions.
4. Instructor should have experience as an instructor teaching adults.

IS-705: NIMS Preparedness

Audience

Federal, state, local and tribal emergency managers; first responders to include incident commanders from all emergency management disciplines; private industry personnel responsible for coordination activities during a disaster; and Voluntary Organizations Active in Disaster (VOAD) personnel.

Course Objectives	*Relation to NIMS Document*	
• Define the preparedness component of the National Incident Management System (NIMS)	Preparedness	
• Define key concepts and principles of NIMS preparedness to include levels of capability and the use of a unified approach to preparedness	I.A	Preparedness Concepts and Principles
	I.A.1	Unified Approach
	I.A.2	Levels of capability
• Identify the key preparedness concepts outlined in HSPD8 to include the National Preparedness Goal, the Target Capabilities List, the Universal Task List, and the National Planning Scenarios.	I.B	Achieving Preparedness
	I.B.1	HSPDs
	I.B.2	National Response Plan
• Identify each agency involved in NIMS Preparedness activities to ensure appropriate implementation of the preparedness cycle in advance of an incident.	I.B.3	Preparedness Roles
	I.B.4	Preparedness Elements
• Identify typical priorities for the NIMS Preparedness activities outlined in the NIMS document to include at minimum the following components: emergency policies, plans, procedures, resources, training, and exercises	I.B.5	Mitigation
	III.B	Resource Management Process
	III.B.7	Inventory
• Describe the importance of personnel qualifications and certification, equipment certification, mutual aid agreements, and publications management to NIMS Preparedness		

Instruction Standards

Prerequisites: IS-700 and ICS-100

Minimum course contact hours: 12 contact hours in classroom; 4 contact hours in distance learning

Instructor Qualifications:

1. Successful completion of accredited ICS-100, IS-700, and IS-800.

2. Service in a mid-level emergency management/incident response position within five years in either real world incidents, planned events, or accredited exercises.

3. Recognized qualifications in techniques of instruction and adult education methodologies.

IS-706: NIMS Intrastate Mutual Aid, An Introduction

Audience

This course is designed for State, local, and tribal emergency response and coordination personnel and takes approximately two and a half hours to complete.

Course Objectives	Relation to NIMS Document	
• **Purpose:** Describe the purpose, benefits, and uses of mutual aid and assistance.	I	Preparedness
	I.A	Preparedness Concepts and Principles
• **Relation to NIMS:** Explain how mutual aid and assistance agreements relate to NIMS.	I.B	Achieving Preparedness
	I.B.3	Preparedness Roles
• **Involved Information** Identify what information should be included in a mutual aid and assistance agreement.	I.B.4	Preparedness Elements
	III	Resource Management
	III.A.1	Underlying Concepts of Resource Management
• **Processes required:** Explain the process for developing mutual aid and assistance agreements.	III.A.2	Five Basic Principles of Resource Management
	III.B	Resource Management Process
• **Elements of Mutual Aid and Assistance:** Identify the elements of a mutual aid and assistance operational plan.	IV	Command and Management
	IV A	Incident Management
	IV.A.1.	Management Characteristics

Instruction Standards

IS-706: NIMS Intrastate Mutual Aid, An Introduction is a web-based independent study module course that explains resource management components, concepts, and principles. The course is divided into 5 lessons. Completion time for each lesson varies but overall the course will take approximately 2.5 hours to complete. A passing grade on the post-test at the completion of Lesson 5 is required for course credit.

Prerequisites: The prerequisite for this course is IS-700: National Incident Management Systems (NIMS), An Introduction.

IS-707: NIMS Resource Typing

Audience

Federal, state, local and tribal emergency managers; first responders to include incident commanders from all emergency management disciplines; private industry personnel responsible for coordination activities during a disaster; and Voluntary Organizations Active in Disaster (VOAD) personnel.

Course Objectives	*Relation to NIMS Document*	
• Define NIMS Resource Typing Definitions	I	Preparedness
	I.A	Preparedness Concepts and Principles
• Use NIMS Resource Typing Definitions to request and receive appropriate resources during disasters	I.B	Achieving Preparedness
	III	Resource Management
• Use resource database management software program in support of response operations	III.A.1	Underlying Concepts of Resource Management
	III.A.2	Five Basic Principles of Resource Management
• Demonstrate understanding of criteria for recommending non-identified resources for inclusion in the *NIMS Guide 0001 – National NIMS Resource Typing Criteria*	III.B	Resource Management Process
	IV	Command and Management
	IV.A	Incident Management
	IV.A.1	Management Characteristics
	IV.A.2	Incident Command (IC) and Command Staff
	IV.A.2.a	Incident Command

Instruction Standards

Prerequisites: IS-700 and ICS-100

Contact hours: 4 contact hours in classroom; or 2 contact hours interactive, web-based course

Instructor qualifications:

1. Successful completion of accredited ICS-100, IS-700, IS-800.

2. Service in a mid-level emergency management/incident response position within five years in either real world incidents, planned events, or accredited exercises.

3. Recognized qualifications in techniques of instruction and adult education methodologies.

P400: All-Hazards Incident Commander

Audience

Individuals who would fill the role of Type-3 Incident Commander.

Course Objectives	*Relation to NIMS Document*	

Course Objectives

- **Managing the Organization**: Describe how to manage an IMT, common management and communication perils, the role of human resource specialists, and union agreements.

- **IMT Administration and Readiness**: Describe the incident commander's responsibilities; identify orientation procedures and methods to measure success and build teams.

- **Kits, Aids, Guides**: Identify the components of a typical incident commander's kit.

- **Command, Coordination, Support, and Oversight**: Describe the purpose and function as related to incident management; define agency administrator.

- **Command Structure and MACS**: Describe the concept and purpose of unified command and area command and the role of PFO and MACS.

- **AA and IC Cooperation**: Describe complexity analyses and clarification of authority and define the responsibility in preparing and conducting an agency administrator briefing.

- **Transfer of Command**: Describe elements of an effective transfer of command and the purpose of a transition plan; identify required forms.

- **Communication, Information, and Intelligence Processing**: Describe primary communication responsibilities, target audiences, and sources to obtain intelligence. Define information and intelligence and ways to enhance internal communications.

- **Objectives, Strategies, and Tactics**: Define incident objectives, strategies, and tactics.

- **Plans and Meetings**: Describe the plans and meetings for which the IC is responsible.

- **Staffing**: Describe the staffing responsibilities and considerations of the IC.

- **Agreements**: Describe agreements united in incident management and the difference between a cooperative agreement and a memorandum of understanding.

Relation to NIMS Document

IV	Command and Management
IV.A	Incident Management
IV.A.1	Management Characteristics
IV.A.1.a	Common Terminology
IV.A.1.b	Modular Organization
IV.A.1.c	Management by Objectives
IV.A.1.d	Incident Action Planning
IV.A.1.e	Manageable Span of Control
IV.A.1.f	Incident Facilities & Locations
IV.A.1.g	Comprehensive Resource Management
IV.A.1.h	Integrated Communications
IV.A.1.i	Establishment and Transfer of Command
IV.A.1.j	Chain of Command and Unity of Command
IV.A.1.k	Unified Command
IV.A.1.l	Accountability
IV.A.1.m	Dispatch/Deployment
IV.A.1.n	Information and Intelligence Management
IV.A.2	Incident Command (IC) and Command Staff
IV.A.2.a	Incident Command
IV.A.2.b	Command Staff
IV.A.2.c	Incident Command Organization
IV.A.3	General Staff
IV.A.5	Incident Complex—Multiple Incident Management with a Single ICS Organization
IV.A.6	Area Command
IV.A.6.b	Area Command Responsibilities
IV.B	Multiagency Coordination Systems
IV.B.1	MACS Description:
IV.B.2	System Elements
IV.B.3	Examples of System Elements
IV.B.4	Primary Functions of Multiagency Coordination Systems

Instruction Standards

Minimum Course Contact Hours: 40 total hours

Instructor standards:

1. Course should be conducted with at least two instructors, one of whom must be qualified as a lead instructor.

2. Instructors should have completed ICS-400 and IS-800.

3. Lead instructor should be fully qualified as Type 1 or 2 for this position and have functioned in that capacity at an incident that required multiagency coordination went beyond one operational period and required a written IAP.

4. Lead instructors must have completed at least 32 hours of instructor training and have previous experience as an instructor on Incident Command System or Emergency Management courses.

P430: All-Hazards Operations Section Chief

Audience

Individuals who would fill the role of Operations Section Chief.

Course Objectives	*Relation to NIMS Document*	

Course Objectives

- **Roles and Responsibilities:** Identify the role of the Operations Section Chief and contrast that with the other divisions and groups.
- **Management Cycle:** Describe the incident management and planning process and operational schedules.
- **Information Gathering:** Describe how to gather, organize, and communicate the appropriate information; incident commander briefing.
- **Strategy and Planning:** Identify the purpose of strategy, tactics, and planning meetings, use of the Operational Planning Worksheet, and the Incident Action Plan.
- **Contingency Planning:** Differentiate short- and long-term contingency planning; name ways to obtain, adjust, communicate, and publicize contingency plans.
- **Demobilization:** Describe early resource monitoring and the demobilization plan.
- **Supervision and Communication:** Identify the supervisor's role in ICS, communicating instructions, effective delegation, and executing an ops briefing and sub-briefing.
- **Managing and Adjusting the Operations Section:** Identify appropriate use of multiple Operations Section Chiefs, responsibilities in planning, staging areas, the Air Operations Branch, and developments that require adjustments.
- **Risk Assessment and Safety Management:** Differences between Operations Section Chief and safety officer duties, partnerships for safety, and information-gathering strategies for safety management.
- **Personal Interaction:** Identify key players, significant events requiring special communications, and external partners.

Relation to NIMS Document

IV	Command and Management
IV.A	Incident Management
IV.A.2	Incident Command (IC) and Command Staff
IV.A.2.a	Incident Command
IV.A.2.b	Command Staff
IV.A.2.c	Incident Command Organization
IV.A.3	General Staff
IV.A.3.a	Operations Section
IV.A.3.b	Planning Section
IV.A.3.c	Logistics Section
IV.A.3.d	Finance/Administration Section
IV.A.3.e	Intelligence/Investigations Function
IV.A.5	Incident Complex—Multiple Incident Management with a Single ICS Organization
IV.A.6	Area Command
IV.A.6.b	Area Command Responsibilities
IV.B	Multiagency Coordination Systems
IV.B.1	MACS Description
IV.B.2	System Elements

Instruction Standards

Minimum Course Contact Hours: 40 total hours

Instructor standards:

1. Course should be conducted with at least two instructors, one of whom must be qualified as a lead instructor.
2. Instructors should have completed ICS-400 and IS-800.
3. Lead instructor should be fully qualified as Type 1 or 2 for this position and have functioned in that capacity at an incident that required multiagency coordination went beyond one operational period and required a written IAP.
4. Lead instructors must have completed at least 32 hours of instructor training and have previous experience as an instructor on Incident Command System or Emergency Management courses.

P440: All-Hazards Planning Section Chief

Audience

Individuals who would fill the role of Planning Section Chief.

Course Objectives	Relation to NIMS Document	

Course Objectives

- **Position:** Describe the function and units of the Planning Section and the roles and responsibilities of the Planning Section Chief.
- **Resources Unit:** Describe the function of the Resources Unit, the roles and responsibilities of the Resources Unit Leader, and the ICS positions that interact with the Resource Unit.
- **Situation Unit:** Describe the function of the Situation Unit and the roles and responsibilities of the Situation Unit Leader.
- **Initial Response:** Describe the information gathered from the initial meetings, briefings and documents, the categories of items to carry in the PSC Kit and items of information derived from Strategic Plan.
- **Planning Cycle:** Describe the purpose, timing and structure of each of the meetings, briefings and documents in the Planning Cycle and the PSC role in the IAP.
- **Interactions:** Identify key strategies for interacting with members of the Planning Section, members of the IMT, and personnel outside of the IMT.
- **Documentation and Demobilization Units:** Describe the responsibilities of the Documentation Unit and Demobilization Unit Leaders and the purpose of the Final Incident Package.

Relation to NIMS Document

I	Preparedness
I.A	Preparedness Concepts and Principles
I.A.2	Relationship of the NIMS to the National Response Framework (NRF)
I.B	Achieving Preparedness
IV	Command and Management
IV.A	Incident Management
IV.A.2	Incident Command (IC) and Command Staff
IV.A.2.a	Incident Command
IV.A.2.b	Command Staff
IV.A.2.c	Incident Command Organization
IV.A.3	General Staff
IV.A.3.a	Operations Section
IV.A.3.b	Planning Section
IV.A.3.c	Logistics Section
IV.A.3.d	Finance/Administration Section
IV.A.3.e	Intelligence/Investigations Function
IV.A.5	Incident Complex—Multiple Incident Management with a Single ICS Organization
IV.A.6	Area Command
IV.A.6.b	Area Command Responsibilities
IV.B	Multiagency Coordination Systems
IV.B.1	MACS Description
IV.B.2	System Elements

Instruction Standards

Minimum Course Contact Hours: 32 total hours

Instructor standards:

1. Course should be conducted with at least two instructors, one of whom must be qualified as a lead instructor.
2. Instructors should have completed ICS-400 and IS-800.
3. Lead instructor should be fully qualified as Type 1 or 2 for this position and have functioned in that capacity at an incident that required multiagency coordination went beyond one operational period and required a written IAP.
4. Lead instructors must have completed at least 32 hours of instructor training and have previous experience as an instructor on Incident Command System or Emergency Management courses.

P450: All-Hazards Logistics Section Chief

Audience

Individuals who would fill the role of Logistics Section Chief.

<table>
<tr><th>Course Objectives</th><th colspan="2">Relation to NIMS Document</th></tr>
<tr><td rowspan="30">

- **Position**: Describe key functions, responsibilities, and units in the Logistics Section.

- **Facilities Unit**: Describe responsibilities and purpose.

- **Ground Support Unit**: Describe responsibilities and purpose.

- **Supply Unit**: Describe responsibilities and purpose.

- **Food Unit**: Describe responsibilities and purpose.

- **Medical Unit**: Describe responsibilities and purpose.

- **Communications Unit**: Describe responsibilities and purpose.

- **Responsibilities**: Describe necessary equipment. Define the role of initial briefings and the IAP and responsibilities in developing them.

- **Planning and Activating the Section**: Identify briefing components; describe how to assess capabilities and limitations.

- **Coordination**: Describe how to work with Command and General Staff; describe the role and responsibility in planning meetings and developing IAPs.

- **Managing and Directing Staff and Contractors**: Describe how to manage personnel, assign work, and monitor progress.

- **Demobilization and Evaluation**: Describe how to evaluate personnel and conduct debriefings.

</td><td>I</td><td>Preparedness</td></tr>
<tr><td>I.A</td><td>Preparedness Concepts and Principles</td></tr>
<tr><td>I.A.2</td><td>Relationship of NIMS to the National Response Framework</td></tr>
<tr><td>I.B</td><td>Achieving Preparedness</td></tr>
<tr><td>III</td><td>Resource Management</td></tr>
<tr><td>III.A.1</td><td>Underlying Concepts of Resource Management</td></tr>
<tr><td>III.A.2</td><td>Five Basic Principles of Resource Management</td></tr>
<tr><td>III.B</td><td>Resource Management Process</td></tr>
<tr><td>IV</td><td>Command and Management</td></tr>
<tr><td>IV.A</td><td>Incident Management</td></tr>
<tr><td>IV.A.1</td><td>Management Characteristics</td></tr>
<tr><td>IV.A.1.f</td><td>Incident Facilities & Locations</td></tr>
<tr><td>IV.A.1.g</td><td>Comprehensive Resource Management</td></tr>
<tr><td>IV.A.2</td><td>Incident Command (IC) and Command Staff</td></tr>
<tr><td>IV.A.2.a</td><td>Incident Command</td></tr>
<tr><td>IV.A.2.b</td><td>Command Staff</td></tr>
<tr><td>IV.A.2.c</td><td>Incident Command Organization</td></tr>
<tr><td>IV.A.3</td><td>General Staff</td></tr>
<tr><td>IV.A.3.a</td><td>Operations Section</td></tr>
<tr><td>IV.A.3.b</td><td>Planning Section</td></tr>
<tr><td>IV.A.3.c</td><td>Logistics Section</td></tr>
<tr><td>IV.A.3.d</td><td>Finance/Administration Section</td></tr>
<tr><td>IV.A.3.e</td><td>Intelligence/Investigations Function</td></tr>
<tr><td>IV.A.5</td><td>Incident Complex—Multiple Incident Management with a Single ICS Organization</td></tr>
<tr><td>IV.A.6</td><td>Area Command</td></tr>
<tr><td>IV.A.6.b</td><td>Area Command Responsibilities</td></tr>
<tr><td>IV.B</td><td>Multiagency Coordination Systems</td></tr>
<tr><td>IV.B.1</td><td>MACS Description</td></tr>
<tr><td>IV.B.2</td><td>System Elements</td></tr>
<tr><td>IV.B.3</td><td>Examples of System Elements</td></tr>
<tr><td>IV.B.4</td><td>Primary Functions of MACS</td></tr>
</table>

Instruction Standards

Minimum Course Contact Hours: 40 total hours

Instructor standards:

1. Course should be conducted with at least two instructors, one of whom must be qualified as a lead instructor.

2. Instructors should have completed ICS-400 and IS-800.

3. Lead instructor should be fully qualified as Type 1 or 2 for this position and have functioned in that capacity at an incident that required multiagency coordination went beyond one operational period and required a written IAP.

4. Lead instructors must have completed at least 32 hours of instructor training and have previous experience as an instructor on Incident Command System or Emergency Management courses.

P460: All-Hazards Finance Section Chief

Audience

Individuals who would fill the role of Finance Section Chief.

Course Objectives	Relation to NIMS Document	

Course Objectives

- **Information Gathering and Sharing**: Identify required reference materials, forms, and supplies. Describe the contents of the Finance Section Chief's kit. Describe use of the unit log.

- **Section Management**: Describe staffing and ordering needs. Define the initial briefing, section operating plan, performance requirements, and standards.

- **Interaction and Coordination**: Identify information to exchange. Define the role of the planning meeting, IAP, and operational period briefing.

- **Demobilization and Closeout**: Describe responsibilities in closeout and the demobilization plan. Identify information to include in the briefing for replacement.

Relation to NIMS Document

III	Resource Management
III.A.1	Underlying Concepts of Resource Management
III.A.2	Five Basic Principles of Resource Management
III.B	Resource Management Process
IV	Command and Management
IV.A	Incident Management
IV.A.1	Management Characteristics
IV.A.1.f	Incident Facilities & Locations
IV.A.1.g	Comprehensive Resource Management
IV.A.2	Incident Command (IC) and Command Staff
IV.A.3	General Staff
IV.A.3.a	Operations Section
IV.A.3.b	Planning Section
IV.A.3.c	Logistics Section
IV.A.3.d	Finance/Administration Section
IV.A.3.e	Intelligence/Investigations Function
IV.A.5	Incident Complex—Multiple Incident Management with a Single ICS Organization
IV.A.6	Area Command
IV.A.6.b	Area Command Responsibilities
IV.B	Multiagency Coordination Systems
IV.B.1	MACS Description
IV.B.2	System Elements
IV.B.3	Examples of System Elements

Instruction Standards

Minimum Course Contact Hours: 24 Hours

Instructor standards:

1. Course should be conducted with at least two instructors, one of whom must be qualified as a lead instructor.

2. Instructors should have completed ICS-400 and IS-800.

3. Lead instructor should be fully qualified as Type 1 or 2 for this position and have functioned in that capacity at an incident that required multiagency coordination went beyond one operational period and required a written IAP.

4. Lead instructors must have completed at least 32 hours of instructor training and have previous experience as an instructor on Incident Command System or Emergency Management courses.

P402: All-Hazards Liaison Officer

Audience

Individuals who would fill the role of Liaison Officer.

Course Objectives	Relation to NIMS Document	
• **Position Concept:** Understand the roles and responsibilities of the Liaison Officer as a member of the command staff.	IV	Command and Management
	IV.A	Incident Management
	IV.A.1	Management Characteristics
• **Agency Representatives:** Understand the function of an agency representative.	IV.A.2	Incident Command (IC) and Command Staff
	IV.A.2.a	Incident Command
• **Stakeholders:** Define, identify, and profile stakeholders. Understand their roles and responsibilities regarding stakeholders and evaluate Liaison Officers' success.	IV.A.2.b	Command Staff
	IV.A.2.c	Incident Command Organization
	IV.A.3	General Staff
	IV.A.3.a	Operations Section
• **Incident Communications and Work Location:** Identify types of communication and work location needs for a given incident.	IV.A.3.b	Planning Section
	IV.A.3.c	Logistics Section
	IV.A.3.d	Finance/Administration Section
• **Information Flow and Use of Assistants:** Understand the process and relevant parties involved in incident information flow, including the role of Assistant Liaison Officers. Know how to obtain status of and information about cooperating agencies.	IV.A.3.e	Intelligence/Investigations Function
	IV.A.5	Incident Complex—Multiple Incident Management with a Single ICS Organization
	IV.A.6	Area Command
	IV.A.6.b	Area Command Responsibilities
• **Planning Process:** Know how the Liaison Officers fits into the planning process.	IV.B	Multiagency Coordination Systems
	IV.B.1	MACS Description
• **Special Situations:** Determine the proper steps to follow in the event of a special situation.	IV.B.2	System Elements
	IV.B.3	Examples of System Elements
• **Demobilization:** Understand the demobilization process as it relates to the duties of the Liaison Officers. Describe Liaison Officers' responsibilities throughout demobilization.	IV.B.4	Primary Functions of MACS

Instruction Standards

Minimum Course Contact Hours: 16 total hours

Instructor standards:

1. Course should be conducted with at least two instructors, one of whom must be qualified as a lead instructor.
2. Instructors should have completed ICS-400 and IS-800.
3. Lead instructor should be fully qualified as Type 1 or 2 for this position and have functioned in that capacity at an incident that required multiagency coordination went beyond one operational period and required a written IAP.
4. Lead instructors must have completed at least 32 hours of instructor training and have previous experience as an instructor on Incident Command System or Emergency Management courses.

P403: All-Hazards Public Information Officer

Audience

Individuals who would fill the role of Public Information Officer.

Course Objectives	Relation to NIMS Document	

Course Objectives

- **Roles and Responsibilities**: Describe the role of the PIO position in incident operations and the elements of an incident information strategy.
- **Incident Information Operations:** Describe the fundamentals of information operations during incident management. List elements of an operations plan for information function, and the types of information the PIO will provide at a planning meeting and shift briefings.
- **Developing a Communications Strategy:** List four elements of a communication strategy; describe the importance of coordination and addressing long-term needs.
- **Effective Media Relations:** Describe the importance of effective media relations and the role of the PIO in developing and maintaining such relationships.
- **Assistant PIO Tasks and Assignments:** Describe the roles and responsibilities of Assistant Public Information Officers for internal and external communication and information coordination.
- **Effective Community Relations:** Identify principles of positive community relations, key individuals and organizations, and understanding when and how to use information and formal meetings.
- **Special Situations:** Describe the role of the PIO as it pertains to handling special situations within incidents.
- **Creating a Safe Environment:** Identify sources of safety hazard information and techniques to communicate the hazards to internal and external groups.
- **Demobilization Summary:** Define the PIO's roles and responsibilities during incident transition and demobilization.

Relation to NIMS Document

II	Communications and Information Management
II.A	Underlying Concepts of Communications and Information Management
IV	Command and Management
IV.A	Incident Management
IV.A.1	Management Characteristics
IV.A.2	Incident Command (IC) and Command Staff
IV A.2.a	Incident Command
IV.A.3	General Staff
IV.C	Public Information
IV.C.1	Public Information Overview
IV.C.2	System Description and Components
IV.C.2.a	Public Information Officer (PIO)
IV.C.2.b	Joint Information System (JIS)
IV.C.2.c	Joint Information Center (JIC)
IC.C.2.d	Organizational Independence
IV.C.2.e	Information Flow to Stakeholders and the Public
IV.C.3	Public Information Communications Planning

Instruction Standards

Minimum Course Contact Hours: 40 total hours

Instructor standards:

1. Course should be conducted with at least two instructors, one of whom must be qualified as a lead instructor.
2. Instructors should have completed ICS-400 and IS-800.
3. Lead instructor should be fully qualified as Type 1 or 2 for this position and have functioned in that capacity at an incident that required multiagency coordination went beyond one operational period and required a written IAP.
4. Lead instructors must have completed at least 32 hours of instructor training and have previous experience as an instructor on Incident Command System or Emergency Management courses.

P404: All-Hazards Safety Officer

Audience

Individuals who would fill a role of Safety Officer.

Course Objectives	*Relation to NIMS Document*	
• **Position Role:** Materials for Safety Officer kit, unit log.	IV	Command and Management
• **Incident Overview**: Information sources, laws, regulations and policies, and technical specialists.	IV.A	Incident Management
	IV.A.1	Management Characteristics
• **Hazards and Risks**: Hazard and safety risks, prioritize mitigation, mitigation and accident prevention methods.	IV.A.2	Incident Command and Command Staff
	IV.A.2.a	Incident Command
• **Incident Safety Analysis, ICS Form 215A:** The purpose, components, and use of Form 215A.	IV.A.3	General Staff
• **Site Safety and Control Plan, ICS208HM:** The purpose, use, and components of Form 208HM.	IV.A.6	Area Command
	IV.B	Multiagency Coordination Systems
• **Incident Safety Action Plan:** Elements of a safety plan, safety message, safety briefing, and assistant safety officers.		
• **Coordination with Logistics:** Interaction with the Medical Unit, Ground Support Unit, and local health department.		
• **Operations and General Health and Welfare:** Promote general health and welfare, describe work/rest guidelines, identify authority to stop and prevent unsafe acts.		
• **Special Situations:** Describe the role of critical incident stress management, accident investigations, and special reports.		
• **Demobilization and Closeout:** Describe demobilization checkout procedures.		

Instruction Standards

Minimum Course Contact Hours: 32 total hours

Instructor standards:

1. Course should be conducted with at least two instructors, one of whom must be qualified as a lead instructor.

2. Instructors should have completed ICS-400 and IS-800.

3. Lead instructor should be fully qualified as Type 1 or 2 for this position and have functioned in that capacity at an incident that required multiagency coordination went beyond one operational period and required a written IAP.

4. Lead instructors must have completed at least 32 hours of instructor training and have previous experience as an instructor on Incident Command System or Emergency Management courses.

P480: All-Hazards Intelligence/Investigations Function

Audience

Individuals who would fill a leadership role within the Intelligence and Investigations Function.

Course Objectives	Relation to NIMS Document	

Course Objectives

- **Nature of Intelligence:** Describe the nature of intelligence as it relates to the responsibilities of the Intelligence/Investigations Function. Define the difference between intelligence, information, and investigations and provide examples.

- **Developing Intelligence:** Identify sources of intelligence and National Security Classification Level and determine what type of information should be included in the intelligence file.

- **Organizational Implications:** Identify each of the four organizational structures of the Intelligence/Investigations Function as well as the benefits and challenges of each. Identify members of IMT to interact with most frequently.

- **Preplanning for Intelligence:** Describe the importance of preplanning activities.

Relation to NIMS Document

IV	Command and Management
IV.A	Incident Management
IV.A.1	Management Characteristics
IV.A.1.a	Common Terminology
IV.A.1.n	Information and Intelligence Management
IV.A.2	Incident Command (IC) and Command Staff
IV A.2.a	Incident Command
IV A.2.b	Command Staff
IV.A.2.c	Incident Command Organization
IV.A.3	General Staff
IV.A.3.a	Operations Section
IV.A.3.b	Planning Section
IV.A.3.c	Logistics Section
IV.A.3.d	Finance/Administration Section
IV.A.3.e	Intelligence/Investigations Function
IV.A.5	Incident Complex—Multiple Incident Management with a Single ICS Organization
IV.A.6	Area Command
IV.A.6.b	Area Command Responsibilities
IV.B	Multiagency Coordination Systems

Instruction Standards

Minimum Course Contact Hours: 24 Hours

Instructor standards:

1. Course should be conducted with at least two instructors, one of whom must be qualified as a lead instructor.

2. Instructors should have completed ICS-400 and IS-800.

3. Lead instructor should be fully qualified as Type 1 or 2 for this position and have functioned in that capacity at an incident that required multiagency coordination went beyond one operational period and required a written IAP.

4. Lead instructors must have completed at least 32 hours of instructor training and have previous experience as an instructor on Incident Command System or Emergency Management courses.

Appendix D: References

National Incident Management System. Washington, DC: Department of Homeland Security, March 2004.

National Incident Management System, revision. Washington, DC: Department of Homeland Security, FEMA 501, Draft August 2007. *http://www.fema.gov/pdf/emergency/nrf/nrf-nims.pdf.*

Federal Emergency Management Agency, *National Incident Management System (NIMS)—National Standard Curriculum Training Development Guidance—FY07,* Washington, DC: Department of Homeland Security, March 2007.

Federal Emergency Management Agency, *NIMS Guide: National Credentialing Definition and Criteria,* Washington, DC, Department of Homeland Security, FEMA NG0002, March 2007. *http://www.fema.gov/pdf/emergency/nims/ng_0002.pdf.*

National Strategy for Homeland Security. Washington, DC: White House, July 2002.

National Strategy for the Physical Protection of Critical Infrastructures and Key Assets. Washington, DC: White House, February 2003.

Homeland Security Presidential Directive (HSPD)-5: Management of Domestic Incidents. Washington, DC: White House, February 2003.

HSPD-7: Critical Infrastructure Identification, Prioritization, and Protection. Washington, DC: White House, December 2003.

HSPD-8: National Preparedness. Washington, DC: White House, December 2003.

HSPD-12: Policy for a Common Identification Standard for Federal Employees and Contractors. Washington, DC: White House, August 2004.

United States House of Representatives. 107th Congress, 2nd Session. *Homeland Security Act of 2002.* Congressional Bills, GPO Access.

National Infrastructure Protection Plan. Washington, DC: Department of Homeland Security, 2006.

National Response Framework. Washington, DC: Department of Homeland Security, Draft, XX 2007.

Emergency Responder Field Operating Guide. Washington, DC: Department of Homeland Security, Draft, 24 May 2007.

Joint Field Office Activation and Operations: Interagency Integrated Standard Operating Procedure. Washington, DC: Department of Homeland Security, Interim Approval April 2006. *http://www.dhs.gov/xlibrary/assets/NRP_JFO_SOP.pdf.*

Joint Field Office Field Operations Guide. Washington, DC: Department of Homeland Security, June 2006.

National Wildfire Coordinating Group. *Wildland Fire Qualification System Guide.* PMS 310-1. Boise, ID: National Interagency Fire Center, April 2006. *http://www.nwcg.gov/pms/docs/PMS310-1.pdf.*

National Wildfire Coordinating Group. *Agency Administrator's Guide to Critical Incident Management.* Boise, ID: National Interagency Fire Center, January 2005 (draft). *http://www.nwcg.gov/pms/pubs/PMS926-DRAFT.pdf.*

National Wildfire Coordinating Group. *Interagency Incident Business Management Handbook*. Boise, ID: National Interagency Fire Center, April 2004. Accessible via: *http://www.nwcg.gov/pms/pubs/large.html*.

National Wildfire Coordinating Group. *GIS Standard Operating Procedures on Incidents*. PMS-936. Boise, ID: National Interagency Fire Center, June 2006. *http://www.nwcg.gov/pms/pubs/GSTOP7.pdf*

Index

A

academic continuity model, 197–200
  recommendations, 199–200
administrative chief model, 200–201
adult learning projects, 181
American Public University (APU),
  degree programs, 183–185
Association of Contingency
  Planners (ACP), 98

B

Blanchard, B. Wayne, 7
business continuity planning, 94

C

callout systems
  fire protection, 3
  scanners, 5
  technological advances in, 4
Centre for National Operation (CNO), 166
  benefits of emergency management, 141
  Incident Commander, 169
  in Sri Lanka, 138, 170, 204
CERT (Community Emergency Response
  Team Program), 97, 173
certified emergency manager (CEM),
  61, 64, 208
Civilian Defense, 6
civilian emergency management, 74
classroom training, 76

Command Post. *See* Emergency Operations
  Center (EOC)
Command Staff, 203
  Liaison Officer, 41
  responsibilities of, 40
  skill sets for, 42
communication models, 84
community adult education courses, 84
Community Emergency Response Team
  Program (CERT), 97, 173
comprehensive emergency management,
  concepts of, 63
crisis management
  activities, 24
  for general managers, 172–173
  in private sector, 94–95

D

department chief
  fire chief, 36
  management skills, 58
Disaster Mitigation Act (DMA) of 2000, 93
Disaster Mortuary Operational Response
  Team (DMORT), 69, 120, 122–124
  emergency management
    FEMA, 150–151
    hurricane Katrina, 147, 150–152
    Incident Command System, 150
  Incident Commander, 166, 171
  tactical response operations of, 147, 149

disaster recovery (DR)
  health professionals, 151
  volunteer with Red Cross, 96
Disaster Recovery Institute International
      (DRII), 75
Disaster Recovery Journal Conference,
      75, 95, 113, 172
Disaster Research Center (DRC), 187–188

E
electronic monitoring systems, 5
emergency and risk communications, 83
emergency management
  college programs
    curriculum for, 77–81, 83
    graduate students, 189
    growth of, 75
    quality review for, 78–79
  competencies, 7–8
  core courses of, 163
  DMORT, 150–152
  entry-level positions in, 92–95
  first responders, 125, 127
  general manager expertise, 172–173
  ICS management, 201–202
  influence of business and industry in, 9–10
  management of objectives (MOB),
      uses of, 160–163
  mitigation planning orientation meeting,
      188–189
  newsletters for, 187
  professional development, 28–29
  in project management, 163
  research conducted for, 86–88
  skill sets for, 2
    abilities, 23–24
    knowledge, 22–23
    students, 81–84
    tasks, 24–25
    technical and functional skills, 21–22

in Sri Lanka, 135–137
structure of
  family assistance center, 126–127
  logistics management, 125
  personnel accountability, 124–125
  planning and public information, 126
  private sector enterprises, 127
supporting operations, 122
in tactical response operations, 188–189,
      207–208
training and education, 27–28
during World War II, 6
Emergency Management Assistance
      Compact (EMAC), 81
emergency management coordinator.
      See emergency managers
emergency management personnel, 14
emergency managers
  administrative and management
      duties of, 50–51
  benefits of college preparation, 180
  career development skills for, 112–114
  career paths to, 2–4
  comparison with chief of first
      responder unit, 7
  as crisis management team leaders, 172
  emergency response personnel,
      206, 209
  vs. first responders, 179–180
  importance of speaking skills for,
      82–83
  incident commander and, 58
  job description of, 50, 62–64
  knowledge and skills, 163, 188
  management competencies of, 60
    factors contributing to, 65
  mitigation planning for, 178
  next generation education of,
      205–206
  in tactical response operations, 179

Emergency Medical Services (EMS), 100
emergency operations
    application, 67
    systems, 94
Emergency Operations Center (EOC),
        43, 68, 189
    Incident Commander, 204
    role at Pier 92, 120, 126, 167–168, 206
emergency responders, 209
emergency response personnel, 206
emergency response planning, 79
emergency services
    coordinated response, need for, 4–6
    fire protection and law enforcement, 2–4
    media response, 6
emergency volunteer organizations,
        declining membership in, 8–9
EOC (Emergency Operations Center), 43

F
family assistance center, 126–127
farm team system, 8–9
FEMA, 150–151
    DMORT operations, effect on,
        146, 150–151, 153, 171
    emergency management positions in,
        103–110
    emergency management training courses,
        27, 88, 182–183
    guidelines for all-hazard mitigation plan
        preparation, 77
    objectives of, 75
fire chief
    factors contributing to competencies of, 65
    and Home Rule, US, 164–165
    job description of, 52–54
Fire Department of New York (FDNY), 126
firefighters, 120–121
    training curriculum, 15–16
    volunteer, 201

firefighting, 2
    fire chief, 5
    source of response, 3
first responders
    actions of, 118–121
    command, concerns to, 43
    and emergency management, 125, 127
    vs. emergency managers, 179–180
    vs. firefighters, 120
    Plectron installment for, 4
    priorities of, 6
    private sector enterprises, 127
    role of chief of, 7
    role of Incident Commander, 165–166
    special skills of, 120
    in tactical operations, 2, 7
    training for tactical response operations,
        16–21
        patrol rifles, operation of, 18–21
        in tactical operations, 16–18

G
general managers, role of, 172
geographic information systems (GIS),
        83, 94
graduate programs, emergency
        management, 81

H
Homeland Security and Emergency
        Management Agency (HSEMA), 100
Homeland Security Exercise and Evaluation
        Program (HSEEP), 93
home rule, US, 164

I
IAEM (International Association of
        Emergency Management), 59–60
ICS courses, 27–28. See also emergency
        management

Incident Action Plan (IAP), 38, 67,
        160–161
    operational objectives of, 171
Incident Commander, 35
    difference between emergency manager
        and, 58
    DMORT, 166, 171
    emergency management, 162
    management roles of, 58–61, 165–166
    role in tactical operations, 39, 42–44
    in Sri Lanka, 166
Incident Command System (ICS), 34, 58,
        69, 84, 92, 98, 122
    Command Staff, 34–36
    in complex incidents, 38
    core elements of, 160
    in DMORT, 150
    goal of, 36
    Incident Manager, 164
    management by objectives (MOB), 161
    management functions, 201–202
    Operations Section Chief, 37–38
    structure of, 35
incident management systems, 83, 85
incident manager, 164
    role and responsibility of, 204–205
Indian ocean tsunami, 169–170
informative magazines, 186–187
International Association of Emergency
        Management (IAEM), 59–60, 113

L
Lanka Jatika Sarvodaya Shramadana
        Sangamaya (Sarvodaya), 134–135
law enforcement
    fire protection and, 3
    officials, responsibilities of, 7
    responder, 5
    training for, 16–18
Liaison Officer, 41

M
management by objectives (MBO), 66–69
    core courses for, 163
    Incident Action Plan (IAP), 160–161
    incident objectives, implementation of, 161
    sales objectives, 162
mitigation planning, requirement of, 178
municipal emergency management, 83

N
National Coordinating Council on
        Emergency Management, 64
National Disaster Medical System
        (NDMS), 123, 167–168
National Fire Protection Association, 65
National Incident Management System
        (NIMS), 58
Natural Hazards Center, 187
New York City Police Department
        (NYPD), 119, 121
NGOs (nongovernmental organizations), 134
NIMS ICS, 34
NY-ALERT, 196–197

O
Office of Emergency Management &
        Communications (OEMC), 100
office of emergency management (OEM), 99
Operations Section Chief
    Command Staff supports, 40–42
    Incident Commander, 165
    responsibilities of, 166
        emergency management, 36–37
        Incident Action Plan (IAP), 38
        law enforcement, 37
OSHA HAZWOPER certification, 112

P
PIO (Public Information Officer)
    communicating with media, 42

responsibilities of, 44–45
tactical operations supports, 41
Planning Section Chief, 42
Plectron, 4
police chief, 55
essential functions of, 56
factors contributing to
competencies of, 65
knowledge, skills, and abilities,
56–57
private sector enterprises, 127
advantages of, 153
private sector managers, 173
professional development, 28
Professional Emergency Management,
competencies of, 59–60
project management, 163
Public Information Officer (PIO), 41
public safety manager, 62
public safety training center model, training
programs, 195–196
public sector emergency responders, 95

Q
Quarantelli's management definition, 206

R
Red Cross Disaster Services, 96
retiring emergency manager, 179

S
Safety Officer, 40
Sahana, free and open source disaster
management system, 138–140
sales management objectives, 162
Sarvodaya (Lanka Jatika Sarvodaya
Shramadana Sangamaya), 134–135
security and crisis management, 94
State Emergency Management Office
(SEMO), 150, 196–197

T
tactical response operations, 2
under command and control, 164
DMORT
management, 171
in morgue operations, 149
emergency management recommendations,
207–208
emergency managers in, 160, 164
firefighters vs. first responders, 120–121
first responders actions, 118–121
security, 121
skill sets for
fire response personnel, 15–16
law enforcement personnel, 16–18
patrol rifle usage, 18–21
in Sri Lanka
first responders, 132–133
military assistance, 133
nongovernmental organizations
(NGOs), 134
training for
developing skills, 28–29
firefighter, 26–27

U
unified command (UC), 203
University-based Disaster Research Center, 187

V
volunteer firefighter, 201
Volunteering, disaster recovery, 98
vulnerability assessment, 195

W
World Conference on Disaster Management
(WCDM), 75, 113
World Trade Center
emergency management, 122–125
tactical response operations, 118–121